HAILE SELASSIE:
The Conquering Lion

HAILE SELASSIE:
The Conquering Lion

Leonard Mosley

PRENTICE-HALL, Inc., Englewood Cliffs, New Jersey

© 1964 by Leonard Mosley

First American Edition 1965

Library of Congress Catalog Card Number: 65-11882

Printed in the United States of America
T 16772

PRENTICE-HALL INTERNATIONAL, INC., *London*
PRENTICE-HALL OF AUSTRALIA, PTY., LTD., *Sydney*
PRENTICE-HALL OF CANADA, LTD., *Toronto*
PRENTICE-HALL OF INDIA (PRIVATE) LTD., *New Delhi*
PRENTICE-HALL OF JAPAN, INC., *Tokyo*

CONTENTS

Introduction   7

Glossary   11

PART ONE: PREPARATION

  1 Harar, 1892   15
  2 Menelik's Court   36
  3 The Arrogant Prince   57
  4 Coup D'état   76
  5 Ras Mikael Strikes   87

PART TWO: PATIENCE

  6 Counter-Revolution   101
  7 Ethiopia Joins the League   116
  8 Negus Tafari   131
  9 Negusa Nagast   139

PART THREE: FRUSTRATION

 10 Lij Yasu Again   155
 11 Misplaced Faith   172
 12 Civilizing Mission   184
 13 The Last Attack   201
 14 Train to Jibouti   215

PART FOUR: EXILE—AND RETURN

 15 A Time for Patience   221
 16 The Road Back   226
 17 State Entry   245

PART FIVE: HARSH REALITY

18 Liberated—or Not?   255
19 Independent Again   264

Epilogue   268

Appendix: The Solomonic Legend   277

Bibliography   281

Index   285

INTRODUCTION

OF ALL THE memories of my youth, none remains more vividly in my mind than the appearance of H.I.M. Haile Selassie I, Emperor of Ethiopia, as he stood at the bar of the League of Nations in 1936 and pleaded with the so-called civilized governments of the world not to abandon his country. I remember him as a pathetic figure, his black cloak hung from drooping shoulders, sick from the rigors and disasters of the Italo-Ethiopian war. And yet dignity still clung to him; he looked both regal and romantic.

I was to discover later, when the accidents of war enabled me to watch him at closer quarters, that this kingly presence never leaves him even in the most uncomfortable circumstances. He is the only man I have ever seen who can put his shoulder to the back of a truck —as he did when we were stuck in the scabrous bushlands of Ethiopia in 1941—and not cease to exude through his sweat a distinct aura of imperialism. Here indeed is a king.

I noted in my diary in 1941 that I would one day write the biography of Haile Selassie, an Emperor in many ways so brave, in many ways so ruthless, in many ways so cunning, in many ways so far-seeing, in many ways so great. It could be said that my Life of the late Orde Wingate, who led the wartime forces which took the Emperor back to Ethiopia, was in some ways a preparation for it. In the years since that project was finished I have been gathering in the facts and filling in the backgrounds, both in Britain and in Africa. It seems to me that the time is now ripe for a study of the life and works of this remarkable man.

This biography is not what is usually termed an "official" or "authorized" Life, though the Emperor is aware that it is being written and he, his family and his Ministers have helped me in many of my researches. The opinions expressed and the judgments made are entirely my own. For my historical background I have been careful not to rely exclusively on Ethiopian sources, since the Court Historians of previous régimes, though not necessarily the present one, have too often succumbed to the temptation to rewrite past events in order to please their present masters. Fortunately, British, American, Italian and French sources have been available to me as well.

I have tried to eliminate Ethiopian words from my text where a clear translation from the Amharic is available, but a short list of those which I have found indispensable, together with their approximate meanings, will be found at the end of this Introduction. I hope Amharic scholars will forgive me for the simplification of many of the names which figure in this story, since there seem to be so many different versions of each one (even Haile Selassie has its spelling variations). I also hope that the general reader will be able to work out the blood ties between the characters who appear in the narrative —sometimes as mortal foes, sometimes as steadfast allies—by studying the family tree of the Royal House of Ethiopia which I have included.

I would like to express my warm thanks to all those who have spent so much time helping me to unravel the tangled skein of contemporary Ethiopian history, and I hope that the fabric I have knitted from it justifies the trouble they took. In Ethiopia itself I am, of course, particularly grateful to H.I.M. the Emperor for interrupting his preparations, on the eve of his State Visit to the United States, in order to renew old acquaintance with me and listen to my needs. After he had departed, his grandson, Prince Iskinder Desta, did his best to supply me with information, records and introductions. Among others who were quick to express their willingness to be of service were H. E. Tsehafe Taezaz Tafera Work, Minister of the Imperial Court, and H. E. Kebbede Mikael, Minister of the Imperial Chronicles; and it was from the latter's staff that I was given the aid of Ato Amaha Walde Sadik on my journeys outside Addis Ababa. He proved to be a witty, intelligent and indefatigable companion and retained his sense of humor sometimes in most remote places and trying circumstances. Of the many scores of helpers in Ethiopia I would also like to single out for gratitude Mr. Geoffrey Wetherell, Managing Director of a British business firm, Mitchell Cotts of Ethiopia. Another who went out of his way, in the midst of a busy life and worrying domestic problems, to smooth the path of my researches was one of the most promising young personalities in Ethiopia today, Ato Abebe Kebbede, who looks after the charitable trusts established by the Emperor, and whose horizons have been broadened and shaped by service at his country's embassies in Britain and America. I am also only too well aware that my travels in Harar and Harar Province would have been impossible—coming as they did on the eve of a crisis between Ethiopia and Somalia over encroachments on Harar territory—had it not been for the willing co-operation of an old comrade of mine from Wingate days, Colonel Tamrat Yegizu, now deputy Governor of Harar. He provided the Land Rover and the armed guard without which travel would have been too hazardous.

In Britain I had the invaluable privilege of being able to talk to H.I.H. the Crown Prince, Asfa Wossen, while he was here on a visit, and a favorite grandson of the Emperor, the Duke of Harar, who is at school at Gordonstoun. I could hardly have proceeded with my researches into the earlier years of the Emperor's career had it not been for the willing help of Mr. R. W. Mason, CMG, the Foreign Office Librarian, who was good enough to open the archives to me; to the Earl of Avon, KG, PC, MC, for talking to me and searching his own records on my behalf; to Sir Edwin Chapman-Andrews, OBE, for looking back with me on a colorful career which was not only distinguished diplomatically but included a close and lasting friendship with the Emperor; to Mrs. Esme Kenyon Jones, the daughter of a famous British Minister to Ethiopia, Sir Sidney Barton, the widow of a splendid friend and fighter for Ethiopia and Haile Selassie, George Steer, and the mother of one of the Emperor's god-children, George Steer Jr., for talking to me about her doughty father, her brilliant husband and her own fond memories of life in Ethiopia; to Mr. Peter Hayes and Brigadier and Mrs. Turnbull for some striking photographs and fascinating memories; and lastly the unstinting help and advice of a great expert on Ethiopia and a tremendous admirer of the Emperor, Mr. P. P. Dunkley, for whom no obstacle was insurmountable—in a land where obstacles are apt to be high and spiky.

Finally I should like to thank Professor Edward Ullendorf, MD, D. Phil, formally of the University of Manchester, who now holds the Chair of Ethiopian Studies at the University of London, a renowned expert on Ethiopian history, for having read the book and made many corrections and suggestions. I hasten to add that he— like all the others I have consulted—is not responsible for any of the opinions in it.

All these deserve especial gratitude, but there are many others who are too numerous to mention by name but have all played some part in adding a fact or a nuance to this book; and I thank them too.

GLOSSARY

of some Ethiopian words used in this book

ABUN — the title of the Head, or Archbishop, of the Ethiopian Coptic Church. Until 1950 he was always of non-Ethiopian origin, being appointed by the Synod of the Coptic Church in Alexandria. Once he arrived in Ethiopia he was traditionally forbidden to leave it in his lifetime; though the last non-Ethiopian Abun, Kyril, who died in 1950, left Addis Ababa for Alexandria during the Italian Occupation.

AMBA — A flat-topped mountain or mesa.

ATO — A polite form of "Mr." rather like the British Esq.

BITAWADED — Prime Minister or senior Minister.

DEJAZMACH — Literally "Keeper of the Door," but equivalent to senior official or High Sheriff.

ITCHEGE — Head of the Monastic Orders; the most senior *Ethiopian* ecclesiastic until 1950.

FITAURARI — "Commander of the Spearhead," a rank below Dejazmach.

GEBBI — Palace or royal compound.

GEBRE — First name. Servant of.

GERAZMACH — "Commander of the Left Wing," a rank below Fitaurari.

HAILE — First name. Power of.

HAPTA — First name. Gift of.

INJERA — Soft, doughy Ethiopian bread.

ITEGE — An Ethiopian queen.

JANHOI — An Ethiopian king.

KANYAZMACH — "Commander of the Right Wing," equivalent rank to Gerazmach.

LIJ — Equivalent of Prince or The Honorable. Son of an aristocrat of royal blood.

MASKAL — A religious feast of the Ethiopian spring, celebrated on September 27 with bonfires, much merrymaking and feasting. It signalizes the end of the rains.

NEGUS	King.
NEGUSA NAGAST	King of Kings, or Emperor.
RAS	The most senior title below that of Negus, roughly equivalent to Duke.
SHAMMA	Cloak of wool or silk, plain or embroidered, black or colored, worn by men and women.
SHIFTA	Bandit.
TALLA	Ethiopian beer.
TESFA	First name. Hope of.
TEKLA	First name. Plant of.
TEJ	A mead made from honey, varying in color from pale yellow to amber, in strength from the mildness of cider to the potency of yellow Chartreuse.
TUKUL	A round Ethiopian hut.
WAIZERO	A lady, the feminine equivalent of Ato.
WALATTA	First name. Daughter of.
WALDO (e) (a)	First name. Son of.
WAT	Strongly spiced Ethiopian sauce; a fiery stew.

A useful word in Ethiopia: Tenastelin! (God be with you!).

part one

PREPARATION

chapter one

HARAR, 1892

THE TRACK WHICH connects Harar with the hilltop hamlet of Ejarsa Gora twists, climbs and tumbles its way for thirty-five miles through some of the loveliest and most fertile country in the Horn of Africa. It is a land where the soil, the color of dried blood, is rich enough to grow two crops of durrah a year, as well as a profusion of wild coffee, figs, olives and aloes. In September, when the great rains are over and the Ethiopian spring begins, the green hills are lavishly daubed with acres of yellow Maskal daisies. In December and in April, the air is sweet with the smell of wild roses and loud with the hum of fat honey bees. Away to the south east, the landscape is dominated by a huge table mountain, Kondudo, on whose plateau of grassland wild Somali ponies graze in packs and are hunted and roped, cowboy fashion, every year by the young bloods of Harar. In that direction the country slopes rapidly towards Jig Jigga and the fiercely hot deserts of Somalia. But the track to Ejarso Gora winds across broad valleys and undulating hills which never drop below 5,000 feet and the climate is kindly to both humans and crops, pleasantly warm by day and cool by night.

This is the land of the Itu Gallas, and their mud and wattle *tukuls* (thatched round huts), protected by huge hedges of the largest succulent, euphorbia candelabra, are tucked into every dale and fold in the hills. They are a people with looks and natures in keeping with their amiable climate, as many a traveler in the past has recorded. Richard Burton, who always had an eye as well as an appetite for a pretty woman, noted on his adventurous journey to Harar in 1854 that the women were slim, arch, graceful and attractive, as well as eager to please.[1] He gave one tobacco and salt, with no sign of resentment from her husband, and she came next morning to bring him milk and help

[1] Though he did not notice that they wear flowers in their hair.

him pack; he did not miss her "warm, rich nut-brown" skin, her "arch look" or her carelessly covered breasts. Lord Edward Gleichen, a member of the British mission to the court of the Emperor Menelik in 1897, was also favorably impressed by the inhabitants of this country. "They are tall and bronze-skinned," he wrote, "rather good-looking on the whole, and with their hair frizzed out all round like a mop. One of their women whom we passed on the road was the most beautiful dark-skinned lady I have ever seen—like a vision of what Zenobia ought to have been, with very clear-cut and classical features and magnificent black eyes."

It was among these people, at Ejarsa Gora—and not, as most record books have it, at Harar—that Lij Tafari Makonnen, later to become Haile Selassie I of Ethiopia, was born on July 23, 1892.

In May each year, the boy's father, Ras Makonnen, Governor of Harar, took his family and retainers to Ejarsa Gora to escape the stuffiness, the typhoid and other diseases which stalked the streets of the walled city of Harar at this time of the year. Here on a green hillside that looked down on the fertile valleys, he had built a large mud-and-wattle house with a refinement that was unusual in Ethiopia at the time—it had a large verandah in front where he could receive the chiefs who came to pay him tribute, listen to grievances and settle quarrels, and, in the cool of the evening, drink his tej (an Ethiopian mead) with his confidantes and watch the lammergeier and ravens wheeling in the sky. In 1892 he came early because his wife, Waizero Yeshimabeit, was with child and he hoped that the fresh breezes and clear air would help her pregnancy to go well. She was the wrong mould for shaping children, and eight of her offspring were stillborn or had died from the diseases lurking in Harar for susceptible infants. So this time she and her baby must be given every chance.

For Ras Makonnen wanted a son. It was true that he already had other children, by consorts or concubines or slaves. He even had a natural son named Yilma, of whom he was fond. But it was not enough. If the Emperor Menelik, who had no son of his own (and who trusted Ras Makonnen as no one else) did as some wiseacres at Court forecast and passed his Imperial crown to him when he died, Makonnen wanted a legitimate son to inherit it from him. So Waizero Yeshimabeit was cosseted at Ejarsa Gora until her time came, and that was not until the first heavy rains had broken over the valleys. As the midwife dragged him clear, Tafari's first yelps were drowned by a spectacular cannonading of thunder and a torrential downpour; a good enough omen, in a land where rain is always welcome, for the women to raise their voices in praise as the babe's lips were moistened with ritual butter, for all the rifles in the village to let go a ragged fusillade, for the cattle to be killed and tej and talla to be made ready, and for the feasting to begin. Ras Makonnen had the son he craved, and there was raw meat, heady drink and two nights of singing, boasting and wenching to celebrate it.

A month later Lij Tafari and his mother were taken back on litters to Harar to prepare for the boy's baptism into the Coptic Church. Though the rains had turned the track into a river of red mud and the rivers themselves into torrents, it was still a ceremonial procession. At its head marched six members of Ras Makonnen's ceremonial fanfare, each sounding a different note on his curved one-note horn. Behind came the deputy Governor, Fitaurari Banti, in crimson coat and violet velvet hat, his pony richly ornamented, a silver shield on the saddle-bow, spear-carriers running at his side. Then the decorated litter of the baby Tafari covered with a silver embroidered canopy, and behind the litter of Waizero Yeshimabeit.

Fanning out from the procession were the young men of Ras Makonnen's entourage, dressed like peacocks in colored shirts, leopard or lion skins flung over their shoulders, lion manes around their heads, curved swords clanking, and their rifles firing madly as they galloped bravely through the mud. After which came the attendants and slaves, running alongside, the men shouting or firing their guns, the women loolooing in their eerie, birdlike Ethiopian way. And at every village en route the chiefs brought out the talla beer for the multitude, the tej for the officers, and every villager bowed his head while the women clapped and screamed.

Just outside the city walls of Harar, Ras Makonnen himself waited upon the arrival of his son. He leaned over from his saddle and took the babe, red with mud stains by this time, in his arms and led the dishevelled but merry procession into the city.

Emperor Menelik had sent gifts. Chiefs had arrived from the countryside with tribute. There were more feasts; and Ras Makonnen said many prayers of thankfulness in gratitude for the safe delivery of his son.

He had reason to be grateful. Less than two years later, Waizero Yeshimabeit was pregnant again, and this time she died in childbirth.

Even today Harar still looks, smells and feels like a medieval city, though it now has its own gasoline station and taxi service, and one is liable to be awakened in the morning by the sound of an Ethiopian

Army band playing its peculiar version of "Auld Lang Syne." It is
still a walled city whose five gates are closed every night to all save
the hyenas, which filter into the labyrinthine streets by the score and
devour the city's garbage, offal and the occasional stray donkey. A
European in the crowded market place or street of the mat-makers
is liable to be followed by the cries of "ferengi, ferengi!" (foreigner!),
as Burton was; though those who do so nowadays cry more out of
fun than resentment, and the owner of the voice is likely to be
young, coquettish and female, a pretty Harari girl in thin silk form-
fitting gown over skin-tight velvet trousers. In Burton's day there
was a superstition that Harar would be safe only until a Frank was
allowed beyond its walls, and all previous attempts by missionaries or
traders to penetrate the city had failed. The ruler was a bloodthirsty
tyrant named Emir Abu Bekr and his people were said to be surly,
suspicious and savage. Burton was warned that he would be killed,
and possibly tortured beforehand, if he ventured to break the prohibi-
tion, but for an infidel who had already traveled to Mecca, this was
more a challenge than a disincentive. In the event, he was to have
more trouble in leaving Harar than he did in passing through its
walls. Unlike those who came afterwards, he found it an unimpressive
town whose walls were uneven and whose only main building was an
unimpressive, "poverty-stricken" mosque with "two broken down
gates and two white-washed minarets." Smallpox was raging in the
town and he was repelled by the men he saw, pock-marked or de-
formed. But at least he shared the opinions of other travelers so far
as the Harari women are concerned, finding their clear profiles, large
eyes, straight noses and "Caucasian mouths" most beautiful to see.

The dreaded Emir Achmed bin Abu Bekr turned out to be "an
etiolated youth twenty-four or twenty-five years old, plain and thin
bearded, with a yellow complexion, wrinkled brow and protruding
eyes." But etiolated is hardly the word for the nature of his rule inside
the city; he was apt to order death or torture, a public hanging or
burning, at a whim; his prisons were full; and he was a keen spectator
when a woman taken in adultery was stripped, doused with water
and publicly whipped. He was removed from his throne by the
Egyptians, with the connivance of the Harari citizens, in 1874. The
Egyptians in turn retreated from Harar a decade later on the advice
of the British, when the Mahdi's insurrection in the Sudan began to
spread. A distant relative of Abu Bekr, Abdullahi, took over as
Emir. He was a much more benevolent and popular ruler; he abolished
punitive taxes, encouraged the outlying Galla tribes to come into the

city for trade; and his remedy for what Burton called "the lax moral habits" of the Hararis was not to whip women for adultery but to force them to cover their slim legs and flanks with the tight-fitting velvet breeches which they still, most attractively, wear to this day. The Emir ordained that they be skin-tight so that they would be difficult to remove.

1887 it was the Emir Abdullahi who was removed and not the breeches of his female subjects. From his temporary capital at Entoto, in Shoa, King Menelik (who was still subordinate at this juncture to Emperor John of Ethiopia) moved on Harar with Ras Makonnen as his second in command and 40,000 cavalry and foot soldiers. On the orders of Emperor John, the town had already been attacked by an expedition under Walde Gabriel, who had been cut to pieces by Emir Abdullahi's Harari and Galla troops. Now Menelik came to avenge the defeat. Menelik spurned the use of his *likamaquas* (an officer who deceives the enemy by impersonating the king) and led his troops in person. A bloody battle took place at Tyalanko in which 11,000 Hararis and Gallas were killed. Abdullahi, who had taken refuge behind the city walls, was captured and brought back in chains to Entoto. As a reward for his gallantry and skillful leadership, Menelik gave his cousin, Ras Makonnen, the Governorship of the captured city. And here it was that the future Emperor Haile Selassie was conceived.

After they had staunched their wounds and buried their dead, the Hararis came first to tolerate and then to admire their new ruler. It is true that Makonnen brought with him from Shoa an entourage of Shoans and Amharas who took over the key positions in the city and the province, but he also invited Moslems and Gallas into his administration and his army. The Hararis and Gallas were expert horsemen, and they formed the nucleus of a magnificent cavalry which was to win great victories for Menelik in the days to come. Ras Makonnen built a Coptic church for himself and his Christian followers in Harar, but he also stimulated the Hararis into erecting new mosques for themselves. In 1889, after the death of Emperor John at the hands of the Sudan dervishes, Menelik crowned himself Negusa Nagast, King of Kings, Emperor of Ethiopia, and sent Ras Makonnen as his plenipotentiary to Italy to spread his fame abroad. It was Makonnen's first visit to Europe and he was impressed with what he saw. The Italians had already signed with Menelik the Treaty of Ucciali, by which (as they read the treaty) Ethiopia agreed to conduct all future negotiations with powers outside Africa through the Italian Government as intermediary, and Rome was by virtue of this confident that Menelik's Ethiopia was all but under its control and well on the way to becoming an Italian protectorate. Makonnen had come to Rome to sign a supplementary agreement for trade, financial, frontier and cultural relations, and he was received with flattering attention by the Italian Government. He enjoyed the banquets and was enchanted with the women (one of whom called him "a brown Garibaldi"), but what he brought back from Italy was an ambition to raise the sanitary and cultural standards of his own people in Ethiopia. What happened in Shoa, where Menelik's new capital of Addis Ababa was still little more than a settlement, was the Emperor's affair, but for Harar Makonnen had his own ideas. One of them was to found a hospital, and for this purpose he imported a doctor who had come from the Caribbean via Italy and gave him the building and the medicines to open a clinic. It was called the Ras Makonnen Hospital and was the first of its kind in Ethiopia. He encouraged the French Mission, under Monseigneur Thaurin (and, later, Monseigneur Jarosseaux) to add educational and medical projects to their proselytizing mission, and welcomed as influences for the good Europeans who came to the city, hoping they would stay not only to trade but to teach.

By the time Lij Tafari was born, Ras Makonnen—a horseman as brilliant as the Hararis—had won his spurs with the people of Harar. He waived his rights and allowed the mullahs to settle quarrels among the Moslem citizens (those quarrels, that is, that were not resolved by the Hararis themselves, according to Harar custom, in a bone-crushing, head-smashing duel with knobkerries). He and his Amharas preferred to drink tej, which is an Ethiopian mead or a barley beer.[2] On the other hand, the local Gallas and Hararis, being Moslem and therefore forbidden alcohol, chewed *chat,* which is a native shrub growing on the terraced hills of Harar; it has strong narcotic properties. Makonnen subsidized a portion of the crop for his Moslem subjects and shipped the rest to Arabis at a fat profit.[3] He did not need to encourage his young Shoans and Amharas to mingle with the nubile natives of the province, but he was more tolerant than

---

[2] Lord Edward Gleichen wrote about tej: "This process produces a strange-tasting drink rather like bitter cider, and intoxicating, distinctly. The brands of tej differ according to the locality. Ras Makonnen's best tastes like sweet, strong old Madeira, and Menelik's like still hock, whilst the inferior kinds vary between bad sherry and sourish water with dead bees and lumps of Ethiopian wax and bark and earth floating in it." He described tallah as "inferior barley water with beery reminiscences."

[3] As Ethiopia does today.

other Shoan Rases [4] in Galla areas in that he insisted that the offspring of these unions were recognized and cared for.

Three years after Tafari's birth, in 1895, his father called the natives of Harar to arms and the response was not only quick but willing. The Italians had established themselves in their new province of Eritrea, having driven the dervishes from Agordat and Kassala back across the Sudan border. Rome's colonial hunger was growing, and the Italian Army was beginning to slaver at the thought of eating up Ethiopia itself, convinced that Menelik would never be able to hold his Empire together. They were furious, therefore, when Emperor Menelik showed signs of negotiating directly with the powers in Europe, in contravention, they hastily pointed out, of the Treaty of Ucciali. Menelik blandly replied that he had agreed in this Treaty that he *might* use Italy as a negotiating power but was under no compulsion to do so. This, the Italians replied, was not what it said in the Italian text of the Treaty, to which Menelik retorted that he had signed only the Amharic text and that gave him the fullest freedom and discretion. To make matters even clearer, he denounced the Treaty of Ucciali in 1893, a move which, in Italian eyes, made war inevitable.

The clash came two years later when Ras Mangasha, a natural son of Emperor John and an erstwhile enemy of Menelik, decided to make amends and demonstrate his loyalty to the new Emperor by assaulting the Italians; and he crossed into territory nowadays known as Eritrea from Tigre with an army of 10,000 men. They were met by an Italian army under General Baratieri and routed. Menelik moved his armies northwards to stem the Italian invasion that followed and Ras Makonnen, with 30,000 eager cavalrymen from Harar, rode to join him. By the time they made contact, the Italians had occupied Adigrat, Makalle and Amba Alagi, all vital towns in Northern Ethiopia.

Makonnen, who had studied Napier's campaign against Emperor Theordore, surrounded the Italians and forced them into the fortress at Magdala, harried them with forays from his horsemen, and laid siege to them all through December and January. Toward the end of January, 1896, out of food and ammunition, they hoisted the white flag on the Magdala heights. Makonnen, as a tribute to a gallant enemy, allowed them to march out with full honors of war and sent the Italian officers and troops south under escort to im-

---

[4] An Ethiopian Ras is a prince or duke.

prisonment. The native troops he released after first branding them on the arm and warning them not to fight against Ethiopia again.

In the next six weeks, disasters hovered like ravens over the heads of the Italians. Amba Alagi was taken, once more by Ras Makonnen. General Baratieri, convinced that well-armed, well-trained reinforcements now pouring into Eritrea from Italy would overwhelm the savage hordes confronting him, decided to advance with 20,000 men in the direction of Adowa. Ninety thousand perfervid, battle-hungry Ethiopians were waiting for them. The battlefield where the vengeful hurricane descended is a vicious and eerie landscape of volcanic rocks that look like giant black, broken teeth, and of waterless valleys and pathless rifts and precipices. The Italians had no reliable maps and no intercommunication. They were shot at from both sides, jammed together into a writhing mass by the cavalry, and then systematically shot or cut down. The Italians fought with great bravery and tenacity and inflicted enormous casualties, but were out-fought and out-numbered. By the time they started their retreat, 12,000 of them had been killed and 4,000 taken prisoner.

Menelik threw his arms around Ras Makonnen's neck and said: "We have fought together like father and son, and like father and son we shall be from this day forth."

The dead and wounded were left to rot or die on the battlefield, for the Ethiopians carried no field ambulances or doctors with them. The prisoners were rounded up and those natives who were found to be branded had an arm chopped off at the wrist or a foot at the ankle, or, in the case of some of their Galla captors, were emasculated.[5] A number of wounded Italians were later brought back to Massawa, in Eritrea, by the Italian Red Cross and were found to have been mutilated, and Menelik's Army was blamed for it; but the culprits were neither the Emperor's soldiers nor Makonnen's but the *shiftas* (bandits) who prey like hyenas on defeated troops in Ethiopia (and were to scavenge on *Ethiopian* wounded in the Italo-Ethiopian War in 1936). Makonnen urged that the Italian prisoners be well treated. They were taken back to Addis Ababa, the men put to work road-making, the officers lodged with Shoan families; and a few months later the Russian Red Cross was allowed to bring in a mission which treated the Italians for wounds and illnesses. Their repatriation began in 1897.

[5] Until recent times, it has been mandatory evidence of the manliness of certain Galla tribesmen to prove they have killed a man by presenting his testicles to the killer's bride-to-be. Nowadays to slay and emasculate a wild beast is considered sufficient.

But though the Italians had no cause for complaint against their Ethiopian conquerors, this did not quench Italy's burning sense of humiliation. The victory at Adowa had important repercussions, one of which was tragic. It planted a desire in Italy for revenge against the savage Empire which had thwarted its colonial ambitions and (as it thought at the time) shamed its troops. Nor was the weed eradicated by Menelik's reluctance to press his advantage. He signed a peace treaty which confirmed Italy's possession of Eritrea and asked nothing in return but recognition by Italy of the independence of the Ethiopian Empire. The Italians had no choice but to give it, but, as the world and Ethiopia discovered forty years later, their signature on a treaty was less indelible than the name Adowa, which was written on their hearts.

The victory, however, had two happier consequences. In a land which admired strength and warrior qualities above all else, Menelik's defeat of the Italians consolidated his claim to be Emperor in fact and in power as well as in title. Even in the dissident South and restless East, rases and chiefs felt it would be wise in the future to bend their knee to the ruler in Addis Ababa; and as a result, Ethiopia in the next few years under Menelik was to become united as never before.

Europe, too, was influenced by the victory at Adowa. Until this event, Ethiopia had been thought of by the Great Powers as a loose and unreliable collection of warlike rases, to be dealt with piecemeal, and Menelik as a merely nominal king. Britain did not even have diplomatic contact with Menelik's court, and had relied upon her allies, the Italians, to keep them in touch. Now it became clear that Menelik spoke for the whole of his country, and that he was a man not only to be reckoned with but to be negotiated with, too. Swarms of traders and adventurers descended upon Addis Ababa in search of concessions and monopolies; the name Addis Ababa means literally "New Flower" and fortune-seekers buzzed around it like bees in search of nectar. In 1897, a year after the victory at Adowa, missions were sent to Menelik's court by the Turks, Russians, Italians, the Sudan Dervishes, the British, with two from the French.

The British was led by Mr. (later Lord) Rennell Rodd and included in its entourage five British officers, two British soldiers and a troop of Aden Cavalry. They landed at Zula, a Somali port on the Gulf of Aden, in March, 1897, and crossed Somaliland by camel caravan to arrive in Harar in early April. Lord Edward Gleichen wrote a report of the journey and it gives a vivid and affectionate picture of the country and environment in which the young Emperor-

to-be (Tafari was five years old at the time) spent his formative
years. The Mission spent some time with Makonnen but his son is
only briefly mentioned by Gleichen, though the present Emperor
clearly remembers their arrival. The Mission had halted for the night
ten miles outside Harar and were bidden by their Ethiopian escort,
who had guided them for the last twenty miles, to ride on to a
rendezvous outside the city walls where Ras Makonnen would "receive us in pomp." They were up at five and struggled shivering into
their uniforms. "Several of us declined to commit our best gold-laced
overalls and varnished Wellingtons to the tender mercies of a mule
for three hours," wrote Gleichen,[6] "and appeared therefore in the
tasteful kit of scarlet tunic, white polo breeches and long brown
field boots. This, although not strictly regulation, produced a brilliant
effect, and the only gloom cast over the proceedings was the refusal
of Bingham to wear his cuirass, he having determined to reserve this
for the capital."

They rode for two hours until they came upon a small group of
Ethiopians grouped by the wayside, in the midst of whom stood Ras
Makonnen. "Mr. Rodd (who, by the way, was riding a magnificently
caparisoned mule, a present from the Ras) immediately dismounted,
and we all followed his example. Then came the ceremony of presenta-
tion, and shaking hands with all of us Makonnen murmured a few
polite words through his interpreter, and begged to take leave of us
in order to receive us with due honour in his capital. He then cantered
off and we followed more slowly."

Gleichen adds: "During this short interview Ras Makonnen had
produced on us a pleasing impression. He is a small dark man with
delicate hands, large expressive eyes, a small black beard and moustache and a most intelligent cast of countenance. His voice is very
gentle and his manners extremely dignified and quiet. What he said
was little, but to the point, and he gave us then and thereafter the
impression of a man who wielded a good deal of power in a quiet way.
His dress was also quiet, consisting of a black silk shirt with narrow
orange stripes, a white robe of fine linen, and a black silk cloak with a
gold throat-fastening, while a broad-brimmed felt hat rather de-
tracted than otherwise from his appearance."

Unlike Burton, the Mission found the view of Harar, with its
white buildings and minarets standing out against the dark-blue
background "made a very pretty picture," and they were suitably impressed when a battery of small guns mounted in a little fort thun-

[6] Lord Edward Gleichen, *Mission to Menelik*.

dered out a salute and white-clad retainers fired rifles in the air. They were led past a "seething and gaily dressed crowd" through narrow streets to Ras Makonnen's house, inside a narrow courtyard.

"Here," writes Gleichen, "there was once more a guard of honour drawn up for us, dark warriors with rifle and silver shield, and dressed in cloaks and silks of all colours of the rainbow. Up the wooden stairs and on the landing above were more of them, mostly coiffed with a strip of lion's mane to denote their valour, and then we found ourselves in a little room, so dark after the sunlight without that at first we hardly distinguished Ras Makonnen sitting by the window and pointing to eight cane chairs arranged alongside the walls."

They took lunch in Makonnen's house, though the Ras did not join them; it was Lent and he was fasting. What they ate Gleichen does not say, except that "the cuisine was European." While the Ras sent out his servants to bring in mules to carry the Mission on to Addis Ababa, Gleichen and his companions explored the town. They visited the head of the Roman Catholic Mission, Monseigneur Thaurin, and watched a class at which the monks were schooling the sons of Ethiopian noblemen. They did not know it, but one of the pupils was Makonnen's son, Lij Tafari, and his elder step-brother, Yilma. Monseigneur Thaurin complained (not the first or last missionary to do so in Ethiopia) that he was allowed to teach but not to preach. But Gleichen noted that if he was proscribed in his missionary work for the Roman Church, he was doing his bit for France. "We noticed several French lay brothers in the Bishop's house," he wrote, "and found to our surprise that they are in charge of the post office, and that the telegraph wire now being laid between Harar and the capital starts from the bishop's courtyard."

There were plenty of other foreigners in the town itself, which Gleichen describes as "a conglomeration of narrow and intricate streets leading between houses built of loose stone or rubble and thatched with horizontal cross-pieces covered with matting or straw." The bazaar was mostly inhabited by Indians "of whom the chief bankers are British subjects and rejoice in the names of Benin and Taib Ali. There are also a good many Greeks and Armenians, who seem to have the power of flourishing in strange places. The natives are a mixture of Galla and R'hotta and call themselves simply Hararis; there are few genuine Abyssinians in the place, except those in authority." And the chief desideratum in Harar while he was there, Gleichen goes on, was hats.

"Pot hats and Italian organ grinder hats," he writes, "would find a ready sale at any time, but the desire of the Ethiopian 'masher' is to possess a comfortable and shady-brimmed felt hat. The present fashion, set no doubt by Europeans, is in the direction of grey Terai hats; but from the avidity which all natives displayed to possess themselves at any price of our weather-worn and doubtfully coloured headgear, I should say that the colour was not so much the object as the actual article. There is no reason, as the demand is universal, why they should not learn to make hats themselves—indeed, a few straw hats of very odd shape and with plenty of ventilation were seen further up country—but they seem to prefer the European make. I therefore present this opportunity of making his fortune, free, gratis and for nothing, to the first enterprising hatter who does me the honour of reading these pages."

The Mission, armed with Makonnen's orders to his chiefs to provide them with sheep, bread and wine en route, and riding the mules the Ras had procured for them, set off on the long trek across country to Addis Ababa. They pushed their mules hard, and left several of them dead on the precipitous tracks over the mountains, but they still took eighteen days on the journey. Most cross-country travel in Ethiopia today is done by plane (except between Addis Ababa, Dire Dawa and Jibouti, by the country's only railway system), and it is difficult to realize the hazards of journeys by land over a terrain which is gashed by gorge after gorge after gorge, many of which drop precipitously for 3,000 feet, and where most roads and tracks are annually washed away by the great rains. It is in the West of Ethiopia that conditions and geography are the most difficult to overcome, but even in 1964 a journey by road from Harar to Addis Ababa is an exhilarating but uncomfortable adventure. In the days when Gleichen (and Ras Makonnen and his son) traveled over the route, it was a long, hard slog. Gleichen compared the trip, with its frequent changes of height, landscape and temperature, with "going upstairs into a different story in a big house—gravel walk and stone flags down below, luxuriant drawing room scenery on the first floor, bedroom scenery on the second and granary in the attics." The country round Addis Ababa, 8,200 feet high, was the granary.

On April 27, 1897, the Mission espied a horseman ("or rather, a muleman") approaching them from the direction of the capital, and he turned out to be a European. Not only that. He was dressed in a frock coat and striped trousers, and was wearing decorations. It was their first sight of a gentleman who was to have a considerable influence in the affairs of Ethiopia during the next few years. He was a certain M. Ilg, a Swiss engineer, who had come to Ethiopia in 1873 to make his fortune. When one considers the turbulent nature of Ethiopia during his quarter of a century in it, one might have congratulated M. Ilg merely on the fact that he had, like Voltaire during the French Revolution, survived. Actually, he had also thrived and not only commercially. In addition to agencies and engineering enterprises (and a scheme for a railway to link Addis Ababa with the coast, which he was, at the moment, promoting with a French colleague) he had so ingratiated himself into Menelik's Court by shrewd advice and guidance on European affairs that he had been created *conseiller d'état* to the Emperor.

M. Ilg had come to prepare the Mission for the ceremonial under which they would meet the Emperor, and it was as well that he did so. They had expected some sort of panoply and were prepared to look and act as if worthy of it.[7] But when M. Ilg urged them to "deck ourselves in our best" there was something in his tone to warn them that in the matter of display they were likely to have competition. They were soon to learn, as has many a more modern visitor to the Court of the Conquering Lion, that Ethiopian Emperors can teach the more upstart monarchies of Europe something new and bizarre in spectacular ceremonial. (It was from Menelik's court that Haile Selassie learned his lessons in pomp and circumstance.)

At 9 A.M. on the day after their arrival in Addis Ababa, the members of the Mission, dressed and burnished as never before (and Bingham's cuirass swinging at his side) were ready and waiting when M. Ilg, in full-dress, arrived and ran a critical eye over them. They must have passed muster, for he became extremely affable.

Shortly afterwards the hillside around the compound in which the Mission had been lodged began to fill with Ethiopian soldiers. There were thousands of them. Some wore red and white shammas. Others had tucked into their white breeches the vividly colored silk shirts that denote the soldier who has distinguished himself in battle. "Hundreds of the traditional green, yellow and red Abyssinian pennons waved in the breeze, and the rapid and orderly manner in which these apparently undisciplined masses ranged themselves in two bodies of from three to four thousand men each, forming the advanced and rearguards, was a most impressive sight."

To command this vast escort, Menelik had sent his Affa Negus

---

7 They had already been warned of the *gaffe* committed by the leader of the French Mission, Prince Henri d'Orléans, who had arrived at the court in riding breeches. "Who is this?" roared Menelik, "that he does not know how to dress for a king?"

("Breath of the King"), or Lord Chief Justice, "a cheery old gentleman" dressed in a huge black hat, green silk handkerchief tied round
his head underneath the hat, black silk cloak embroidered with gold,
purple silk shirt underneath and "continuations of the fairest linen."
He was armed with a long sword in a red scabbard and his squires,
running alongside, carried his rifle and gold-mounted shield.

The Emperor, like Makonnen before him, had sent a mule for
Mr. Rodd, richly caparisoned with silk and gold embroideries, and
it was on this that the Head of Mission led his companions to their
first audience of the Emperor. In the van were horn and flute players
and horsemen; then a detachment of the Imperial Palace Guard,
their rifles covered in red cloth; then four sowars of the Aden Cavalry,
Mr. Rodd and the Affa Negus, Bingham in the full dress of the
1st Life Guards, Cecil in levee dress of the Grenadiers, and the others
in full uniform. Behind came the Ethiopian rearguard.

In this order the procession moved forward at a slow pace across
the mile of ground separating the Mission camp from the palace.
"As we passed along," noted Gleichen, "our escort of something like
10,000 men was swelled by crowds of other people who ran out of
their huts to see, and were every now and then chased off the track
by perspiring policemen with long sticks. The stick seemed to play
a considerable part also in keeping the escort in order, for officers and
non-commissioned officers ran backwards and forwards shouting out
orders and enforcing them and the direction of the march by liberal
application over the heads and shoulders of the rear ranks."

He added: "It was a curious sensation to be borne along in the
hot sun amid a dense crowd of shouting humanity, dressed in all
colours and every variety of garments, and all anxious to do us
honour; and it will be a long time before any of us forget that morning."

The great procession at last approached the palisade that screened
off the royal enclosure and here, noted Gleichen, "the sheep were, as
at Ascot, separated from the goats." It was then that they became
aware of "a quaint sound of a symphony of drums in different pitches.
The noise grew louder until it throbbed like thunder in their ears—
and then into sight came the King's Drums. There were fifteen or
twenty of them—a row of red-capped, red-shirted Gallas each with
two drumsticks and a big kettledrum on the ground in front of him.
"One drumstick was thick and heavy like a club, and the other was
a thin switch, so that two notes could be produced out of the same

drum. 'Trrp trrp BOOM BOOM BOOM trrp trrp trrp' went the drummers in rhythmical cadence, and of all the sights that we saw that day this was the quaintest."

The members of the Mission were led past a formidable array of nearly seventy guns (most of them captured from the Italians at Adowa) and brought at last into the Emperor's presence. Menelik "was seated at the farther end [of the dark hall] in Oriental fashion on a dais covered with silks and carpets, and under a canopy ornamented with silken hangings. He wore on his head the usual white muslin handkerchief, fastened across the brow with ribbons of pale greenish blue, with streamers hanging down the back; a purple velvet cloak richly ornamented with large silver plaques on each side was thrown across his shoulders, and he bore on his breast and around his neck the orders of Catherine of Russia and the Legion of Honour."

Mr. Rodd advanced to bring him greetings from Queen Victoria "and his powerful, dark and small-pox pitted face lit up with a pleasant smile." As their contribution to the Emperor's foreign decorations, the Mission had brought Menelik the insignia of GCMG. At a later audience, they also brought gifts: a giant polar bear skin, "one of the finest we had ever seen"; [8] a tiger skin and the skins of black bear, snow leopard and jaguar. (The snow leopard "he did not think much of—it was too much like the ordinary Abyssinian beast.") Then came two silver salvers with the Lion of Judah engraved on them, four silver branch candlesticks, two gold-inlaid double-barrelled rifles, a silver gilt ewer and basin, four silver-gilt rice bowls, a pair of field glasses, some silk embroideries, a Persian silk carpet and "a life of Alexander the Great printed in Ethiopic. This was a reproduction of a manuscript found in Magdala, and was printed in London by the generosity of Lady Meux."

Menelik was delighted with his presents. "Other nations," he said, "have given me musical boxes and magic lanterns and mechanical toys. But you have given me what is really useful and valuable. I have never seen such things before."

Since this second audience was less formal, Gleichen had a better chance to study the Emperor, and he was impressed. "In height he stands about six feet without shoes, and is stoutly built. His skin is very dark, and he wears a short curly beard and moustache. His face is heavy in cast but is redeemed from positive plainness by an extremely pleasant expression and a pair of most intelligent eyes.

[8] It lies today in front of his desk in Haile Selassie's study, and is truly magnificent.

His smile is very wide and shows an excellent set of teeth. He generally wears a large black Quaker hat over a white silk handkerchief tied round his head, and a black silk gold-embroidered cloak over a profusion of white linen underclothing."

Rodd had brought presents for Queen Taitu, Menelik's consort, but the Emperor insisted that they should be presented personally. So the Mission made its way across the palace compound to a two-storied building with red tiles where the Empress, seated on a white-canopied dais, awaited them. It was whispered to them that they were being greatly honored, since Taitu never showed her face to anyone outside the court; but, as it happened, all they saw of it was one eye and part of a cheek, for the rest was veiled, though they did see enough to realise that she was a large plump woman, of very fair complexion with tiny hands and feet. She got as presents, a diamond and emerald necklace, a large silver looking glass and some silk embroideries. "Queen Taitu has a reputation of being a woman of much ability," Gleichen wrote, "and it is generally understood that the King owes much of his success to her counsels."

For the next three weeks, Rodd, Gleichen and their companions were lavishly wined, dined and otherwise entertained. Gleichen refers to some of his Ethiopian meals as "déjeuners sans fourchettes" and wryly noted that the maid who served his meats first took a bite herself "to show that they had not been poisoned." On May 14, 1897, a Treaty of Friendship was signed between Ethiopia and Britain and the Mission took their leave of the Emperor. The following morning a messenger arrived from Queen Taitu bearing a double gold necklace as a present for Queen Victoria, though one doubts if that staid monarch was anything but repelled to find that it was a copy of one the Queen of Sheba wore—but precious little else—during her first assignation with King Solomon, the assignation from which the first Emperor Menelik of Ethiopia is supposed to have resulted.

The following day the Mission were taking a last luncheon with M. Ilg before setting forth when they heard drums beginning to beat in the Gebbi, the King's palace. "From every direction," Gleichen wrote, "and as far as the eye could see, white-robed masses were pouring into the town, all making in the direction of the palace. The crowd of troops grew larger and larger, and at last we heard the sound of one-note flutes and of many voices just outside the fence of M. Ilg's garden."

The Imperial Guard had arrived to see them away. "We therefore

bade adieu to our kind hostess and were escorted by the Negus'
Household Brigade to the open space in front of the palace enclosure.
Here our attention was called to two figures sitting in the balcony
of the *elfin*, which proved to be King Menelik and his consort."

They climbed the stairs, bowed solemnly three times, and then
mounted their mules and rode away. And it was then that a familiar
sound smote their ears. It was the throb of the King's Drums. "To
our amazement and gratification, they pushed their mules through
the crowd and took up a position in front of us. This was an unheard
of honour for never before had they played for anyone except kings
and royalties. No other Mission had been similarly treated, and,
swollen with pride and satisfaction, we marched on to the sound of
'BOOM BOOM BOOM trrp trrp trrp BOOM BOOM BOOM trrp
trrp trrp', etc."

The Mission was back in England that autumn and reported to
the Foreign Office, strongly recommending the establishment of
permanent diplomatic relations with Ethiopia. As Gleichen wrote:
"Verily, Menelik is a great man ... The future of Abyssinia, as long
as Menelik is on the throne, may be (barring accidents) predicted,
I think with some confidence. The Negus will devote his time and
talents to consolidating and welding into a nation the heterogeneous
elements which now go towards forming his kingdom. It will take
time, for his people are of a retrogressive and not progressive type,
and internal jealousies and factions are rife. As long as foreign
nations keep their hands off, Menelik will proceed in security with
his task, for he has no intention of further expansion at the present.
Whether his object will be attained under these conditions depends
entirely on the length of his reign."

They were shrewd words, as young Lij Tafari found when he
took his place at the Imperial Court.

From the age of seven, when he first started to read and write
well in Amharic, Lij Tafari seems to have become aware that he
would one day succeed Menelik on the throne of the King of Kings.
It must have been premonition, for there was no logical reason why
he should assume that such an august elevation would be awaiting
him. It could have been no secret in the household at Harar, of
course, that his father, Ras Makonnen, was being spoken of among
the influential at Court as Menelik's likeliest heir. Queen Taitu had
given the Emperor no children—though she had borne several to her

four previous consorts—and Menelik's own previous wives had given him two daughters and a son, but the son had died.[9] As his beloved cousin and the only Ras at court whom he really trusted, Makonnen seemed the obvious successor—but there would be no certainty about it until Menelik officially proclaimed him heir. And even so, it did not necessarily follow that Lij Tafari would be the successor to his father. Ras Makonnen was treating Tafari as the Emperor was treating him, and had made no declaration of his preferment. In Ethiopia a son does not inherit his father's titles but has to earn them, by services to the king; nor does a father have to nominate his eldest son, or even any one of his sons, as his heir. It might be anyone. It might be his step-brother, Yilma. It might be his own favorite cousin, Imru Haile Selassie, who was also fondly regarded by Ras Makonnen.

Yet Lij Tafari, the way those who remember him then tell it, "knew" at the age of seven that he would one day be king, and began to study for the job. He badgered his tutor for all the books of Ethiopian history that he could find (there were not many) and listened avidly to tales of the Solomonic dynasty of which he was an offshoot; he believed implicitly in the legend of Solomon and Sheba. At the age of five he had been a shy little shrimp of a fellow, clinging to the robes of the women in the kitchen; but with learning and knowledge came a composure that astonished the household and his friends. Pictures of him at this period show a face that is touchingly good-looking, but the chin is held high and the eyes are aloof and the quiet confidence is evident. There is a regal look about him already.

By the time he was eleven years old he had learned enough French to converse in it with his young tutor, Aba Samuel, who had been recommended to his father by the monks of the French Mission in Harar. Ras Makonnen came back from a journey to England—where he represented Menelik at the coronation of King Edward VII— to find him so fluent that he mentioned his son's accomplishment to the Emperor, and was told to bring him to Court. He made the journey in 1903. It was the first time the boy had been on a long journey away from home—though he had shot his first lion in the Ogaden and helped to capture his own pony on Mount Kondudo— and he never forgot it. The mule caravan, with himself and his father riding at the head, wound its way through green groves of

[9] There were at least three other sons by other, more casual liaisons, but these did not count; at least not in Menelik's eyes or those of his rases.

chat, from Harar's cool and equable tableland, 6,000 feet high, to the heat of the scrublands at sea-level and here, at a new settlement called Dire Dawa, he saw a railway train for the first time and had a ride on a locomotive. The railway for which M. Ilg and his French colleague, M. Chefneux, had been dreaming and scheming since 1895 had finally come into being and the first leg had reached Dire Dawa from Jibouti.[10] The caravan moved on across the Ahwar Mountains to the Awash River, where Lij Tafari and his father took baths in a hot stream flowing into the main river and watched a herd of twenty complacent hippopotami wallowing in the waters of the confluence fifty yards away.

Tafari's appearance at Court a month later is still remembered. He was not much taller than a mannikin. He wore a rakish velvet hat, an embroidered cloak of black and gold silk pinned at the neck, white breeches and a ruffed shirt beneath. He recited a story from La Fontaine, and the Emperor, who did not understand a word, shouted: "He has learned it off by heart!" But when Tafari proceeded to exchange polite words with M. Ilg, Menelik was convinced and the whole court applauded. With two exceptions. Queen Taitu did not think he was charming at all. She could not bring herself to like anyone who was a member of Ras Makonnen's family, for whom she had an antipathy. The other was a member of the court circle almost equally powerful, Ras Mikael, who had married one of Menelik's daughters and also had a son, named Lij Yasu.

These two had ambitions, one for herself and the other for his son, that Ras Makonnen and his son could only embarrass. But if Makonnen was aware of this, he did not mention it to Lij Tafari, who went back to Harar and his books. In 1905, at the age of thirteen, he learned from the Emperor that he had been given the title of Dejazmach—roughly the equivalent of High Sheriff—and his father followed this by officially proclaiming him his heir. He did so in the knowledge that the Emperor would make his announcement very soon of his own choice of heir, and that Ras Makonnen would be confirmed as his successor.

But in April the following year, Ras Makonnen died. He was taken ill at his estate of Kolobi, as he was on his way from Harar to Addis Ababa at the urgent behest of the Emperor. Sudden death has never been infrequent among the Ethiopian nobles, and it is usually

[10] It was M. Ilg's hope that it would one day link Jibouti, Dire Dawa and Addis Ababa with the Sudan. In fact it halted for several years at Dire Dawa and did not reach Addis Ababa until 1915. Beyond there it has never penetrated.

from excess rather than old age that they die—from over-exposure in battle, from over-indulgence in food, wine and sexual intercourse, from too rigid adherence to the frequent fasts which are ordained by the Coptic Church, or from an overdose of poison. Ras Makonnen had survived his battles and could never have been described as a libertine; and though he was an extremely religious man, his constitution was robust enough to withstand the rigors of abstinence. Could it have been poison? So far as Tafari was concerned, his death could not have been more untimely, but for Makonnen's enemies at the court it was most convenient. By one death two claimants to the throne were wiped out. Since death took place in his own household, no one suggested that there was something sinister in his demise; but it certainly could not have been more pleasing to Queen Taitu, who knew that his accession would have meant the end of her influence at court, and it was most convenient for Ras Mikael, who could now press the claims of his own son.

The rases came to offer their sympathy to the young Tafari, and his advisers comforted him with the thought that, as Ras Makonnen's legal heir, he would be able to win his spurs as a ras, if not a ruler, by taking over from his father as Governor of Harar. It seems almost certain that Menelik intended to confirm Tafari in his inheritance, and not only as a gesture in memory of his old friend; he had already made it clear that he liked the boy and was impressed by his burgeoning abilities. But it was just about this time that he suffered the first of the strokes which would eventually incapacitate him, and though this was a comparatively mild one it was sufficient to give Queen Taitu the opportunity to exercise an even stronger influence over her husband. It was announced from the court that Tafari's step-brother, Yilma (the natural son who had been passed over by Ras Makonnen), and not the young legal heir would become Governor of Harar, a choice which proved to be painfully unpopular with the people of the province. The reason given was that Tafari was too young to control such a large and prosperous state as Harar, a particularly lame explanation in Ethiopia, where young governors were and are often appointed with an older deputy to help and advise them.[11]

It was an uncomfortable situation and could have been a hazardous one for Tafari. The step-brother, who had been rejected in Tafari's

11 The present Governor of Harar (1964) is the Emperor's grandson, the Duke of Harar, who is sixteen and a pupil at Gordonstoun in Scotland. A deputy, Colonel Tamrat, runs the province in his absence.

favor by Ras Makonnen, had not only been allowed, by Court decree, to usurp him but was also his legal guardian so long as he remained in Harar. Fraternal feeling between Yilma and Tafari was warm enough to eliminate any possibility that the new Governor would harm his step-brother, but in Ethiopia there have always been intriguers and schemers ready to trick, cheat and, if necessary, kill to ingratiate themselves with their overlords.

The peril in which young Tafari stood became apparent to Menelik as soon as he recovered from his illness. He summoned the boy to Addis Ababa and there announced that he had appointed him Governor of the small province of Solali. But it was to be an absentee appointment. Tafari was to remain in the capital at the Emperor's side and learn some of the arts of government.

In the Imperial circle in 1906, when he arrived, there were more devious skills to be acquired as well. The Court was filled with schemers, connivers, plotters, deft practitioners of dark intrigue. For the next few years, as a squire at the Court of Emperor Menelik, young Tafari learned not only how to govern but also how to survive.

chapter two

MENELIK'S COURT

WHEN THE BRITISH MISSION arrived in Addis Ababa in 1897, it so little resembled a capital city that the members referred to it in their reports as "a camp." They fully expected it to be deserted within a year or two and a new seat of government chosen.

"The King's headquarters are never for many years in the same place," wrote Lieut.-Col. (later Sir Reginald) Wingate, a member of the Mission. "Ankober, which was the former capital, is now practically deserted; Entoto succeeded Ankober; and this place was deserted for Addis Ababa (or 'the new flower') in 1892; but sooner or later a new spot must be chosen, for gradually all the wood in the vicinity is being cut down and consumed, and when the distance from the forest becomes inconveniently great, the capital must be removed elsewhere." [1]

In 1906, when Tafari took his place at Menelik's court, Addis Ababa had become the permanent capital of Ethiopia, chiefly because afforestation projects (particularly the planting of the fast-growing Australian eucalyptus) had solved the problem of providing fuel for the population. The temporary look, the resemblance to a gigantic encampment, remained. The town was a great sprawling mass of thatched round huts, or tukuls, covering the lower slopes of the blue Entoto mountains, with only a few square buildings intervening and even fewer erections two stories high.

In the center, on a small hill, was the great compound in which Menelik had his palace or Gebbi. In the European sense of the word, it was not a palace at all but a collection of hutments and houses obviously thrown up according to the needs of the moment and with no thought that they should meld into the landscape or match or

[1] Report to the Foreign Office, 1897.

36

complement each other in their shape or the color with which they were painted. Menelik's dwelling house where he lived with his Consort was a two-storied whitewashed building, called the *elfin*, which had what was at the time the only red tiled roof in Ethiopia. It was hung with balconies and exterior staircases painted in violent shades of yellow, red, blue and green. Beside the *elfin* was a huge oblong dining hall and the principal hall of reception. A little further away was the *saganet* or clocktower where Menelik dispensed justice, and a huge white building in which the Emperor kept his personal stores of food, arms, and, it was reputed, chests of silver dollars (though it is more likely that these were secreted in the vaults which had been tunneled into the hill beneath the *elfin*). There were several other buildings within the compound; workshops, barrack rooms, administrative offices, a private chapel and a night-den for the palace lions, which were allowed to roam on long chains during the day. As a royal enclosure it was a mess, but less so than the litter of dwelling places surrounding it.

On the lower slopes below the palace were the enclosures of the Emperor's advisers, the size depending on the importance of the official, and, beyond them, the compounds of the rases. These were all but deserted when the ras was away in his province, but seething with retainers and surrounded by tents when he had been summoned to court.

There were no roads but only mule tracks leading into the town, nothing but beaten paths and open spaces between the huts, and no bridges across the streams and rivers which divided the settlement. In the dry season this did not matter. In spring Addis Ababa, in spite of its squalid huts, was a lovely place to be, a flawed stone in an idyllic setting, its surrounding mountains and hills covered with yellow daises and crinum lilies and wild orchids, its streams filled with fresh water, its air fresh and its sun brilliant but (because of the town's 8,000 foot elevation) never trying. Even in the brown and dusty days of summer it was tolerable, because the populace could easily get out to the plains or the volcanic lakes nearby on mules or donkeys. But in the rainy season the streams flooded and the rain lashed down, sometimes for two or three days almost without cease, and the town became a cold, miserable, unhealthy quagmire; and only the pungent tang of eucalyptus smoke from the fires and the nightly infiltration of the scavenger hyenas prevented it from becoming one great garbage heap, and smelling like one.

It is true that there was a telephone system in Addis Ababa and a telegraph line to the outlying towns. There was a power system which provided electric light for the palace and the houses of the chief officials, European residents and foreign legations.[2] Menelik, himself a victim of smallpox in his youth, his face ridged and pitted as a result, had imported vaccine from abroad at his own expense and opened a clinic to which the citizens could come (or, during an epidemic, were driven) to be vaccinated. (They could get precious little else in the way of medicaments, however.)

But this was a superficial veneer on a city which was the medieval capital of a feudal kingdom, and looked it. A ras in his lion's mane and crimson cloak would gallop down the lanes, his squires at his side with his spears, his retainers behind, and woe betide anyone who got in the way of his curved sword or rifle butt. A nobleman's wife on her donkey, sheltered from the sun's rays by a scarlet, blue or golden umbrella, would have a way cleared for her by her attendants, armed with sticks and staves. Menelik had published ordinances abolishing slavery, but there were few households which did not have them, few rases who did not keep a regular supply of slave concubines, and though public slave auctions had been abolished, the places outside the town where every kind could be bought from a Galla girl to a Dankali boy and his father were well known and well attended. Through the streets and in the bazaar it was a normal sight to see a man strolling about with another man attached to him by a chain; though the manacled man was no slave but a debtor sentenced to be chained to his creditor until his dues were paid. Each Friday, in a clearing just below the palace, was punishment day when men and women (and only too often, children) were mutilated or executed for their crimes or misdemeanors. It was usual to sentence a thief to the amputation of a hand or a foot, or, in lesser cases, an ear, and this rarely attracted much attention among the throng. For more serious crimes such as murder, the relatives of the dead man or woman had the right to carry out the sentence themselves, and to do it in exactly the same way as the murderer had dispatched his victim. This was an eye for an eye, tooth for a tooth with a vengeance, and it carried the biblical ritual to the extent of considering accidental death to be murder too—so that a man who rode down and killed a child with his donkey could be trampled to death, and a boatman who lost his passenger could be ceremonially drowned. The law did allow the relatives of a victim to accept blood money

2 These had for the most part established themselves in compounds on the outskirts of the town.

in lieu of execution, and it is perhaps natural that someone who had hacked, burned, scalded or strangled his victim usually preferred to pay up (or accept servitude and chains) rather than suffer a similar fate.

It is only fair to Menelik to say that he had ambitions to bring his people some distance (but not too far) along the road to the twentieth century, and had he kept his health great changes might well have come about during his reign. He had conquered and pacified the Galla tribes, he had occupied Harar and the Ogaden, he had thwarted Italian ambitions and demonstrated to the world the independence of Ethiopia. His writ ran from the Sudan border to the Danakil Desert, from the Kenya frontier to Eritrea, and wherever a man travelled in this domain Menelik's was a name to be respected or (if it was not) reckoned with. No doubt had he lived and kept his strength, he would have pushed through edicts to diminish the power of his feudal rases and brought them more firmly under the control of his administration in Addis Ababa; and it is even possible that he would have done something to alleviate the lot of the serfs, who were mostly Gallas and were bled and tyrannized by their Amhara overlords. He was well aware that an Emperor would never really control his country until he had a national army under his direct command, instead of having to rely upon coalitions of his rases, and the private armies which they brought with them. It was one of his ambitions to station a garrison of Imperial troops in every province in the country, paid from Government coffers and subject only to Imperial discipline and command. The need for it became clearer with the death of Ras Makonnen, whose army he knew would always be on his side: with the new Governor of Harar he could not be so sure.

But these were not so much reforms as bulwarks to strengthen his own position and consolidate his rule; and, in any case, he did not have time to bring them into effect. Whatever schemes he planned to initiate in order to modernize his country did not include any weakening of his own power and influence. He hoped to remain a despot, if an increasingly benevolent one, to the end of his life.

Tafari was to discover that there were those at court who had other plans, and that the despot would soon be in danger of becoming a puppet.

1906 is probably the last year in which the Emperor Menelik remained in possession of all his faculties. The privilege of watching

him at close quarters left an impression on Tafari for life and influenced him in many important ways. Menelik was an indefatigable worker and he expected his courtiers to be equally industrious.
He rose each morning well before dawn and went across to his private
chapel to hear Mass said for him either by the Abun (the head of
the Ethiopian Church) or the Itchege (the head of the monasteries).

Thereafter, for the next three hours, he dictated letters on matters
of State and listened to reports from the outposts of his Empire.
There followed a succession of visitors, rases, courtiers, merchants,
concessionaires and M. Ilg. From all but the last he cocked an ear
to the gossip they brought him: which of his rases was plotting or
intriguing, and against whom; which marital liaisons in the court
were breaking up and which new alliances were being formed; who
had been extorting bribes and for what services; and who had been
cheating by holding back from the king the tribute that was his due.
From M. Ilg he extracted information about the foreign legations and
concessionaires (he was particularly sensitive to French infiltration
at this time, and had halted the railway at Dire Dawa because he
felt it would strengthen French influence). As a result of these
sessions, he made his decisions: a restless ras in Tigre must be summoned to Addis Ababa, where Menelik could keep an eye on him;
the Sultan of Kaffa must be warned that punitive action might
follow if he delayed any longer with the Emperor's share of his
taxes; the wife of Dejazmach . . . must be told that it would be
dangerous to continue her seductive assaults upon Ras . . . , for the
Ras's marriage had been solemnized in Church and was therefore
indissoluble; and Fitaurari . . . must be informed that it was no use
accepting bribes from the French to supply woollens since the Emperor
himself had already given the contract to the British, but that he
had better hand over the bribes he had already received to the
Treasury.

On two mornings a week, Menelik proceeded to the *saganet* where
he was lifted on to his royal dais (it looked rather like an extremely
opulent four-poster bed). Tafari and the other young nobles of the
court, wearing their best silk court-dress and curved ornamental
swords, stood behind him. In front was the Affa Negus and, pressing
at the door, the people of the town. These were Justice Days during
which the Emperor was available to his subjects to hear their grievances, listen to their quarrels and adjudicate, to decide on pleas for
mercy from convicted criminals. The plaintiffs and intercedents fell
on their knees before the Affa Negus and banged their heads on the

ground, and then began to speak; and though no one is more loqua-
cious than an Ethiopian, especially when he has a complaint, Tafari
noted that in every case the Emperor heard him or her out. Behind
him the squires were busily taking notes. They knew that they would
be questioned about the cases they had heard, and asked to make
their own judgments, later in the day; and it was not necessarily
an easy way to Menelik's favor, Tafari found, to agree implicitly
with every decision he had taken.

The Ethiopian Church has probably more fast days than any
other in the world, and the Emperor followed them rigidly; at these
times he would eat no animal foods—and take no food or drink at
all at Easter—and expected his courtiers to be equally abstinent. At
least two of the other courtiers, Imru Haile Selassie and Lij Yasu,
found this hard to follow, particularly when a fast day also included
one of the long church ceremonials (Lij Yasu kept a piece of raw
meat in his shamma to chew during the ritual dancing, and pleaded
toothache when the Emperor once asked him about the blood on
his chin). Tafari found that he could fast without too much discomfort; it was the feast days, almost as frequent as fast days, which
he found literally difficult to stomach, for he had a small appetite
and an abstemious nature, qualities which marked him out in a
court where appetites of every kind were gross. Even Menelik himself, though rigidly obedient of fast days, let himself go when there
was an excuse.

Gleichen noted that "an Abyssinian's stomach seems to be very
elastic, for he can put away in it a wonderful quantity of food at
a sitting." It was not unusual for two men, after going for two or
three days uncomplainingly without any food at all and only an
occasional sip of water, to eat a whole sheep between them, and
imbibe the equivalent of a barrel of beer. "He prefers [his meat]
raw. . . . Taking a large hunk in his left hand, say the hind leg of
a sheep or half a dozen ribs of beef, he draws his sword and carves
off a manageable slab. This he crams into his mouth—with his sword
—close to his lips. Then he masticates the piece, an operation of some
difficulty, for the mouthful is fairly large—and repeats the process.
Liquid assistance to wash it down is afforded by drafts of tej or
tallah out of a horn cup." [3]

Gleichen thought that the upper classes took their food more
tidily, but that was probably because the palace feast which he and
the Mission attended was organized especially for them by the

[3] Gleichen, *op cit.*

Emperor and the guests were obviously on their best behavior. On
arrival in the banqueting hall of the Gebbi they "found the Emperor
seated on the dais, while on his right was a table laid for eight
persons laid in the European fashion, spotless tablecloth and service
of Sèvres china, bearing the Lion of Judah burned in colours." They
were given a European luncheon "spiced with Abyssinian delicacies
of which red pepper formed the principal ingredient," and they
drank Burgundy, "very superior" tej and powerful araki. Menelik
himself, enveloped in silken cushions, was fed injera (soft bread made
of durrah) dipped in *wat* (a red Ethiopian hot spice) followed by
cooked meat. Each mouthful was tasted by a courtier before he ate
it, and another wiped the drips from his mouth.

"Soon after he had begun to eat," wrote Gleichen, "his principal
men of State, ministers, priests and generals entered, and, seating
themselves on the floor, the most important guest nearest the Emperor,
were served with dishes out of which the Negus had just eaten, each
individual being also provided with a flagon of tej covered with a
piece of silk. During the meal, Menelik, his officials and ourselves
were shut off from the rest of the hall by closely-drawn curtains,
and when the King drank, sneezed or coughed, or blew his nose, his
attendants were ready with their robes to screen him from the public
gaze."

Once the Emperor had finished eating, the Englishmen were even
invited to smoke—an insult to his presence that would normally
have been punished by the slicing off of the offender's lips—and
then the curtains were drawn aside and the lesser officials of the
court allowed in to eat. The entry of the retinue, 500 at a time,
was heralded by stentorian blasts from Ethiopian shawms. They
squatted before great baskets of bread and bowls of spice, and were
served slices of cooked meat and horns of tej; and then filed out
for the next batch. The Englishmen saw no great gluttony and no
drunkenness, and they were led away before the raw meat, "to be
consumed while still palpitating," was brought in and fed to the
hungry masses who now came in, with slopping gombos of beer.
Gleichen appears to have believed that raw meat was a dish confined
to the "inferior" classes, but Menelik was partial to it and Queen
Taitu preferred it to cooked meat; as a result of which an Italian
doctor who examined them in 1909 discovered that both of them
were regular sufferers from worms (a common ailment among
Ethiopians, who usually purge themselves by eating the bark of the
kousso tree).

It was the considerably more relaxed behavior of Ethiopians feasting alone, when appetites were not stinted and behavior at least in the body of the hall, became more incontinent,[4] which Tafari found distasteful. He had inherited his father's revulsion for raw meat; he was never a roisterer by nature; and the drunken horseplay, the noise of braying laughter and belching bodies, combined with the combined stench of raw meat, spices and sweat (especially during the rains, when the doors of the hall were closed) he found hard to bear. After a big feast in the banquet hall, the smell from the Gebbi had the pungency of an overflowing cesspool, until an alert Armenian concessionaire got a monopoly from the Emperor to supply the palace with disinfectant.

It was perhaps natural that all the filial affection which Tafari had held for his father should now be transferred to Menelik, and lacking a son of his own the Emperor warmed to this slim and rather pathetic youth of fourteen who had come under his wing. There was no doubt in anyone's mind that he preferred him to any of the other young nobles he had summoned to the Imperial court, and thought much more of his acumen and administrative abilities. In temperament there was a vast difference between the Emperor and his relative. Menelik had a temper sometimes so violent that his eyes would all but start out of his head with fury; he bellowed like a bull and roared like a lion. It had not gone unnoticed by him that even when baited by members of the Court, mocked for his abstemiousness, ridiculed for his shyness with concubines and slaves, Tafari showed no sign of temper other than a freezing of the features and an icy glitter in the eyes; nor did he need to be told that Tafari had one quality which he himself lacked but is a necessity in the mental knapsack of all great statesmen, patience. He knew how to wait—and he showed no sign of anger when he was thwarted. Toward pain, as toward disappointment, he had a stoic implacability. Once, when out riding with the Emperor on the plains outside the city, Tafari's horse had stumbled in a rabbit hole and flung him into a blackberry bush, from which he emerged scratched and dishevelled. The ten-year-old grandson of the Emperor, Lij Yasu, already an arrogant boy with a cutting tongue, laughed at Tafari's discomfiture and rode away to persuade the Court minstrel to make up a song to mark his cousin's "clumsy horsemanship." As the minstrel's mocking verses started the royal retinue tittering, Tafari (who had re-

---

[4] It was not unusual for women to be present at the feasts.

mounted) urged his pony ahead and was immediately challenged to a race by Lij Yasu. Tafari not only easily outrode the boy but treated the entourage to a dazzling display of horsemanship, jumping streams, stopping short, wheeling round and rearing up his mount on its hind legs before the Emperor—and doing it all with one hand. It was not until the cortège reached the palace that it was discovered Tafari had broken a wrist in his fall and must for some time have been in considerable pain. The less observant members of the Court nicknamed Tafari "The Shy One" and jeered at his lack of words, but Menelik was one of the few who realized that he had all the qualities of a hawk, and sighed at the thought that he would never see him pounce and on whom it would be.

For the next three years, Tafari and the other squires at the Imperial court combined the duties of lieges of the Emperor with studies at Addis Ababa's first school. To run it Menelik had brought from Cairo an Egyptian savant who had studied in Paris, and he ordered that the sons of all the rases be enrolled to study modern languages. Tafari had not much more to learn in French (and he had, in any case, brought his young tutor, Aba Samuel, with him), but he widened his range of reading and branched out into mathematics and economics, geography and history. He was the school's star pupil, and not simply because he wanted to please the Emperor; he found a stimulating and exciting new world emerging from his books and lectures, and his hours in the classroom whetted an appetite for education—and for educating others—which has never left him.

There were those at court who were not exactly pleased at the affection which had grown up between Tafari and the Emperor, but there was little that anyone dared do about it so long as Menelik was in full possession of his faculties. In particular, both Ras Mikael and Queen Taitu feared that the bonds between the two were such that the Emperor might be tempted to name him his heir. In fact it is doubtful whether it was ever more than a sentimental dream which Menelik toyed with but knew only too well could not be made a reality. To name Tafari as his heir could have put the young man in dire peril. So long as the Emperor remained alive, he could protect him; but with the Emperor dead, Tafari's own mortality would become an imminent possibility unless it was made clear that he was making no claim to the succession. For this truly was a medieval court, and once the Emperor was dead the struggle for the throne would begin: and Tafari had no powerful allies to fight for his cause, no army to pit against his opponents and no money to buy over supporters at court.[5] Menelik was only too well aware of the seething ambitions with which he was surrounded, and knew that with his death all the plots and intrigues and clandestine pacts would come to the boil. Weak, young and inexperienced, it would have been cruel to make Tafari more vulnerable than he was already. So there was actually no danger at all, so far as the Queen and the ambitious rases were concerned, that Tafari would come between them and the throne, but it did not stop them from continuing to regard him with the gravest suspicion.

During these years, in fact, life at Menelik's court was not unlike an Ethiopic version of *Macbeth*. In the circumstances, the Emperor could hardly be compared with the Thane of Cawdor, for it was in connection with his demise or removal that the plots were being hatched, but Queen Taitu had all the drives, ambitions and ruthlessness of a Lady Macbeth.

In many ways she was a remarkable as well as an indomitable woman whose temper was quick, nature lubricious, passions easily aroused and quite unashamed, and was consumed with a dream of one day becoming—or controlling—the first important female ruler of Ethiopia since the Queen of Sheba. Inside the massive, gluttonous and almost inert oval of flesh which she had now become was the vestige of what was once one of the most beautiful women in all the Empire. She was the daughter of a former ruler of the ancient city of Gondar and she came from a family renowned for its ravishing looks and pale skins. At the age of thirteen she was a slim child of such aching loveliness that she was seen, wooed and won in the same year by Fitaurari Walde Gabriel, a general attached to the armies of the Emperor Theodore. This was in 1867, the year that General Napier landed at Zula and began his march, with 13,000 troops and a herd of elephants, to avenge Theodore's defiance of Britain by besieging and defeating him at Magdala. Walde Gabriel did not take part in the battle because he had quarrelled with the Emperor, by this time mad with a *folie de grandeur*, and had been flung in fetters into the dungeons. After Theodore's suicide, Taitu did not stay to see the entry of the British or the release of her husband, but found her way back to Gondar and, before she was fourteen years old, was married again. It was the second of several marriages.

It would perhaps be advisable here to mention in passing some-

[5] He had inherited a sum of money which Ras Makonnen had prudently deposited with the Bank of England, but he had lost both Makonnen's army and the taxes and tributes from Harar to his step-brother.

thing about Ethiopian marriage and divorce, for otherwise a study
of the period and personalities could well become confusing. Most
of the men and women whose names figure in these pages will be
found to have been married two, three, four or even more times, and
these do not include liaisons with slaves or concubines. (The Emperor
Menelik himself, for example, had been married three times before
his union with Queen Taitu,[6] and Ras Makonnen had a previous
wife before marrying Waizero Yeshimabeit, Tafari's mother.) But
in Ethiopia there is marriage and marriage. The most solemn and
binding union is called *qurban* and not only takes place in a church but
is accompanied by holy communion. From its bonds a couple cannot
easily be freed—although divorce by special church dispensation is
possible. Most Ethiopian couples have preferred *semanya*, which is
marriage by a civil contract which is nowadays written but hitherto
has been a simple declaration before a responsible official that a man
and woman intend to live together. Third is hardly a marriage at
all but a *liaison de convenance* called *damoz* in which a man and
woman simply set up temporary house together for purely sexual,
social or economic reasons, the sort of arrangement that in the
Western world might be of great convenience to traveling salesmen
with a regular route. As has been mentioned, divorce *is* possible
from *qurban* but is difficult to obtain. Divorce from *semanya* needs
only a formal declaration to a public official by either wife or husband,
for reasons of cruelty, adultery, non-support by the male spouse or
slovenliness, immorality, laziness or barrenness on the part of the
female. *Damoz* is just a question of kissing or waving good-bye.

It has been said that the Ethiopians prefer *semanya*, and flit from
spouse to spouse with confusing frequency, because the menfolk yearn
for the Solomonic harems of old. But if the marriage pattern is a
substitute for polygamy it must also be nostalgia for polyandry, too,
for Ethiopian women (particularly Amharas of the ruling classes)
have never been reluctant to declare themselves divorced from their
husbands the moment they begin to bore them, or whenever a new
marital prospect seems more likely to rise in the Imperial circle, or
even for lust. Queen Taitu's motives were no doubt mixed, for she
was both a passionate woman and an ambitious one.

Her second husband was Dejazmach Tekla Giorgis, a general who
appears to have lacked both marital and martial prowess, and she
divorced him shortly afterwards for a Tigrean governor. This was
during the reign of Emperor John, a monarch who seems to have been

---

[6] One of his earlier wives took to the field in battle against him after he divorced her.

as dazzled by her lissom beauty and fiery nature as was Theodore before him. He sent her husband to the dungeons in chains, and for self-protection Taitu took refuge in a convent. From this she emerged, aged twenty-eight, a little plumper but still attractive, to marry for a fourth time, her new spouse being an officer in the army of Menelik, then King of Shoa. It was in the following year that Menelik saw her and at once fell in love with her, so passionately that he willingly banished his slave girls and concubines from the court so that she should have no cause to be jealous. She swiftly slipped the shackle that bound her to her fourth husband and, in 1883, became the wife of King Menelik, a union which was shortly afterwards solemnized by the Abun in a ceremony that was to make her legal Empress when her husband was crowned Emperor of Ethiopia. She bore him no children but of that he did not complain, for she brought him other gifts both pleasurable and practicable which he soon learned to appreciate. Nor were her accomplishments confined to the arts of the bedchamber and the council room, though it was here that she was at her most supple. She was a woman who had not only slept with kings and counselled kings but also studied them in battle, and she was no amateur in the arts of warfare too. In one of the campaigns against the Northern rebels in the Tigre in 1902 she rode into battle at the head of a regiment of cavalry and put the insurgents to rout, and, subsequently, to the sword. Earlier, at the battle of Adowa, she had appeared among the troops just before the attack began and knelt down, a stone on her back, her face pressed into the ground, as she prayed for their victory; and she was never far away from the fighting.

Now the burnished beauty was no more; Queen Taitu was sixty and fat. She rarely left the palace but stayed in her *elfin*, surrounded by her womenfolk and a bevy of young men. Mentally, however, she was as active as ever, and even more ambitious. She had always been a great admirer of Queen Victoria and dreamed of emulating her and becoming a ruling Empress too. Failing that, she had ambitions that would give her the throne in fact if not in name: she had taken great pains to win the affection of Menelik's daughter, Zauditu, by one of his previous wives.[7] Zauditu (the Ethiopian version of Judith) was far from being her stepmother's equal in mental capacity or ambition; much more important, from the Queen's

---

[7] Menelik's other daughter, Shoaragad, had married Ras Mikael and died in 1897 after bearing him a daughter and one son, Lij Yasu. Menelik's only recognized son had died in 1888.

point of view, was that she was amenable and ever willing to listen to Taitu's advice. She too had been married at thirteen and was about to divest herself (she was thirty) of her third husband. Taitu had a favorite nephew on hand, Ras Gugsa, ready and willing to become husband number four. After which, if she could not have the throne herself, Queen Taitu schemed to have Zauditu declared heir, with herself, of course, power behind it.

Could she persuade the Emperor to declare himself in her favor—or in favor of his daughter?

The danger to her plans came from Ras Mikael. He was laying siege to the Emperor too, not on his own behalf but in the cause of his grandson, Lij Yasu. Ras Mikael, King of the Wollo Gallas, was a formidable foe. Gleichen met him with the British Mission in Addis Ababa and described him as "a man of pleasing address, of strong character and many rifles.[8] By the time the struggle for the throne was under way, his "many" rifles amounted to at least 20,000, most of them smuggled into the country through Jibouti in French Somaliland, and his troops (a third of them highly trained cavalry) numbered some 50,000.

Ras Mikael had been born a Moslem and remained one until his adult years. He too had been at Magdala when it was stormed by General Napier, and like Queen Taitu he escaped after Theodore's suicide. But he fled North to join the forces of Ras Kassa, the chief who had cooperated with the British army in the defeat of Theodore. Kassa accepted him as one of his officers so long as he renounced Islam and was baptized into the Ethiopian Church, and this he appears to have done without any hesitation. Thereafter, he rose with his chief. Kassa inherited from the British the batteries of brass cannon and many other guns and supplies which Napier's expeditionary force left behind when they withdrew from Ethiopia, and with these powerful shots in his locker he felt strong enough to crown himself King of Kings and become Emperor John. Ras Mikael fought at his side until John was killed by the dervishes on the Sudan border in 1889.[9] He then retreated to Dessye with his Wollo Galla army and declared himself King of the Tribes, meanwhile watching closely the situation in Shoa. When Menelik emerged as

[8] Gleichen, incidentally, has him married to the wrong daughter of the Emperor and is confused about his progeny; but then so are most writers about Ethiopian princes.

[9] Ras Mikael was, in fact, about to lead a victory charge against the dervishes, who were all but defeated, when a stray shot killed John. The Ethiopians promptly panicked and fled, as they always do when they lose their leader.

unassailable Emperor he rode South to Addis Ababa to pledge his allegiance to the new ruler, and shortly afterwards the relationship was cemented by marriage to Menelik's daughter (who first quickly divorced her first husband). One of the results of that union was the birth of his son, Lij Yasu, and Ras Mikael was determined that when Menelik died it was this son who would become the new Negusa Nagast, or King of Kings. He was prepared to put his armies in the field to make sure of it.

The first sign that the Emperor Menelik's faculties were failing had come shortly before the death of Ras Makonnen. There had been another sign of weakness in the same year, and the watchful rases at the court had not missed its significance. The three powers with colonial territories on Ethiopia's frontiers (Britain in the Sudan and East Africa, Italy in Eritrea and France in Somaliland) were beginning to be perturbed by rumors of Menelik's failing health and, to their suspicious eyes, one of the confirmations that his guiding hand no longer gripped so strongly was an increase of German influence in the court; Queen Taitu was known to be pro-German. The French redoubled their efforts to get control of the railway (which was still a concession shared between the Emperor, M. Ilg and a French colleague M. Chefneux), and complete the section between Addis Ababa and Dire Dawa, where it had been dawdling ever since 1902.[10] Meanwhile the powers met in secret and, without consulting Menelik, concluded a Tripartite Treaty which, while acknowledging Ethiopian independence, proclaimed their right "in the event of rivalries or internal changes in Ethiopia" to intervene in protection of their nationals, and to act always in concert to safeguard their respective interests, these interests being: Great Britain's in the Nile basin and round Lake Tsana, in whose vicinity the Blue Nile springs; France's around the railway linking their port of Jibouti in French Somaliland with Dire Dawa and, eventually, they hoped, Addis Ababa; and Italy's over a crescent of territory linking Eritrea and Italian Somaliland.

In normal circumstances the Emperor would have reacted to such interference in his domestic affairs with reprisals. To adumbrate the dismemberment of his country while he was still alive was something which the Menelik of Adowa would not have stomached. It is true that he angrily demanded details of the Treaty which the powers

[10] They did succeed, a year later, in persuading Menelik to sign a new concession giving effective control of the railway to purely French interests.

had secretly signed, and a copy was hastily sent to him—with a reassurance that it dealt with purely hypothetical contingencies. But the
outburst of furious retaliation which the British, Italian and French
ministers in Addis Ababa apprehensively awaited did not come. Instead there was a long hiatus and it was not for several weeks that
Menelik sent his response. It was surprisingly mild.

"We have received the arrangement made by the Three Powers,"
the Emperor wrote. "We thank them for their communication, and
their desire to keep and maintain the independence of our Government. But let it be understood that this arrangement in no way limits
what we consider our sovereign rights."

It was the response of a man who seemed to have lost his will to
fight.

So indeed he had. The following year, 1907, he had another stroke,
and, as if anticipating that he would soon lose all control, he appointed
a Council of Ministers to advise him and to take responsibility in the
event of his incapacity; it was the first time in his life he had ever
delegated responsibility, and to all intents and purposes it was the
end of his autocracy. That year, Tafari's step-brother, Yilma, died
suddenly and the Governorship of Harar was once more vacant.
Tafari was now sixteen and remarkably mature, and he made it clear
to the court that he considered that now was the time to give him
his dues and award him the province for which his father had named
him heir. Unfortunately he was not allowed to press his claim with
the Emperor himself, who from this moment on was blocked from
callers and interceders by the formidable bulk of Queen Taitu herself.
The Council met and decided that Tafari was still too young to
acquire so vast and rich a province, and after some delay it was
awarded to Ras Balcha, Governor of Sidamo province; and Tafari
was informed that when he came of age, at eighteen, he would take
Balcha's place in Sidamo.

From that moment on, Menelik became a ghostly skeleton in the
palace closet from which, in the next few years, only vague and
sinister rattlings were heard. In 1908 the Emperor had another stroke,
this one more violent than all the rest, and both Queen Taitu and
Ras Mikael, convinced that his end was imminent, became frenetically
busy. The Queen summoned her cousin, Ras Gugsa, from Gondar,
and her brother from the Tigre, and they camped with their followers
outside the palace. Ras Mikael rode in from Dessye with his magnificent bodyguard, resplendent in crimson, and his Wollo Galla army.

Just before the end of the year, the council of ministers summoned the rases to the palace to hear an announcement from the Emperor, and they gathered in the *saganet* in tense expectancy. When the shawms sounded his imminent arrival the concourse fell to their knees and brought their foreheads to the ground; but presently someone risked a sidelong glance, and then another and another, and a murmuring sigh shivered through them. Menelik had been carried in by six huge Negroes on a canopied throne upon which poles had been slung. In front of him came the Affa Negus and then the Abuna. Beside him stood the Queen.

Was this the great Emperor who had unified Ethiopia for the first time for centuries, whose name was feared and respected by every race in the Empire, before whom the most arrogant rases had quailed? He had turned into a doddering old man. His beard was gray and ragged and spittle was oozing down it from his half-open mouth. His hand shook and his neck was twisted. It soon became apparent that he could not speak, though there were evidences that he was trying to do so—quivering of his lips, vague froglike sounds from his throat and desperate inhalations of breath.

It was the Abuna who spoke instead. The shawns sounded again and then the archbishop stepped forward to read the Imperial edict. The Emperor had considered and had decided that the time had come to name his heir. He had chosen his grandson. Lij Yasu, son of Ras Mikael, would follow him as Negusa Nagast, King of Kings, Emperor of Ethiopia.

The gaze of the rases was riveted on the Emperor until this moment, and they saw that if he could not speak at least he could make it clear how he was feeling, for he had begun to nod his head violently. But now their eyes moved first to Queen Taitu, from whom they got little enlightenment, for her smooth fat face was placid and she was staring, as if humbly, to the ground. After which they glanced around for Lij Yasu. He had entered the *saganet* at that moment with Ras Mikael, and with a self-confidence that belied his thirteen years, he moved up to the throne, flung himself down before it, and kissed the Emperor first on the foot and then on the knee. This done he moved to the other side of Queen Taitu and stared, with an arrogant smile, at the assembled rases.

But there was still time for Queen Taitu to recoup for herself or for her step-daughter. Menelik, though obviously dying, was not dead yet and Taitu still had his ear in his lucid moments. In the next few months she whispered into it busily, though not always with the success for which she hoped. The failing Emperor allowed her to push through the Council of Ministers various appointments that put her relatives in positions of power in the provinces. (She also got his consent to the appointment of Tafari as Governor of Sidamo. She had summed up Tafari as so loyal a subject of Menelik that he would accept without question the Emperor's nomination of Lij Yasu as heir to the throne, and might well resist any attempt to prevent its implementation. He was therefore better away, and he could hardly go further than Sidamo.) [11] But sometimes Menelik struggled through the enveloping coils of paralysis to the extent of being able to speak for a few moments. In May, 1909, he rallied sufficiently to summon yet another assembly of the rases in the *saganet* and here, through the Abun, he reaffirmed his decision to appoint Lij Yasu as his heir. "Cursed shall be he," went the proclamation, "who shall refuse to obey him and he shall have a black dog for a son. If on his part he shall betray you in an unworthy manner, he himself shall be accursed, and he shall beget for his son a black dog." Then, however, came a further announcement that cannot have given either Lij Yasu or Ras Mikael much pleasure: Menelik, convinced that his days were numbered, had decided to appoint a Regent to rule the country until such time as Lij Yasu reached an age of discretion. Nominated as Regent was a former general in Menelik's army, "our strong-armed, brave and incorruptible" Ras Tesemma.

The two years between 1909 and 1911 in Ethiopia seemed, to foreign observers, to bring that country to the nadir of chaos and corruption, but that was because they could not envisage what was going to happen in the years to come. At the time, however, it was difficult to see how much worse things could get. Regent Tesemma soon showed himself, in the words of the British Minister, Mr. Wilfred Thesiger, "to stand for everything that was most corrupt in officialdom." He did demonstrate some sense of discrimination, for though he made it clear that he was prepared to take bribes from everyone, it was only on behalf of Queen Taitu that he was really prepared to corrupt himself. For her he did everything possible to consolidate her position and to help her prosecute her ambition to rule the country, conniving at the appointment of her relatives to positions of power and the banishment of anyone likely to interfere with her

[11] On the Southern frontiers of Ethiopia.

plans. In 1910 Ras Mikael persuaded the Council of Ministers to protest against the powers which she had arrogated to herself—for by this time Tesemma had become a willing puppet in her hands—and he promised to back any action which they took with his own army. The Council hesitated. Then the British, French and Italians intervened with expressions of concern at what was happening at court. German influence was growing. Queen Taitu had even called in a German "adviser" and banished the Francophile M. Ilg. Arms were pouring into the country from smugglers anchoring off the Somaliland shore. The slave trade, which had at least been kept undercover during Menelik's days of power, had come out into the open and long lines of fettered Gallas, Sidamos and Sudanis could be seen shuffling towards the auction blocks in the market place.

At last the Council plucked up its courage. The Abun denounced both the Queen for her arrogance and Tesemma for his laxity and lack of loyalty to his oath to the Emperor. Taitu decided that discretion was the watchword for the moment and retired to her *elfin* with her all but moribund husband. Her only activity for the time being was to get her step-daughter, Zauditu, free from her marital entanglements and into the marriage bed with her cousin, Ras Gugsa. As for Ras Tesemma, he promised that he would in the future be loyal to his oath and impartial in all his rulings, and that no one would have cause to mistrust him again.

This may have been enough for the Council of Ministers but it was not enough for Ras Mikael, and he demanded that Tesemma be dismissed and banished. But while the council havered and hesitated something happened which would have been a fantastic coincidence anywhere else but caused no particular surprise in Ethiopia. Ras Tesemma too, like his Emperor, had a stroke and Ras Tesemma, too, was paralyzed so that he could no longer move or speak.

He did not, however, live through it as long as Menelik. He was stricken on March 2, 1911 and he died four weeks later. His body was smuggled out of the palace and transported to Debra Libanos where, it was announced, he had gone to take a "cure" at the mineral baths. It was not until the end of May that his death was announced.

That was when chaos really came to Ethiopia.

Galvanized by the news of Tesemma's demise the rases began to move in on the city, bringing their armies with them. "Addis Ababa is like an armed camp," reported the British Minister, Mr. Wilfred Thesiger. "There is a great difficulty in doing business with anyone

for no one is willing to take responsibility." He speculated whether
the Council of Ministers would now appoint another Regent and
listed the possibilities. He thought that the most popular choice
(among the Shoan chiefs, at least) would be a veteran chieftain from
the North, Ras Walda Giorgis, "who is possibly the only man whose
authority is generally recognised." Walda Giorgis, a cousin of Menelik
and extraordinarily like him in appearance, "is a devout churchman,
a heavy drinker and distrusts all foreigners." But he added, he was a
chief of great influence with the Shoan rases, most of whom found
little to choose between the two main protagonists at Court. They
had resented Queen Taitu's nepotism and they feared Lij Yasu and
Ras Mikael would curtail their privileges in favor of the Wollo
chiefs.

Unfortunately, Thesiger went on, Ras Walda Giorgis "hasn't arrived yet" (he was fighting rebels in Tigre) but might well, if he
came in time, be not only a candidate for Regent but "a possible
claimant to the throne. His nephew, Fitaurari Tanje, is another
hope, but he is now a prisoner at Dessye, his health ruined by prison
and dope. Walda Giorgis has demanded his release." In the circumstances, that seemed unlikely since Dessye was Ras Mikael's capital
and he controlled the dungeons; he was hardly likely to unlock the
door to a rival to his son.

Who else was in the running? There was, went on Thesiger, a
powerful member of the Council of Ministers, Fitaurari Hapta
Giorgis (no relation to Walda Giorgis, Ethiopian names work dif-
ferently). But no, that was unlikely, since he was not of royal blood.
In any case, he had thrown in his lot with Lij Yasu and Ras Mikael.

Ah, but what about Ras Abata? He had moved into the city from
the South with a large army and was now encamped on the slopes
outside the palace. It was rumored that Abata had a daring plan.
He had once been on intimate terms with Zauditu, the Emperor's
daughter, even, it was said, to the extent of entering a *damoz* or
temporary marriage with her, from which Zauditu had been wrenched
by her father. Now in Ethiopia it has long been recognized that a
suitor who cannot persuade the parents of the bride he desires, is
justified in kidnapping her—providing he can penetrate the parental
defences and persuade the girl to elope. This, reported Thesiger on
June 2, 1911, with admirably controlled excitement, was what Ras
Abata seemed to be planning. "He arrived at the gates of the palace
and demanded admittance. . . . It is rumoured that he wants to marry

Zauditu, proclaim himself Regent" and make Zauditu Queen, "seeking as far back as Sheba for precedents."

The gates of the palace remained closed and Abata was instructed by Queen Taitu to go on his way. Instead, he called on the soldiers waiting a little distance away to bring forth a tent. This he had erected in front of the palace gates and inside the tent went Ras Abata, while his army of 3,000 men encamped around him.

It was not only the Legation which was watching him now but all Addis Ababa, and all the rases. What would happen next? Would Ras Abata storm the gates and snatch his bride?

Suddenly it was all over. A horseman flying Ras Abata's pennon galloped up to his master's tent and disappeared inside. Then came three robed figures on mules, one of whom was seen to be the Abuna. He too went into the tent. A few minutes later Abata emerged and ordered the tent to be struck. He did not wait to see it done but mounted his horse and, the Abuna with him, led his troops away. The watchers did not have to wait long to discover why. From the distance came the sound of one-note horns and over the brow of the hill came a vast army of excited soldiers, firing their guns in the air and shrieking battle cries. At their head was Fitaurari Hapta Giorgis, and, beside him on a bucking Arab pony, the small figure of the tiny heir to the throne, Lij Yasu in a violet hat, white breeches, violet shirt and red and gold silk robe.

This time the palace gates swung open and Lij Yasu and Hapta Giorgis rode inside. It looked as if it was all over and that the Heir had overawed his rivals and made them recognize that, with Menelik a sick and helpless man, he alone was powerful enough to act as Emperor-designate. Even the British Legation seemed ready to accept him as the winner of the trial of strength and influence. On June 23, 1911, the British Minister, Mr. Thesiger, invited Lij Yasu to dine with him as the Emperor's representative at a Legation banquet to celebrate the Coronation Day of King George V. It was a spectacular occasion. Among the other guests were the Abuna and the Itchege, thus giving the Church's blessing to Lij Yasu, and all the rases with the exception of Ras Abata (who had taken refuge in the Abuna's house, loudly denying he had ever planned to kidnap Zauditu). Tafari came too (for he had been in Addis Ababa for the past month), and he hastened to make friendly overtures to his cousin, Lij Yasu. The British Minister made a speech in which he toasted the health of Lij Yasu and wished prosperity and unity to

Ethiopia.[12] And then everyone—200 guests in the house, 1,200 soldiers in the compound—settled down to eat and drink.

It was the first occasion that the British Minister was to see Lij Yasu get helplessly drunk, but it was certainly not the last. The heir to the throne was just sixteen, and he had other vices too.

[12] He had intended to present a GCVO (Grand Cross of the Victorian Order) to the Ethiopian Foreign Minister, Igazu, but the telegram authorizing it was delayed. It was just as well. A few days later Lij Yasu arrested the Foreign Minister on a charge of high treason.

chapter three

THE ARROGANT PRINCE

TAFARI WAS in Addis Ababa at the moment of Lij Yasu's apotheosis because, at long last, he had come into his father's inheritance. In one of his last moments of clarity before the shutters came down over his mind, the Emperor Menelik had signed a decree nominating his kinsman to be Governor of Harar, and enlisted the aid of the Abun to drive it through the Council of Ministers. But it would not have gone any further had not Lij Yasu now confirmed the arrangement. In return he extracted a *quid pro quo* from Tafari which was to have an important effect upon future events. "I give you Harar, cousin," he said. "But I want you to swear on oath in return that so long as I sustain you in Harar, so long will you give me your undivided loyalty." To this Tafari agreed and formally took the oath.

Ras Balcha was to exchange provinces with Tafari and once more take over Sidamo, and he too was in the capital. Tafari had only to look at Balcha's legions to realize that many months of repair and maintenance lay ahead once he reached Harar. The soldiers must have stripped the province bare; they carried with them vast stores of grain, of tej and *chat* (to which many of them had become addicted), and every man seemed to have brought with him at least one Galla girl as concubine. "A rearrangement of provinces is always a popular move with soldiers," Thesiger wrote about this time. "For those that leave a province sweep up all they can and those that enter it take the rest. After which the poor province rests for a few years to prepare for a new Governor." In fact Tafari had left Sidamo with plenty of flesh clinging to its carcass; the natives had been sorry to see him go, for though he had regularly sent to Addis Ababa the tribute which the Imperial Government demanded and had not stinted himself or his troops, he had been careful to leave an adequate margin for the villagers. He had learned from his father's administration in Harar that a village taxed of only half of its produce grows more and pays more than one left with only ten percent of its crop. Never of his soldiers, he was determined, would it be said, as it was of Balcha's and Walda Giorgis's and Mikael's that "they come among us like a plague of locusts and pick us clean."

The eighteen months in Sidamo had been good for Tafari and matured him in more ways than one; he was nineteen years old now and manhood sat easily and securely on his shoulders. He had learned to run a province with a population of nearly a million people and run it, moreover, with no trained administrators to help him, for they did not exist. It was he who assessed the taxes, judged the disputants, sentenced the criminals, led punitive raids against the slave traders and ivory poachers; it was his first taste of autocratic power and he would not have been human, or young, if he had resisted all its temptations. "The Governor of a Province in Ethiopia," wrote M. Zaphiro, a famous Oriental Secretary at the British Legation in Addis Ababa, "is paid no salary, and he and his officers and soldiers must live off the land they administer. He is all powerful as nowhere else in the modern world with the possible exception of China. It is a position not without its dangers to a weak, dishonest and even normally susceptible man, for it is unlikely that any form of corruptive influence will be overlooked by those anxious to curry favour. The average Ethiopian is not known to lack an appetite for the pleasures of the flesh and many of the rases are gluttons for it. This is a land where the currency of bribery is more likely to be a man's nubile daughter than this chest of Maria Theresa dollars."

To judge how a nature less firmly based than Tafari's could be twisted by the intoxicating potentialities of power in this country will be seen when this narrative deals further with his cousin, Lij Yasu. For Tafari himself it was a baptism (or perhaps one should say a marination) which taught him many lessons and ripened him in experience. He committed his youthful follies and he made his mistakes, but he emerged the richer for it. (It must be admitted that he did not do so badly in material ways, too; he had managed well in Sidamo *without* paring the natives to the bone.) Now he was on his way to the province and the position for which all this had been a preparation; and after the depredations of Ras Balcha, Harar would be glad to see its native son.

But first there was a personal matter to be attended to in Addis

Ababa. Lij Yasu had asked him, with a sly smile: "Is the gossip true, cousin? Have you fallen in love with Menen? Then," airily, "take her. I give her to you with my blessing. She will bind us closer together."

Waizero Menen was Lij Yasu's niece (the daughter of a much older half sister) and one of the loveliest girls at the court, but hardly his to give away. She was already married to Lul Seged, a Southern war-lord, to whom she had been given as a bride—with the approval of Ras Mikael, her grandfather, and her father, a Galla chief—at the age of thirteen. After two years with him, she had run away and gone into hiding in Addis Ababa—for Lul Seged was furious at her desertion and determined to get her back, by force if necessary. It was at the palace that Tafari had first seen her and fallen in love, a passion that was more than reciprocated by Menen. Now plans were in train for her divorce and her departure for Harar, where she would be safe with Tafari's relatives until a Church marriage could be arranged.

Tafari made his discreet arrangements with the Abun. By the time Lul Seged discovered what was afoot he was on his way to Harar with his bride-to-be, and it was too late for Lul Seged to follow them. He stayed behind and plotted revenge against Lij Yasu, for having "given away" his wife, as he believed. He was reported shortly afterwards by Thesiger to be "involved in a plot against the prince with Ras Balcha. Lul Seged is offended because he believed Lij Yasu gave away his young wife to Dejaz Tafari." But when this plot was discovered, Lul Seged made his peace with the prince (Ras Balcha was deprived of Sidamo and flung into jail) and turned his resentment in Tafari's direction. Ethiopians are usually a broadminded and forgiving race, but Lul Seged never forgave Tafari and never ceased to hanker after his lovely young wife. The time would come when he would be in the position to exact a very sweet revenge indeed.

But that was later. Meanwhile, Dejazmach Tafari Makonnen and Waizero Menen were married by a bishop in 1912. It was a union that was to prove both fruitful and happy—though not without its moments of mortal danger for both of them.

It is time now, I think, to write in more detail about the character and activities of Tafari's cousin, Lij Yasu, for it was his behavior and his attitudes of mind that were shaping Tafari's future.

One of the strange facets of Ethiopian character is its capacity for forgiveness. There are exceptions, as has been mentioned in the case of Lul Seged, but on the whole Ethiopians just do not seem to cherish hatred and resentment, even against their enemies. It is quite usual for a victim to come before a court of law in Addis Ababa or Harar or Gondar and publicly forgive the man who has robbed or tried to kill him. The result is that the culprit is immediately set free. Time and again in Ethiopian history, cases are recorded of traitors pardoned, their crimes forgotten and their fortunes restored. Among foreigners living in Ethiopia today none is more popular than the Italian; their poison-gas bombs, their massacre of Ethiopian youth, may not have been forgotten but they have certainly been forgiven.

This amiable trait is nowhere more surprising in its effect than in the case of Lij Yasu. In his lifetime he was a shabby tyrant with hardly a discoverable virtue. Between 1911 and 1916 he broke up the Empire which Menelik had painfully put together and brought Ethiopia to a state of chaos in which she was all but taken over by the colonial powers. He tortured, massacred and raped his people and enslaved them in thousands. Yet Ethiopians remember him today with a gentle sigh rather than the heavy groan which his misdeeds would seem to merit. Such a clever young man, they will tell you; so full of promise and ideas. What a pity he dabbled with Islam and had such venal advisers; he might otherwise have made a great Emperor.

This is arrant nonsense which is in danger, if it is not corrected, of getting into Ethiopian history books, and that would be carrying sentimentalization too far. It is true, however, that Lij Yasu could probably not help acting in the way he did and should not be held entirely responsible for his misdeeds, since he was almost certainly an epileptic and was subject to violent brainstorms.[1]

It seems certain that Queen Taitu was aware of his proneness to fits and decided to profit from his infirmities, either by driving him completely mad or by sapping his strength until he became a willing puppet. From the moment that he was proclaimed heir by Menelik, in 1908 (when he was barely thirteen), she set about systematically debauching him. He proved to be a willing victim, but the appetite for wine and sex which she cultivated in him did not, as she hoped, put him in her power. In the business of procuring there were

[1] On August 21, 1911, Mr. Wilfred Thesiger, the British Minister, reported that Lij Yasu was ill in the house of Fitaurari Hapta Giorgis. It was said "that a devil comes by night and shakes him, so that he wants to kill people, but in a little time he falls insensible."

practitioners in Addis Ababa with rather more exotic specialities than Queen Taitu had available, and they quickly began to develop and refine the taste which she had stimulated. So that, far from being grateful to her, Lij Yasu became suspicious of her willingness to pander to his whims and guessed, rightly, of course, that her motives were ulterior. Matters came to a head a few days after he and Fitaurari Hapta Giorgis had driven off Ras Abata and stormed the palace. Queen Taitu made haste to make Yasu welcome and organized a series of banquets in his honor; but after a few days he departed hurriedly with a stomach-ache to the house of Hapta Giorgis, complaining that the Queen had tried to poison him. She had, in fact, contrived to give him something rather more complicated and far-reaching than poison, as he was to discover a few weeks later.

The day-by-day diary of the British Legation in Addis Ababa during 1911 and 1912 gives a succinct picture of life at this time and it reads like the twilight of a régime, of an Empire crumbling into chaos. With the exception of Harar, where the return of Tafari had been joyfully received, the country was rapidly being torn apart by rival rases. Ras Mikael himself was waging a bloody campaign in Wollo to put down a pretender to his province. There was revolt in the Tigre. Arms smuggling was so rife that the British, French and Italians decided to protest in the name of the Brussels Act, which had been signed in 1890 to control arms traffic and slave-trading in Ethiopia. But they knew before they made it that their approach to the Shoan Council of Ministers could not possibly be effective, since the Council had no control over the rases.

"There is an epidemic of robbery in Addis Ababa just now," reported Thesiger on August 21, 1911. "Armed raiders wait until the fall of darkness and then attack houses, and even the compounds of the foreign legations. Last night they fired into the Italian Legation. The raiders are believed to be the soldiers of discontented chiefs (Ras Abata's, mostly) who wish to embarrass Lij Yasu. The peasants are frightened of coming into the town, and no food is arriving, and this increases the restlessness. The country is full of hungry soldiers slave-raiding and poaching ivory." He added: "Lij Yasu is still in the house of Hapta Giorgis full of caprice and in indifferent health. . . . The boy demanded that the Emperor and Empress be sent away and that he be crowned Emperor immediately. He was followed by a mixed crowd of Armenians, Turks, Greeks, and Abyssinians who are said to have encouraged him in various silly orgies. He beat Menelik's officers with a stick and struck Ministers, in full public view, on the polo ground."

On September 30, Thesiger noted that Menelik's soldiers had not been paid and were in an ugly mood. They were reported to have sent a delegation to Lij Yasu and threatened to take over the city if the money were not forthcoming. "Lij Yasu tried to borrow from the Bank of Abyssinia, but there was no cash there. It had all been spent on Japanese rifles." So Lij Yasu decided on drastic action. He marched a battalion of his father's troops to the palace with the object of forcing Queen Taitu to reveal the whereabouts of Menelik's treasure chest, which was rumored to be hidden somewhere in the cellars. The commander of the palace guard, Gabre Mariam, with foolhardy ideas of loyalty, slammed the gates in Lij Yasu's face and prepared to resist; but his determination was stouter than that of his men, and after a few bursts of fire from Lij Yasu's machine-gunners, the gates were opened. Gabre Mariam was carried off in chains. Lij Yasu and Hapta Giorgis began a search of the palace, and eventually penetrated to the cellars beneath the *elfin*. There they found a blubbering Menelik and a defiant Taitu cowering beside three great chests filled with Maria Theresa dollars and a storehouse filled with animal skins and bars of silver and gold.

The soldiers were paid off and, in Addis Ababa, at least, the situation improved. "The robberies have been put down by reprisals," reported Thesiger in September. "One thief who was wounded in an attack on a house was forced to walk around bleeding and shouting his crime until he fell dead. Several have been hanged publicly or cut in pieces by swords, or had their legs cut off, or flogged—and forced to recite their thefts between lashes." But a few weeks later he was writing that conditions had once more deteriorated. "Lij Yasu has left Addis Ababa and there is no immediate prospect of his return. He is reported to be only four days away from the capital but he refuses to return until the Council of Ministers allows him to be crowned at once. The majority feel this is impossible so long as Menelik still lives.... Trade is at a standstill and there is no money in the exchequer. The Government has practically ceased to exist. Any change will be an improvement on the present chaos." But change for what or whom? "The last nine months," wrote Thesiger, "have proved the incapacity of the Council of Ministers. So long as Menelik continues to live and Lij Yasu cannot be crowned, his position remains uncertain. At the moment he is at the mercy of the Council, who are his masters at the art of intrigue. Will he come to power, aided by Ras Mikael and Ras Walda Giorgis? And if so, shall we (the British, Italians and French) support him?

Thesiger must by this time have been well aware of the nature of Lij Yasu, for now his excesses were common knowledge. He had embarked, with ferocious enthusiasm, on a series of slaving expeditions and was doing a thriving business selling his victims to the Danakils and Somalis "men for eighty dollars, virgins (what few of them he leaves) at one hundred dollars, and children for thirty dollars each. He treats them with abominable cruelty." He was making little or no effort to rid himself of the syphilis with which Queen Taitu had arranged to have him infected. He had developed a considerable taste for blood, the more spectacularly shed the better, and did not consider a day well started until he had watched a flogging or two. But his most considerable crime so far had been committed in April, 1912, in the Danakil desert, whither he had gone with two ostensible purposes—to shoot lion and to bring to heel a number of Danakil tribes which had been raiding Ethiopian settlements. The news of the approach of Yasu and his troops preceded him and the tribesmen disappeared into the fastnesses of the desert. Thereupon, the prince decided that he would not be cheated of blood and ordered his horsemen to put to the sword the inhabitants of three villages, none of which had any connection with the raiders. About one hundred Danakil maidens, who are famed for their looks, were reserved for the attentions of Yasu and his officers before being sold on the slave market, but the rest of the inhabitants of the villages were massacred—3,000 in all. "It was simply because he likes the sight of blood," Thesiger wrote. There were one or two of his officers, sickened by the slaughter, who reported that he also had acquired a taste for mutilation.

"There was one maiden who struck out at Lij Yasu when she saw him swing her baby brother by the feet and smash his head against a rock," wrote one of the officers, in a report to Count Colli, the Italian Minister. "Her nail scraped the prince's face and caused it to bleed, and he was infuriated. He had the girl pinioned to the ground and stood over her, whipping the buttocks of his men as they successively raped her. Then he took his sword and sliced off her breasts, leaving her to lie and bleed in the sun. I crept over to her at nightfall and killed her before the hyenas got to her."

Knowing of these atrocities, Thesiger could still write: "This country can be ruled only by autocratic power resting in the hands of one man. Shall we counteract his youth and inexperience and back him?" And added, of the Danakil expedition: "What his real nature may be remains yet to be seen, but there is no doubt that his character has developed very much during the past year, and the fact that he has killed his man in battle and shot his elephant (both necessary proofs of manhood in Abyssinian eyes) will have given him assurance and self-confidence, and it may be taken for granted that the boy who left Addis Ababa earlier this year will return a man to be reckoned with." But not, it soon became clear, in the way that Thesiger was thinking.

For the moment, so far as the British, French and Italians were concerned, Lij Yasu was still the best bulwark they had against the lapping tides of German and Turkish influence in Ethiopia, for both those countries were busy buying all the support they could at Court, and seemed to prefer, for the moment, to put their money on the Shoan chiefs in Addis Ababa.

But they hastily changed their tactics when, on December 12, 1913, the Emperor Menelik died at last. The living corpse of a once great ruler had revived sufficiently on one occasion during the past two years to realize the humiliation of his situation; two priests arrived from Greece and laved his head, face and neck with holy water they had brought with them from Mount Athos, at which he is supposed to have whispered "God help my people!" and burst into tears. Now the life had gone at last from his rotting body; but though the rumor of his passing soon spread through the city, no official announcement was made of his death. Crowds who gathered outside the Palace were driven away with staves, and Queen Taitu and Princess Zauditu, her step-daughter, were packed away to a convent on Mount Entoto. As for Lij Yasu, he consented to return to the capital at last and an orgy of feasting and wenching went on for several days, until the arrival in Addis Ababa of Ras Mikael, "the only one who has any control of the prince," wrote Thesiger. The British Minister had been to see Yasu to talk about the Emperor's death but found him "too intoxicated to take in what was said." But so long as his father was in the city, Lij Yasu behaved himself and obeyed his orders; and the old man (Ras Mikael was now nearly seventy) outlined plans whereby his son could make himself and his position secure. For the moment Menelik's death should remain unannounced (there would even be occasional appearances of the Emperor's *likamaquas*, or double, to create the impression among the people that he was still alive) and, in the meantime, anyone with the remotest chance of challenging Yasu's claim to the throne

Emperor Menelik II (1844-1913)

H.I.M. the Emperor, eleven years old, with his father, Ras Makonnen

An Ethiopian rock church

would be summoned to Addis Ababa, ostensibly to discuss plans for the coronation. Ras Mikael let it be known in diplomatic circles that his son would probably be crowned in October, 1914, at the end of the Maskal celebrations.[2] In fact, the Archbishop (Abuna Mattheos) had made it clear that he would refuse to officiate at any crowning ceremony until Lij Yasu was at least twenty years old and had shown evidence of settling down (he would not be twenty until 1916). The ruse worked, however, and Menelik's blood relations gathered in Addis Ababa in April, 1914, for the bogus conference. Among them was Tafari. Fortunately for him, his intelligence system was superior to that of his cousins; for they were swiftly rounded up, chained and dispatched to be immured in remoter parts of the land, where they would do no harm and offer no threat to Yasu's succession.[3] It might have been simpler to kill them, but an ancient Ethiopian law forbids the execution of any prince of royal blood. Tafari was warned in time that Ras Mikael was planning to arrest him and take him back with him to Dessye, where he would no doubt spend the rest of his days in chains in a dungeon. He summoned his horsemen, left behind an announcement that his wife had been taken seriously ill, and departed under cover of darkness for Harar. He was well into the mountains before news reached the palace that he was gone.

There was still no announcement of Menelik's death, and until that came, plus at least forty days of official mourning, there could be no question of a coronation for Yasu, even should he insist upon it over the opposition of the Abun. But if his son was not yet in a posture to put a crown on his head, Ras Mikael saw no reason why he should not give himself some royal preferment. On May 30, 1914, he caused Bishop Petros of Axum to crown him King of Wollo, Tigre and Begemeder in the Cathedral at Dessye. It was a promotion that was not without its risks, for Begemeder was part of the territory over which Mikael's erstwhile enemy, Ras Walda Giorgis, held sway; and the populace nervously waited to see whether Walda

---

[2] News which caused something of a convulsion at the British Legation, where the minister had been told by the Foreign Office that HM Government's coronation present must not cost more than £500. The Austrians, Germans and Turks were all planning to give presents costing at least £2,000 each. (It was finally decided to offer Yasu an extra £10,000 as a personal present if he would sign an agreement giving control of Lake Tsana to Britain.)

[3] A throwback to an old Ethiopian royal custom. In olden times, an Emperor would banish his immediate male relatives to a remote mountain-top fortress, where they were given every comfort but never allowed to leave.

Giorgis would put his armies into the field to avenge this insult to him. But the wily old war-lord made no move. His inertia may have been due to sickness among his troops (3,000 of whom had died from typhus in the past few months) but it was more likely to be because, though Mikael had taken Begemeder for his title, Walda Giorgis still held it as part of his territory. So the coronation took place without martial interruptions and was the occasion of great feasting and bizarre celebration in which the latest batch of captives taken by Lij Yasu on a slave-raiding expedition played their part.

Mikael himself is said to have produced a new Queen for the occasion, having divorced his wife in favor of a thirteen-year-old daughter of a Galla chief from Gojjam. Ras Hailu, King of Gojjam, came to Dessye as one of the honored guests, and he announced that as a gesture of friendship to Mikael he would divorce his own wife and marry one of Mikael's daughters.[4] Lij Yasu's coronation present to his father was the bulk of Menelik's treasure chest (with the exception of the Maria Theresa dollars) from the vaults under the palace consisting of great quantities of skins, jewels, ornaments and some bars of gold. But the son, having promised, failed to appear for his father's great occasion. He was "at Filwaha with his too numerous concubines and refused to see anyone," reported Major J. H. Dodds, the British chargé d'affaires. He added, coldly: "Lij Yasu spends his night in revelry, or rather debauchery, and often lies abed until midday while chiefs hang around till he gets up." Some of them were beginning to grow restless, Dodds believed, "and I doubt that he will mount the throne without some opposition." But it was not all revelry for Lij Yasu. There were days when he locked himself in darkened rooms and would see no one and eat and drink nothing; he had been told that the wife of a murdered chief had put a curse on him, and he was afraid for his life. He loathed Addis Ababa and was in process of concocting a plan to leave a viceroy in the capital and move his own headquarters either to Ankober or somewhere beyond the Awash River where he felt freer. One of the things that most disturbed him in Addis Ababa was the imminent arrival of the railway, for "he has superstitious fears about the changes it will bring." He was hoping that the enmity between his father and Ras Walda Giorgis would be ended if he gave the Northern half of the country to Mikael, and made Walda Giorgis viceroy (with control from Addis

---

[4] He seems to have changed his mind later. What he did, instead, was present his own daughter to Lij Yasu. The unhappy girl, somewhat the worse for wear, was returned to her father in 1916.

Ababa) of Shoa and the south. "This would, in effect, give the country two governments," wrote Thesiger, "thus enabling Yasu to hold the balance between the two and live a life of ease, which is what he wants to do."

The outbreak of the European War in August, 1914, made, at first, little impact on Ethiopia; there were too many rumors about that the country was about to have a war of its own. The rains had begun early that year and were exceptionally heavy, a sure sign to the superstitious that war was imminent. Then, too, it was said that the Shoan chiefs in Addis Ababa had at long last stirred from their torpor and were discussing what steps could be taken to curb Lij Yasu's excesses. Thesiger reported, during a trek from Addis Ababa to Nairobi via Moyale, that the chiefs in the South were beginning to talk of revolt and that they were mentioning the name of Tafari as the man who should lead them. Ras Mikael appears to have heard the rumors himself, for "he is buying all the arms he can lay his hands on, and instructed his troops to be ready after Maskal (mid-September). Lij Yasu has also ordered his troops to be ready after Maskal, and to fatten their mules." In fact every chief in the country was busy buying arms, which were pouring in despite the decision of the colonial powers to close Jibouti to the trade; they were coming in, instead, by Arab dhows which landed along the coast.

The rains came to an end and the Ethiopians lighted their Maskal bonfires with a certain apprehension, for they might well turn into the signal fires for an uprising. Nothing happened. The Shoan chiefs had lost their courage, after quarrelling among themselves; and, in any case, Tafari had made it clear that he was unwilling to join in any conspiracy. He was convinced that it was too soon and that the conditions were not yet ripe for his cousin's usurpation. In any case he had sworn an oath of loyalty. But he had already begun to realize on what grounds, when the time came, Lij Yasu would be driven from his positions of power if and when someone was bold enough to unseat him. They would not be the grounds of sexual excess, barbarous cruelty or lack of interest in the affairs of government, faults which the Ethiopians had long since come to accept as normal in their rulers. Lij Yasu was making himself vulnerable by indulging in something much more dangerous in a land with a powerful as well as an Established Church: apostasy.

It will no doubt be remembered that Yasu's father, Ras Mikael, has been born a Moslem and was forcibly converted to Christianity by Emperor John. But it should be emphasized that Mikael never gave any sign afterwards that he regretted his own apostasy or that he sought to urge his son back to the religion of his ancestors. Far from it. When the fact became apparent to him that Yasu was contemplating a conversion to Islam, he bombarded him with messages beseeching him to remain a Christian and, later on, publicly prayed in the Cathedral at Dessye that he remain steadfast to the Ethiopian Church.

What was it that finally turned Lij Yasu toward Mecca? Until 1914, most of the Shoan chiefs (and the Allied diplomats) had continued to believe that his sole interest in Moslems was confined to flogging Danakil tribesmen, raping Galla girls and selling Somali children. It was Tafari who warned them that the tyrant was in imminent danger of being converted by his victims. Tafari, as Governor of Harar, had for some time been troubled by the activities of marauding tribesmen in the Ogaden, a great tract of desert country which marches from Harar down to British Somaliland. Most of the raiders were minions of an anti-British Moslem leader known as the Mad Mullah.

These tribesmen, when captured by Tafari's men, pleaded to be set free. "We are all brothers, now," they said. "Soon a prophet will rise in your own country and free you from your infidel masters, and then we will all be as one, from the Nile to the Red Sea, true believers in the One God." Tafari's men, though most of them were Moslems themselves, did not take too kindly to this kind of haranguing from the Somalis, and the prisoners were brought into Harar for more rigorous questioning. There they implicated a certain Mr. Ydlibi, the Turkish consul-general in Harar, in what Tafari at first believed was a conspiracy to involve Lij Yasu without his knowledge in intrigues against the Allies. Ydlibi,[5] the prisoners claimed, had visited the Mad Mullah in the Ogaden and promised that the Ethiopian Government under Lij Yasu would send him arms and aid him in his campaign against the British.

Tafari hastened to send this news to Addis Ababa and asked permission to expel Ydlibi from the city and lead an expeditionary force to drive the Mad Mullah's legions from the Ogaden. He was astounded by Yasu's reaction to his message. The prince sent a telegram warning him to make no move either against the Turkish consul or into

[5] A suave entrepreneur of great culture and charm, by birth half-Syrian and half-English. He had been brought up in Woking.

the Ogaden, which, Yasu told him, was from that moment on no longer under his control. The governorship of the area was being transferred to someone whom Thesiger was later on to refer to as "a notorious Harar Arab" named Abdullai Sadik.

Even now Tafari had still no inkling that Lij Yasu was about to espouse Islam. Not until later did he learn that Sadik, well subsidized by the Turkish and German Legations in Addis Ababa, had been working hard at his subornation for some time with every kind of temptation—worldly and spiritual. He had weaned the young prince away from wine but introduced him to the more aphrodisiac promises, if not realities of, hashish. He had "given him one of his own daughters and supplied him with other women," as Thesiger reported, and these women were enjoined to give him not just sexual service but spiritual reassurance by convincing him that true believers—but true believers only—went to a paradise where sensual delights never ceased. But Abdullai Sadik also promised something else if he followed his inclinations and turned to Islam: power. Power not only over Ethiopia but also over a large slice of Africa. Did he not know the prophecy among Moslems that the new Mahdi would arise from an unexpected quarter, but would be descended from Mahomet's daughter, Fatima? And had it not already been confirmed by the Vali of Yemen that Yasu's genealogical table showed him to be a descendant, on his father's side, of Fatima? The Moslems of Somaliland, Eritrea and the Sudan were waiting for him to liberate them, and Constantinople and the Central Powers would bless him for it.

All this Tafari did not know for the moment. Nor did he guess that Lij Yasu's reaction to his protest against Ydlibi was to presume his awareness of the prince's intrigues with the Turks. Through the British Consulate in Harar, Tafari received a friendly warning that Yasu, in an extremely angry mood, was on his way to Harar and that he should beware—he was in danger. Tafari was never one to ignore a warning of this kind, but he did not believe for a moment that in this case it was true.

On February 25, 1915, Lij Yasu left for Harar with his followers. "He has an attack of syphillis," reported Thesiger, and added: "He is practically crippled by venereal disease and quite unfit to travel but he insists on going. So far as can be ascertained there is no important purpose for the journey, but a certain apprehension exists lest he may be tempted to take some action against Dejaz Tafari, generally regarded as heir to the throne if anything happens to Lij Yasu."

On arrival in Harar, the prince behaved quite recklessly and no longer concealed his sympathy with Islam. "He spent three hours in the Mosque and has since been intimate with Abdullai Sadik and other Moslems. . . . This friendship with Moslems has naturally given rise to very severe criticism."

Thesiger commented: "In Addis Ababa comments on the prince's debauched habits are even more outspoken, and many of the officers are openly saying that if Tafari does not seize the opportunity now of chaining up Lij Yasu and putting himself on the throne it will be a pity." Thesiger added that he did not think Tafari was ready to move "or will be strong minded enough to take this course, but it is fairly certain that these reports will come to the ears of Lij Yasu and considerable anxiety is felt for Tafari's safety. It is reported that Lij Yasu will go from Harar to Dessye and wants Tafari to go with him. If he does, he will almost certainly be put in chains once he reaches Ras Mikael's country."

Tafari was far too wise to leave the protection of his own troops in Harar, and since Lij Yasu's overt espousal of Islam during his visit, his feelings of loyalty toward his cousin had undergone considerable change. But he was still not ready to lead, or even take part in, any conspiracy against his rule: he felt himself still bound by his oath; he still had to be convinced that Yasu was truly evil beyond all redemption; and that he could not be dissuaded from his apostasy. It needed a tragic event to change his mind and stir him into action.

One of Tafari's pleasures when the weather got too hot in summer was not, like his father, Ras Makonnen, to make for the cool air of the mountains of Ejarsa Gora but for the cool breezes of Lake Aramayo, some ten miles outside the city on the road to Dire Dawa. The lake is broad, deep and fringed with pleasant woods. It is a favorite gathering place for pelicans, coot, Egyptian geese and many game birds, which, since the Ethiopians do not much go in for duck-shooting and such, are quite tame. On Lake Aramayo Tafari had a small boat which he, Ras Imru and his friend and tutor-companion, Aba Samuel, liked to row about on the lake while they discussed problems of administration. Lij Yasu was aware of the pleasant habit of his cousin, had himself been out to the lake and knew that Tafari was going there on the day that he himself left for Dessye. That afternoon, in the middle of the lake, the boat sprang a leak and quickly sank. Tafari and Imru struggled ashore, dragging Aba Samuel, who could not swim, between them; but by the time they got there, Aba Samuel was dead.

He had been a beloved friend and a close confidant of Tafari's since childhood and his death affected him deeply. Did he blame Lij Yasu for the tragedy? There are stories in Harar that a Moslem servant later confessed. He said he had been paid by one of the prince's attendants to make a hole in the boat and fill it with mud which would soften and fall out after a time in the water. Whether this is true is something that will probably never be known. What is certain is that after the death of Aba Samuel, Tafari's attitude towards Lij Yasu changed and he no longer held out any hope of the prince's conversion to saner and more civilized ways. This is not to say that Tafari took immediate and precipitate action against his cousin, but he hesitated now not so much because of his oath. It has been stressed before in this story that one of his most admirable qualities was patience; he was always willing to wait his opportunity. He had a strong instinct for self-preservation and an uncanny knack of knowing just when to strike.

From the viewpoint of the Allied Legations, the striking time had come long ago, and in their dispatches to London, Paris and Rome one can sense their impatience with the Shoan chiefs and with Tafari. "There is a vague feeling among people," Thesiger reported, "that thanks to the disorder in which the Government has fallen Abyssinia is slowly drifting towards a crisis." But he added: "The Council of Ministers in Addis Ababa is divided into factions, with the prime minister, Haile Giorgis, and Fituarari Hapta Giorgis on one side and Bargena (Minister of Foreign Affairs) and Telahoun (Minister of Justice) on the other. The former are for the Allied cause and the latter are pro-German. Each side is afraid of making any decision lest their enemies use it against them by misrepresenting it to Lij Yasu. So all questions are referred to Lij Yasu, who doesn't answer them."

He had earlier written: "Each week offers fresh evidence of Lij Yasu's sympathy with Islam and with Moslems, whom he goes out of his way to propitiate, even at the expense of politeness to Abyssinian Christians of far higher standing. Since his visit to Harar he makes no secret of his pretensions. The plain fact is that the heir to the throne of Solomon is at heart a Moslem and is entertaining dreams of one day putting himself at the head of the Abyssinian Moslems— who outnumber the Christians—and of producing a Moslem kingdom which will stretch far beyond the frontiers of the present Empire."

He had no doubt, he went on, that Lij Yasu now believed in a Turco-German victory and his envoys (chiefly Abdullai Sadik) had already begun to discuss tactics with the Mad Mullah in British Somaliland for the occupation of the colony. Arms were already passing in ever-growing numbers to the Somali rebels and they had carried out several successful forays against the British troops. If Lij Yasu allowed the tribes in the Ogaden to join in the *jihad*, the position for Britain might well become untenable.

One could almost hear Thesiger saying: "Why don't Tafari and the Shoan chiefs *do* something?"

But aside from his oath, who could blame Tafari for his caution at this stage? Suddenly everyone had begun to look in his direction and talk of him as the potential savior of his country. But when it came to the crunch, upon whom could he rely? The rases? They were as divided, jealous and treacherous as ever. The Council of Ministers in Addis Ababa? Tafari knew them for a craven and a mendacious rookery of thieves and self-seekers who would not hesitate to betray him. The Allies? Not them, either, in spite of their fears. When Major Dodds, the British consul in Harar, who had formed a close friendship with Tafari, suggested to the Legation that it might be wise for the British to intervene on his side, Thesiger declined with a shudder of distaste: "Not when the power of the Government (he appears to have meant the Shoan chiefs) is based on the lowest and most fanatical elements of the population, whose support is sure only as long as the soldiery are allowed to loot under the pretence of restoring order, the police to extort blackmail in return for protection, and the whole corps of officers, spies and hangers-on, who form part of the retinue of every Abyssinian officer, to commit any villainy with impunity. Dejaz Tafari, Dejaz Kassa and others sincerely deprecate this state of affairs, but they have not the courage to speak out nor the strength to resist the corrupting influences even in their own provinces."

There was some truth in this, particularly in Harar. Lij Yasu's growing fervor for Islam had had its effect upon the Moslems of the province, who had begun to petition to the prince for positions in the administration, and Tafari was being bombarded with orders to replace his Amhara officials with Moslem Hararis, Gallas and Somalis. He described them to Dodds as "undesirable riff-raff" and admitted that it was true when the British consul complained that Harar was now a principal center through which dervishes were passing into Ethiopia to join Lij Yasu and Ethiopian guns were going to the Mad Mullah in Somaliland. But he would not promise to take action and Dodds (wrongly, as he afterwards freely admitted) put his reluctance down to craven-heartedness. "Had Tafari inherited the strong qualities of his father," wrote Dodds, "he might have had a chance of putting things together, but he hasn't and I doubt if anyone in Abyssinia has."

But for the moment Tafari did not take him into his confidence about his plans, possibly because he thought he might be compromising a foreign diplomat—but more likely because he considered that the situation was Ethiopia's own affair to be settled by Ethiopians. Like most of his countrymen, he has always had a desperate determination to keep foreign governments out of his problems whenever possible. But he left Dodds in no doubt of his anxiety not only over the situation in Harar but throughout the country.

"Never have our courts been so busy," he told the consul. "Every soldier, every chief, every trader is tired of the condition of the country. Trade has diminished, prices have increased, revenue has decreased and there is no security. I view the situation with the greatest concern."

Dodds commented: "Whenever I see Tafari he leads the conversation to the topic dearest to his heart, the condition of Abyssinia. It is most apparent that he imagines the days of the kingdom are numbered. His reiterated expression is that the men who hold the reins of power are throwing the country away. Lij Yasu, according to him, is an idler from whom one can expect no assistance to rectify matters, and he describes the Bitawed as 'a man with one thought, to fill his pockets, with not a thought for the good of the country.' "

On March 7, 1916, Mr. Wilfred Thesiger, the British Minister, left Addis Ababa on a trek to the game ranges outside Gore where Lij Yasu had gone on an elephant-shooting expedition. Thesiger had been briefed by his Italian and French colleagues (Count Colli and M. Brice) to talk to the Emperor and make a last effort to bring him to his senses. After some days traveling by mule and camel he came to a village where a number of Government officers were rather disconsolately squatting; they reported that Lij Yasu had shot and wounded several elephants during his safari and these animals were trumpeting angrily about the bush, but they went on to complain that no animal was running so berserk as the Emperor himself. In his entourage now were only "five Abyssinians," as Thesiger termed them and that the rest were "Arabs, Danakils and Somalis." The Government officers said sadly that they were continually receiving messages from Addis Ababa asking them to consult Lij Yasu on matters of state, but that they dare not do so: any official who had the temerity to come to his encampment was publicly flogged. Even an emissary from the Emperor's father, Ras Mikael, carrying a message urging him to return to the capital, had been beaten and driven into the bush. The only personages welcome at the camp, they said, were chieftains bringing their daughters for Lij Yasu's amusement. ("Lij Yasu has now taken to himself the daughters of eight Moslem chiefs in Wollo, Galla, Danakil and Jimma," reported Thesiger, "and he is expecting a daughter from the Mad Mullah. These temporary alliances, though accompanied by no religious or civil ceremony, are intended to take the place of more regular treaties of friendship—and Lij Yasu is now connected informally by marriage with all the Moslem tribes in Abyssinia.") Oh, yes, the Government officials said, nodding morosely, there could be no doubt of it now—the prince had decided that he was the new Mahdi come to bring Ethiopia back to Islam. They pointed to a number of slim, bare-breasted Danakil girls who were giggling in groups about the village and said, not without a touch of envy: "He has already known all of these. At least he is making sure that he will not lack heirs to succeed him." One of the Danakil chiefs rubbed his daughter's belly with happy pride and boasted that there was the seed inside it of a future ruler of the kingdom, uncaring that there was also the seed of something else planted in the girl. "He is one of us now," he said. It seemed that Lij Yasu had shaved his head like a Danakil and was living as they did, and that for each chieftain's bride with whom he had formed a union he had followed the Danakil law and produced the testicles of "an enemy slain in battle." [6]

Whether it was from disgust or despair or sheer inability to reach the Emperor, Thesiger returned to Addis Ababa without having talked to Lij Yasu, but the report he subsequently wrote leaves no doubt of his feelings.

"The prince," he reported on April 14, 1916, "is now feared and detested by the chiefs and hated by the priests, whose daily prayer is: 'Since we can do nothing, may God kill him soon!' But he is still the only source of authority here. Nothing of the slightest importance can be done without his permission, and as he is entirely occupied with his own pleasures and such business as interests him, such as punitive raids against offending villages, all the urgent matters of the kingdom are brought to a standstill. Lij Yasu allows no remonstrances, accepts no advice, and the older officers of Menelik's time are frankly in despair as to the future of their country. When

[6] The Government officials hinted that "slain in battle" was a euphemism for Lij Yasu's emasculation of a prisoner who was held down by members of his retinue.

in the low countries, the prince makes no secret of his sympathies for Islam, living solely in the houses of Moslems and adopting openly Moslem dress and custom. . . . At the same time, considerable resentment is also aroused by Lij Yasu's intimate associates, who consist mainly of the lower class of Europeans and Moslems."

He ended: "As to character: cruelty and arrogance seem to preponderate in him. He wields despotic power. The country would hear of his death with satisfaction. There is no hope that he will improve."

These were different sentiments indeed from those Thesiger had used, four years before, in urging the British Government to give the prince their backing.

chapter four

COUP D'ETAT

IN MAY, 1916, the Shoan chiefs in the Council of Ministers, egged on by both the priests and the Allied legations, summoned Tafari to Addis Ababa urgently for consultations. They were profoundly disturbed by two reports which had reached them through the Allies —they got most of their news of happenings outside Addis Ababa these days from the legations—indicating Lij Yasu's total adherence to Islam. The French Minister reported that on May 12 the prince had suggested, through Mr. Ydlibi, the Turkish consul in Harar, that a Treaty of Alliance be signed between Ethiopia and the Otto-man Empire. At the same time, he was said to have presented the Consul with an Ethiopian flag decorated with a Turkish crescent.[1] The Italian Minister, Count Colli, reported that Lij Yasu was now wearing a new Islamic seal on his finger and that he claimed in his letters to the Somalis (which the Italians had intercepted) to be "descended from Hosein, son of Fatima, daughter of the Prophet." Colli went on to say that he had taxed Lij Yasu about his Islamic ambitions and that he had admitted them, but maintained that this was no evidence of his antipathy to the Allies.

The Ministers were not really concerned with the prince's senti-ments toward the Allies—they themselves veered from pro-British to pro-German as the fortunes of war swung one way or the other —but they were desperately afraid for the future of the established religion of the State. Not since the Moslem *jihad* of the sixteenth century had the Christian Church and the Solomonic Legend been

[1] Lij Yasu came to the British Legation a few weeks later to express his regret at the death of Lord Kitchener and took the opportunity of denying this story. The flag, he said, had been presented by one of his sheikhs, Mohamet Farris, "and I have put him in chains."

in such danger, and it was to Tafari that they turned for advice. It so happened that it was an awkward moment for him to leave Harar, for unrest in the city and the province was growing; moreover his young wife, Waizero Menen, was pregnant for a second time (she had already borne him a daughter) and too near her time to travel, for the little rains were on and the route across the mountains was a quagmire.[2] He called in Major Dodds and extracted from the consul a promise that he would keep him in touch with her welfare, and at the same time he appointed his good friend and cousin, Imru Haile Selassie, as the commander of her bodyguard. Then he took his own picked squad of horsemen and rode off across the muddy hills to the capital. He discovered on reaching it that the situation had gone even further than he had calculated; in open collaboration now with the Turks and the Germans, Lij Yasu was energetically working out his plans for the Islamization of Ethiopia, arrogantly ignoring the antagonism of the Shoan chiefs and the Ethiopian Church. As guests at the Palace he had representatives of most of the Moslem chiefs from the Ogaden and two envoys of the Mad Mullah of Somaliland, and great feasts were held in their honor to which only Moslems were invited ("plus a sordid and motley crew of women of many nationalities, together with their Armenian, Greek and Turkish panderers," M. Zaphiro reported).

"The situation grows more complicated," wrote Thesiger, on May 20. "Tafari has just arrived here and will probably not return to Harar, which will leave power in the hands of the Moslem party there. When the Somali chiefs now in Addis Ababa return to their tribes, trouble may break out on the frontier." He cabled urgently advising the movement of British troops in Somaliland from Berbera to the Ethiopian border. He also suggested to the Foreign Office that as chiefs and priests alike were now bitterly opposed to the Emperor's pro-Moslem policy "the only solution would be for the Entente Legations at an opportune moment to denounce the prince as a Moslem. We would then make a proclamation of the firm determination of our Governments to maintain the integrity of Abyssinia, asking the country to proclaim a new Emperor and decline all further dealings with the present Government until this is done. In this way we would have the support of Church, chiefs and people."

---

[2] The station at Dire Dawa, from which trains were now running to Addis Ababa, was only fifty miles from Harar, but Dire Dawa was now controlled by a Danakil nominee of Lij Yasu with a mixed administration of Arabs and Turks. Tafari was not prepared to risk his wife to their mercies.

This was a complete turnabout with a vengeance from his previous inclination toward non-interference, and it undoubtedly was a direct result of the arrival of Tafari. The young man's quiet determination and complete calm he found very impressive indeed.[3] But Thesiger's conversion to intervention in Ethiopia's affairs seemed too precipitate to HM Government in London, who had enough embarrassments on their hands in German East Africa and Europe without wishing to become involved in Ethiopia. Thesiger was advised to consult his colleagues again. Eventually it was decided that they should make yet another approach to Lij Yasu and put four demands to him. First, they would insist on the return to the British authorities in Somaliland of a machine-gun, captured from the British by the Mad Mullah, which had been sent as a ceremonial present to the Emperor in Addis Ababa; second, they would demand that he receive no further delegations from the Somali tribes; third, that Abdullai Sadik be removed from his post in Harar as Governor of the Ogaden; and fourth, that the municipal offices at Dire Dawa be completely reorganized and all Turks and pro-Turkish Arabs removed.

The note was duly dispatched to the palace and the Ministers sat back to wait for the reaction. All they got was a heavy silence. Or rather, all they heard as they waited in their diplomatic compounds were the shouts of the Moslem feasters in the Gebbi and the worried murmurs and scurryings of the Shoan chiefs and priests, as Tafari tried to galvanize them. He was aware now that a head-on clash between himself and Lij Yasu could not be delayed much longer; the prince no longer bothered to conceal his antipathy toward his cousin. Tafari, informed by his friend Imru Haile Selassie that Waizero Menen's labor pains had begun, but were difficult and protracted, informed the palace he was leaving to return to Harar for a short visit. A curt note came back informing him that permission to leave the capital was refused. The following day a cordon of troops from the royal household was flung around his house: they made no attempt to prevent his movements so long as he did not leave the city, and some of the troops accepted beer and meat in the feast which he threw, a week later, to celebrate the birth of his first son. He rejoiced that he had an heir, but he did not have to be told that in making sure of his line he had only increased the rancor which Lij Yasu now felt for him. It was about this time that he smuggled a message through to Thesiger asking him to come to see him. "Tafari expects daily he will be imprisoned," the Minister reported, "which

3 Tafari was not yet twenty-four.

he believes would be the equivalent of a death sentence, and accordingly he confided his will and all his available money to me, in order that I should arrange for its transmission to the Bank of England in trust for his children." Thesiger added that Tafari, though conscious of his danger, was quite cheerful about it. "If they come for me," he said, "they will find me waiting for them with a gun."

Lij Yasu, however, evidently feared that his cousin had now gathered too many friends together and was too strongly entrenched in his house to be arrested. He had thought up a more subtle plan to upset Tafari's equilibrium. The Allied ministers had been pressing the Emperor to reply to the four-point Note which they had sent him in May, but it was not until the middle of July that he got into touch with one of them. Perhaps aware that Thesiger had been seeing Tafari and would mention it, he sent a note through to the British Minister asking him to attend him at the palace on August 1, when he would discuss the complaints of the legations. But on the night of July 28 he and a small band of horsemen left Addis Ababa and rode across the plain to Akaki, a wayside halt along the railway ten miles from the capital. At dawn next morning they stopped the train for Dire Dawa and boarded it, and the Emperor was among his Moslem allies before anyone in the capital was aware that he was missing.

On arrival in Dire Dawa Lij Yasu went to the local mosque (it was the time of Bairam) and prayed for three hours, after which he presented the mullah with a gift of three camels. It was while he was there that a runner brought news to Imru Haile Selassie that the Emperor was in the vicinity and was planning to visit Harar. He telegraphed Tafari (using a British commercial code) asking "How shall I treat him if he comes here?" Tafari replied: "Treat him with politeness but guard the child."

But it was through the British Legation that he received, two days later, a much more ominous message. Major Dodds cabled Thesiger and asked Tafari to be informed that Ras Lul Seged—Waizero Menen's former husband—was with Lij Yasu. He was said to have asked the Emperor for his ex-wife to be returned to him, and had been promised her.

"I went to see Waizero Menen," Dodds wrote, "and found her in good heart though well aware of her danger. She is desperately anxious not to lose her husband and asks me repeatedly to give her news of what he does in Addis Ababa." As for her own situation, Dodds reported that she smiled calmly and said: "My house has three doors. They are guarded by three brave chiefs whom I trust, Imru, Abba and Deneker. They will stop even Lij Yasu from entering. And they will kill Lul Seged if he tries."

The next few days must have been the most anxious of Tafari's life for he loved his wife deeply and cherished the son and heir he had not yet even seen. But the movement against Lij Yasu in Addis Ababa was at last beginning to gain momentum, and it was vital he stay with it.

He could do nothing personally to help his wife and children. Instead he dispatched a good friend, Petros, by train to Dire Dawa and told him to make his way secretly to Harar. There he must consult with Imru and Major Dodds and make arrangements for the clandestine evacuation of Waizero Menen and her son and daughter.

The operation was effected just in time. Disguised as a Harari woman traveling with her children, Menen was smuggled out of the house and taken to the South Gate in the city wall where a guard, well-bribed, let her through before the dawn opening, and thence she made her way to a rendezvous with Petros and a mule train. The party reached Dire Dawa and boarded the train for Addis Ababa without being recognized. Not long afterwards Thesiger was reporting: "(Tafari) has now given me a further and most embarrassing proof of his confidence in me, by asking me to take charge of his son and heir. Both Tafari and his wife are very anxious and nervous about the child, and I felt it impossible to refuse without risking his friendship. It is a grave responsibility and very inconvenient."

Mother and child had left only just in time. On August 13, a troop of Lij Yasu's cavalry, commanded by Lul Seged, surrounded Tafari's house in Harar. Simultaneously, an announcement was made from Lij Yasu's headquarters and telegraphed to Addis Ababa that Tafari had been removed as Governor of Harar, and that the Emperor would personally rule the province with a Moslem administration. Lul Seged's men called upon Imru and his companions to throw open the house; and after a token show of reluctance (for they now had nothing to protect) they did so. While they were being taken off in chains, Lul Seged rushed to the women's quarters where the crying of a baby could be heard. But all he found was Menen's wet-nurse suckling her own child.

Now, at last, Tafari was free from his oath. He set to work to start fires in the bellies of at least some of the Shoan chiefs. He rallied the priests to his side (the Abun reluctantly, the Itchege more enthusiastically). Most of the members of the Council of Ministers agreed to stand by him in his denunciation of Lij Yasu—but only so long as the Abun agreed to excommunicate the Emperor. That old gentleman was in a considerable state of nerves and kept repeating: "But what will Mikael do if we repudiate his son? He will march his armies against us and then things will be worse than ever." Tafari did not trust him and therefore could not tell him that he had already been in communication with two powerful chiefs, Ras Walda Giorgis and Ras Hailu, both of whom had agreed to watch Mikael's movements and block any attempt he might make to march south. (Walda Giorgis was on the side of the conspiracy for both spiritual and practical reasons: as a perfervid member of the Ethiopian Church, he was incensed by Lij Yasu's apostasy; and he was also ready to join any plot that might bring him Mikael's territories. Ras Hailu had turned against Mikael when Lij Yasu "insulted" him by returning the daughter he had given in marriage.) To the Abun and to the chief Minister—whom he suspected of being in the pay of the Germans—all Tafari could give were vague promises that everything would be all right when the time came. In the meantime, he arranged for thousands of leaflets to be printed denouncing the Emperor as a Moslem, and a rendezvous was fixed for a great meeting at which the Shoan chiefs would register their solid opposition to Lij Yasu's régime.

To the Foreign Office in London the British Minister cabled in code on August 30, 1916: "Movement begun among Shoan chiefs to depose Lij Yasu." But the next day he sent a second message: "Reported movement to depose Lij Yasu has collapsed."

Like many another conspiracy in Ethiopia, this one had gone off at half-cock. As Thesiger reported later: "The proclamations were printed and everything was in readiness. On August 30 a general meeting was to be held at one of the churches, when speeches would be made by the Abun and the Itchege, the latter being one of the principal conspirators. The chiefs were to be released from their oath to Lij Yasu."

But on the morning of August 30 there was a heavy downpour of rain. Tafari and one or two other chiefs who had arrived early at the church were staring disconsolately at the downpour when a messenger sloshed through the mud, bringing notes from the Abun and the Itchege. Both made the same excuse: they were old men, they said, and could not possibly come out in such weather. Tafari and the chiefs, realizing that their bombshell had become a damp squib, hurried back to their homes to await developments.

They were now in a tricky and dangerous position. As Thesiger commented: "Practically the whole town knows all about the conspiracy and the chiefs, compromised in Lij Yasu's eyes, are uncertain of their next step. The conspirators seized the telegraph office, but the trains to Dire Dawa are still running and the Turks and Germans will inform Lij Yasu."

He added: "It is typical of Abyssinia that a thunderstorm should overthrow a conspiracy. . . . All the chiefs lacked was courage."

As it turned out, what the Abun and the Itchege had lacked were neither umbrellas nor courage. Their failure to arrive at the rendezvous was due not to craven hearts but to the chief Minister, who had decided at the last moment (no doubt at the behest of the Germans) to sabotage the plot. He threw cordons of troops around the houses of the two ecclesiastics and warned them that they would be thrown into prison if they did not excuse themselves. At the same time he told an uneasy meeting of his Ministers that he needed their endorsement of an order he was about to issue for the immediate arrest of Tafari; he was obeying instructions he had just received by messenger from Lij Yasu, who wanted his cousin delivered to him in chains in Dire Dawa. But this was going too far even for the discomfited Ministers, who protested that to deliver Tafari to the Emperor would be tantamount to signing his death warrant. Fitaurari Hapta Giorgis suggested that if the Prime Minister was determined to carry out Lij Yasu's commands he should do it with his own troops, but wryly added that it might prove a costly adventure, for Tafari had been warned of his danger and was waiting with an armed bodyguard and his own loaded gun, ready to die rather than be taken.[4]

Nevertheless, it seemed as if it was all over, that the revolt was still-born. Lij Yasu seemed to think so. In Harar on September 14, he attended a long service of thanksgiving at the Indian mosque. There were 3,000 Moslems present and the Emperor spoke to them, telling them to rejoice with him and promising that an Islamic Ethiopia had been brought nearer by the discomfiture of his enemies. Then his servants brought a great chest into the courtyard of the mosque and when it was opened the crowd saw that it was filled with Maria Theresa dollars. Lij Yasu handed one to each man present and

---

[4] It was at this time, as has been mentioned, that Tafari put his son and heir in the care of the British Minister.

then the Mufti ordered them to kneel down and pray "for the long life of Lij Yasu, our King."

In Addis Ababa it was said that the Emperor had assembled 20,000 troops at Doba and Dire Dawa in readiness for a march on the capital, and an uneasy gloom settled over the city as the inhabitants watched the plains for signs of the vengeance they feared was coming. But if the populace was afraid and some of the Ministers downhearted, Tafari was not even dismayed; he had gone on with his plans, and this time he had taken steps to see that they should not fail. Not only were the troops of Ras Walda Giorgis and Ras Hailu in position to block Ras Mikael should he try to come south; he had also dispatched Ras Balcha, an old enemy of Lij Yasu's, across the River Awash with an army of several thousands of men. Balcha's instructions were to surround Harar and, at the appropriate moment, enter the town and imprison the Emperor.

This time the chiefs involved in the conspiracy kept quiet about their plans, and the rumors in the bazaars lacked any *semblance* of the truth of what was really happening. (Tafari and his fellow plotters took only Thesiger and Count Colli, the Italian Minister, into their confidence; they did not trust the French.) On September 28 Tafari and the Itchege called a meeting of the Council of Ministers and all the Shoan chiefs to be held in the banqueting hall of the Palace, but no mention was made of the purpose of the meeting. Neither the chief Minister nor the Abun was invited—in the case of the Abun because his house was still cordoned off by the Chief Minister's troops. But the Chief Minister was not going to allow himself to be absent on such an occasion, and he rode up to the Palace and demanded to be let in. Tafari informed him that he could attend only if he brought the Abun with him, and this presently he did.

Once in the hall, he discovered that the Ministers had taken matters into their own hands and that vital decisions had been made without his knowledge. Tafari rose and introduced Hapta Giorgis to the assembly, and this Minister then began to read out a long proclamation detailing the acts which had convinced the ministers that Lij Yasu had become a Moslem. He made reference to the Note from the British, Italian and French legations warning Lij Yasu of the dangers of the situation and of his cavalier treatment of it. Hapta Giorgis's recital of the Emperor's crimes and of proof of his apostasy stimulated a rising murmur of resentment among the chiefs in the hall, and an attempt by the Chief Minister to leave by a side door was halted abruptly when several of them jabbed him roughly with their rifle butts and told him: "The time has come to vote, for Ethiopia or for Lij Yasu. Which is it to be—a live yea or a dead nay?"

The Chief Minister resumed his seat. All around him now chiefs were rising to denounce the Emperor. Finally Tafari called out: "But what has the Abun to say?" Archbishop Mattheos, a woebegone picture of abject terror, was pushed forward; as he made his way to the middle of the throng, where Tafari and the Ministers were gathered, the palace shawms sounded a fanfare and the royal drummers beat a tattoo on their drums, preparing the assembly for what it presumed would be the final blow to Lij Yasu's position. Instead, in the silence that followed, there was for a long pause nothing but the sound of the Abun's heavy breathing, after which he cleared his throat and said slowly and hesitantly "I have listened to the charges which have been made against Menelik's heir. If these things be true . . ."

At this angry protests rose from the chiefs that he should still be sceptical, and finally the Itchege came forward, put his hand on the Abun's shoulder, and as if he were thus getting a message through by physical contact slowly pronounced Lij Yasu's excommunication. "From this day forth, oh chiefs," he intoned, "you are freed from your oath to the apostate Lij Yasu. Let us all take a new oath, to be true to our religion." At this the Abun picked up his courage and also pronounced excommunication. There was a burst of fervid applause as the chiefs fell to their knees, but the murmuring hush was suddenly broken by a cry from somewhere among the throng. A voice was heard to shout: "It is the Abun's right and his only to excommunicate. But what right have you, Itchege, to absolve anyone from his oath to the Emperor?" Someone had not heard the Abun's words.

At this (reported Thesiger later) a certain minor chief, Bayena, waved his rifle above his head and passionately declared that the complaint could only have come from a Moslem. "Let those who are Moslems stand on one side and we shall see," he cried.

There followed "a scene of indescribable confusion. A shot was fired and immediately the excited crowd of soldiers began to fire their rifles in all directions. In the congested space few bullets can have missed their mark. The slaughter would have continued but for the presence of mind of the officer-in-charge of the war drums, who ordered them to beat the signal for silence. The madness ceased.

But many were dead and the casualties were afterwards numbered at more than a hundred. In the heavy silence that followed most of the chiefs were seen to be in tears, and the council was dissolved until the afternoon."

That afternoon when the chiefs reassembled the deposition of Lij Yasu was formally announced amid frenetic acclamation. The royal drums throbbed. Guns boomed from the perimeter of the palace. But when the people heard the news they were puzzled. What had happened to Tafari? Why were they not called upon to acclaim him as their new Emperor—for was he not the architect of the revolt and the symbol of stability in a rapidly crumbling kingdom?

They could not know that the Shoan chiefs had demanded and got their price in return for their support of the conspiracy. That price was Tafari's agreement not to demand the throne for himself but to consent to a formula that would split power and influence in the palace, and thus allow the Ministers to control it. They had backed Tafari in his plot to remove Lij Yasu, but in some ways they feared him as much as they had feared the Emperor—the one for his passion for Islam, the other because of his zeal and enthusiasm for reform. Lij Yasu had tried to drag Ethiopia back into an Islamic barbarism, but Tafari wanted to push the country forward into the twentieth century, and to an oligarchy of rapacious rases for whom feudalism meant wealth and power, that was almost equally alarming.

So at the last moment they had blocked his path to the throne that he had so surely demonstrated he was worthy to occupy. The official proclamation, as issued to the Ethiopian people on September 29, 1916, read:

Hear, oh Christian people of Abyssinia: Our religion and Government were suffering and were being destroyed. Therefore, for the protection and benefit of our religion and Government, the people of Ethiopia assembled and appointed the daughter of the Emperor Menelik as Empress and Ras Tafari as Heir to the Throne. Because this has been done with the consent of all, go and rejoice.

Princess Zauditu, now to be crowned Empress of Ethiopia, was brought down from her exile in the convent of Entoto to be welcomed by the populace. She made a tearful speech telling of her suffering at the hands of Lij Yasu. But it was to the appearance of the slight, dignified, bearded figure of Ras Tafari [5] at her side that

[5] He had been promoted to Ras at the same time that he was made heir to the throne.

the crowd reacted with excited enthusiasm. The warmth of his reception was not lost upon the Council of Ministers, but they were not worried. As a counter-balance to Tafari's popularity, they had already made another appointment. As a woman, Zauditu would not be allowed by the Constitution to rule alone—and therefore Tafari had been named as Regent as well as heir. But the Council pointed out that he was very young for such responsibility; and they nominated Fitaurari Hapta Giorgis as War Minister to form a triumvirate, well knowing that he was a conservative of the old feudal school and would curb the young heir's enthusiasm for modernity. So long as Empress Zauditu, a conformist, and Hapta Giorgis worked together, the rases had no fear that Tafari would meddle with their medieval privileges and perquisites.

Or so they thought.

chapter five

RAS MIKAEL STRIKES

"Because this has been done with the consent of all," read the proclamation deposing Lij Yasu, "go and rejoice."

But, of course, it had not been done with the consent of all, and there were many in the country who did not rejoice. Moslem hopes and ambitions had been fired, and those fires must be doused quickly if the country was not to be plunged into bloody civil war. Ras Tafari, who had been accepted as head of Government in fact if not in title, dispatched the new War Minister, Fitaurari Hapta Giorgis, to take charge of the largely Moslem provinces of Jimma and Gurage, where some public scourging of the ringleaders and the hanging of two *mullahs* soon quelled incipient revolts. Tafari also accepted the advice of the British Minister and flung into jail two important sultans in Western Ethiopia who were said by the British to be German agents. So far so good. As soon as they realized that there was a new régime in Addis Ababa obviously determined to rule, the rases began to arrive in person—or sent emissaries with gifts—to signify their allegiance to the new Empress.

The big questions to be answered now were: What will Ras Mikael do? And what will happen to Lij Yasu?

It was too much to expect that the Shoan chiefs' rejection of his son would be taken supinely by Mikael, but for a few days the new régime had wild hopes that even he might be persuaded to accept the *fait accompli.* The Council of Ministers had sent to him (as, indeed, to all the rases) news of their proclamation coupled with a demand for an expression of allegiance to the new Queen. They had expected a bellow of defiance to come back from Mikael, but they received instead a note couched in reasonable language in which he admitted that his son had committed grievous wrongs against his

87

country and that he had been sinful in abandoning his Church, but asserting that this was no excuse for his excommunication and deposition, that he could have been dealt with less harshly. Was Mikael then going to toe the line? Hopes were dashed when news filtered through from Dessye, Mikael's capital, that their emissary from Shoa, Ras Abata, had been imprisoned, and that the telegraph line connecting Addis Ababa to Europe (which passed through Dessye) had been cut.

One of the rases to swear allegiance to the Empress with commendable promptitude turned out, to Tafari's surprise, to be his wife's former husband, Lul Seged, who appeared with his army outside Addis Ababa a few days after the *coup*. He hastened to see Tafari and offer him his congratulations and to explain that he had been associating with Lij Yasu "under duress," but had left him before he had been deposed because "I was disgusted at his excesses."

It was no time to conduct a post-mortem on Lul Seged's activities (he appears, in fact, to have been dismissed by the Emperor after a quarrel), and Tafari told him that he would have an immediate opportunity of proving his loyalty to the new régime. He told him to take his army north to the frontiers of Mikael's kingdom and block any attempt he might make to march on the capital. Neither Tafari nor Lul Seged could have known at the time what a test of loyalty it would prove to be.

And what of Lij Yasu?

In his case, Tafari's plans had gone disastrously wrong. In order to consolidate the position of Empress Zauditu and her two chief advisers it was, of course, vitally important that the deposed claimant to the throne should be apprehended and incarcerated as speedily as possible. So long as he remained at large he would be a rallying point for dissidents. Well aware of this, Tafari had, as will be remembered, dispatched Ras Balcha and an army of several thousand men to surround Harar. On September 28, immediately the deposition was decided upon, he sent off a telegram to the deputy Governor of Harar informing him of what had happened and instructing him to arrest and chain the Emperor. But things went wrong. Gerazmach Bellati, the chief of the telegraph office, delivered the message instead to Lij Yasu, who promptly cut the telegraph wire. Yasu then dispatched his soldiers to round up all the priests in Harar and bring them back to the public square. The trembling clerics were driven into the square and told to get down on their knees, and some of them were so afraid and so anxious to demonstrate their allegiance to the Emperor "that they bowed their trembling heads to the ground," wrote an eyewitness afterwards, "and when they raised them again their beards were all brown with dust." But it was not an oath of allegiance Lij Yasu was asking from the priests, but an oath swearing that they would excommunicate any chief or soldier who was unfaithful to him. This, after a glance at the grinning soldiery surrounding the square, they fervently promised to do.

At that Lij Yasu too flung himself to his knees. From the hands of the Bishop of Harar he took an ornamental cross and a Bible, and these he passionately kissed, swearing at the same time—with tears starting in his eyes by now—that he had always been and would remain a true Christian. That evening he sent an emissary to Major Dodds, the British Consul in Harar, with a surprising message. He asked whether Dodds would transmit a message to London asking the British Government to take Ethiopia under the protection of its troops. Dodds, hardly able to believe his ears, told the emissary that he would like to talk to Lij Yasu himself before transmitting any such message.

The next day there were sounds of gunfire from all around Harar and the city quivered and rumbled with panic. The forces of Ras Balcha, ranged outside, had begun their attack upon the city walls. Just before noon, Lij Yasu and a few horsemen galloped up to the British Consulate and the Emperor entered. His eyes were rolling with panic and he was obviously desperately afraid. He began by telling Dodds that he had always entertained the liveliest admiration for the British people and wished to establish close ties of friendship with them. He admitted that his minions had been instrumental in stirring up unrest among the Somalis and shipping arms to the Mad Mullah, but swore that Ethiopia would pay compensation. And then he repeated his request that the British Government should take Ethiopia under its protection.

Dodds made a noncommittal reply. It was obvious now that what Lij Yasu wanted was not British protection for his people but for himself. Dodds did not need to be told that the tide of anti-British, pro-Turkish feeling in the city had already turned. Posters attacking Britain, which had been posted all over the place for the past week, were now torn down; M. Ydlibi, the Turkish consul-general, suddenly discovered an urgent reason for departing for Jibouti "on business," taking his daughters with him; and Abdullai Sadik had disappeared into the Ogaden.

Because the Ethiopians are inclined to equate acts of cruelty with strength, the legend has persisted to this day that Lij Yasu was a person of great personality and power, a flawed hero. It is true that he was, in his more stimulated moments, a great ravisher of Galla and Harari virgins, an enthusiastic corrupter of small boys, with an unquenchable appetite for exhibitions of flogging and mutilations; but for an Ethiopian normally to accept these as the attributes of one of their heroes, he must also display tremendous bravery in battle and loyalty in emergency. It is impossible to discover—at least in this period of his career—a single example of the Emperor's willingness even to face an enemy at the head of his troops, let alone stay to fight; and when a crisis came, he was almost always the first to desert.

When the Somali chiefs whom he had called to Harar from British Somaliland heard of the action of the Shoan chiefs in deposing him, they attended upon Lij Yasu. They asked him to proclaim a *jihad* and call upon every Moslem in his kingdom to rally round; and they asked him to lead them in resistance to Ras Balcha and his besieging troops.

Lij Yasu's answer was to slip out of the city, with a handful of mounted horsemen, on the morning of October 1, 1916. His was the last party to leave by the city gates that day. When the usual time for opening the gates came, they remained padlocked. The Moslem guards had been replaced by Amharas. When the Somalis heard that Lij Yasu had deserted them, they swarmed down to the gates, eager to make their escape back to the deserts of the Ogaden. They found the Amharas waiting for them, and they were shot down in the narrow streets or torn and cut to pieces as they tried to scramble up the walls to the safety of the scrub. When Ras Balcha rode into the city in triumph later that day, he found the alleyways clogged with bodies, and for many days afterwards the stink of Harar could be smelled for miles around. Attracted by the tantalizing stenches, the hyenas came into the city in their hundreds and did not bother to wait until the fall of darkness; but even so, it was many a long day before Dodds could go into the streets without a nose-cloth, and even longer before the scavengers were back on a diet of garbage and animal offal.

Lij Yasu was at Dire Dawa when he heard of the massacre in Harar, and the news completed his panic; all he wanted to do now was reach the protecting arms of his father, for there, it seemed, he would find salvation. Ras Mikael had decided to move at last to revenge the humiliation of his son, and at first his crusade was most bloodily successful. It will be remembered that Lul Seged had been sent out by Tafari with his troops to block any move southwards which Mikael might make; and this force, which did not number more than two thousand, made contact with the enemy's cavalry south of the ancient capital of Ankober, which Mikael had already occupied.

His men were fresh and his horsemen were in good condition, in contrast to those of Lul Seged, whose animals were bleeding and footsore from their forced march from Harar.[1] Mikael ordered a swift encircling movement and surrounded Seged's forces, trapping them in a small valley from which there was no escape. They were cut down, their commander killed, their wounded mutilated. Only a few score escaped to bring back the news of the disaster to Addis Ababa.

"Ras Mikael is on the rampage," reported Thesiger, and went on to add that he had called Tafari in to see him and urged him to mobilize his forces and march out to meet the threat from the North. But before he could do so, there were complicated arrangements that Tafari had to make: he needed to sign and seal agreements he had been secretly negotiating with two chiefs who might otherwise tip the scales in Mikael's favor, Ras Demissie, whose son was married to one of Mikael's daughters, and Ras Seyoum, who was his son-in-law. He must convince Ras Hailu of Gojjam and Ras Walda Giorgis of Gondar that they would receive a rich reward if they gave practical support, instead of just lip-service, to the Shoan armies. He had to make sure that while he was fighting in the field there was no treachery in Addis Ababa that would stab the new régime in the back.

To give him time while he made his arrangements, Tafari sent the War Minister, Fitaurari Hapta Giorgis, forth with an army of some 10,000 men to delay Mikael's army "at all costs." To a European general, this may have sounded like a clarion-call for a last stand, a fight to the death, a Charge of the Light Brigade. But Hapta Giorgis was a wily old gentleman with a warm regard for the safety of his own skin and a veteran's awareness that, in Ethiopia, anyway, there are more ways of winning a battle than by mounting an attack. He encamped his men in a pass overlooking Debra Berhan, some eighty miles northeast of Addis Ababa, and then sent a runner across the valley to Ras Mikael's headquarters suggesting an armistice. As two veterans who had fought side by side in Menelik's wars, he wrote, it

[1] Ethiopian horses and mules, until quite recent time, have never been shod.

was surely madness to fight against each other; he would prefer to parley. He calculated that Mikael would consider the overture a sign of weakness—as it was, practically if not psychologically—and would consent to talk. He was right. Mikael was taken in by the strategem, but he did demand in return that Hapta Giorgis should give him some token of his good faith. Hapta Giorgis considered this and then decided to take a calculated risk. He informed Mikael that as a demonstration of his unwillingness to make war on an old comrade, and as an earnest expression of his hope for a settlement between the two of them, he was sending him a mule train of ammunition for his guns.

The load was duly delivered, and, in the circumstances, it was a hostage to fortune indeed. But Mikael fell into the trap. He not only did not attack, he relaxed his guard. Hapta Giorgis had won time for Tafari to complete his arrangements and to move northwards with his reinforcements. Now he was on the march at the head of a troop of gaily-decked Harar cavalry, and from all over the hills soldiers swarmed out of their villages to join him. He no longer feared that intriguers and plotters would usurp him while he was away in the field, for he had brought the whole of the Council of Ministers—and the Abun and the Itchege—with him so that he could keep an eye on them; while behind in Addis Ababa he had left Ras Balcha in command with a small but crack force, well knowing that Balcha was Lij Yasu's bitterest enemy.

On November 3, 1916, Tafari and his forces joined those of Ras Kassa and Hapta Giorgis at a small junction of mule roads called Sallale, on the Sendafa plain some fifty miles north of Addis Ababa. It was to this point that Hapta Giorgis had withdrawn after his negotiations with Mikael. It was only a question of time before the old warrior discovered that he had been tricked; so while they waited for the first furious reaction, the generals met and concerted their plans.

The Sendafa plain in November is a heart-warming sight to see. This is the spring of the year on the Shoan uplands; the grass is green from the rains, and the Maskal daisies, crinum lilies and Ethiopian orchids are in bloom. The ground undulates northwards toward a chain of small lakes and grassy fens in which teal and widgeon and Egyptian geese collect and breed, and since no Ethiopian would think of shooting them for food—though occasionally for target practice—the game were at first undisturbed by the military preparations that were going on around them. It had been decided that Ras Tafari should have control of tactics (as he had so far controlled strategy) in the coming battle, and for this purpose would establish his head-quarters just to the rear of the main formations with a bodyguard of Harar cavalry and a team of runners to keep contact. Ras Kassa and his army (most of them Galla tribesmen armed with spears, stiffened by Shoan infantry and half a dozen machine-gunners) would hold the left flank, and the War Minister, Hapta Giorgis, would be out in front with both horsemen and foot-soldiers, ready to exploit any weakness in the enemy's lines. Right until the moment of contact, tribesmen continued to pour over the hills in readiness for the battle—and for the looting that would follow. Once Tafari and his reinforcements had arrived, there was no longer any question of camouflage or concealment. By day the bright colored tents, green, gold, yellow and red, glittered in the sunshine, and the number of gaudy pennons waving in the light breeze was almost as numerous as the blossoms in the grass. By night bonfires flared and around them the soldiers feasted, drank and told tall tales of previous brave ex-ploits, or listened to the songs of the minstrels, who are as much part of an Ethiopian military formation as, in the Western world, a bat-talion band. The three senior commanders were arrayed in their battle-dress of colored tight jodphurs—Tafari's yellow, Kassa's red and Hapta Giorgis's green—silk *kamis* (or shirt) and silken cloak, their heads swathed in a cloth head-covering that rather resembled, with its knots at each corner, the handkerchief protector of bald sun-bathers at Edwardian seaside resorts. When the actual fighting began, they would top this with an ornamented *kufta* (a sort of brimless topper richly embroidered and a sign of great distinction and bravery) and hang an encrusted, ornamented sword at their waists, with squires running alongside with their shield and rifle. In addition, Hapta Giorgis would be accompanied, as a rallying sign and badge of rank, by a green ceremonial umbrella carried by an attendant.

Unless it cannot be avoided, an Ethiopian army rarely attacks first —and then only if it is confident that it has overwhelming superiority in men and arms, or if the country in which it is encamped is running short of food. The Shoan Army had the advantage that the battle ground it had chosen was home ground, well-stocked with cattle and sheep, and near enough to its own villages for the soldiers' wives and camp-followers to bring them sustenance and entertainment of every kind. It could afford to wait. Ras Mikael could not. His armies had been longer in the field and were beginning to go hungry; nor had Hapta Giorgis, in his retreat, left them much to feed or forage on.

Moreover, news had reached him from his rear that Ras Walda Giorgis had at last decided to come off the fence and support the new régime; he had occupied Dessye, Mikael's capital, and was now marching south.

It was inevitable, therefore, that Ras Mikael should launch the attack. It was now or never. If he could overcome the Shoan Army, Addis Ababa would be open to him and he could swiftly come to some arrangement with Ras Balcha and Walda Giorgis to divide up the kingdom—with Lij Yasu restored to power, of course. He had no doubts about the outcome. He and his Galla horsemen, a crack force of daredevil riders equally adept with javelins, rifles and short spears, had triumphed before over bigger armies than the one confronting him now. In a harangue to his soldiers, he told them that all that was needed was boldness and speed—and all the riches of Shoa would be in their hands.

Not only do Ethiopians not like to attack, they also believe that war is a daytime occupation and should cease with the fall of darkness. Mikael decided that he might well rout the Shoans if he not only made the first thrust but did it by night. With a squadron of cavalry and two companies of infantry, therefore, he waited until darkness had fallen and the Shoan bonfires were blazing, and then began a flanking movement designed to take the enemy, while wenching and carousing, in the rear. He might have succeeded had the scouts of his attack bothered to give him an adequate map of the route to be taken. But this they failed to do.

In the early hours of the morning, the Shoan camp was aroused by the sound of the wild squawking of geese and ducks, long before they were normally away on their dawn flights. Tafari was roused and ordered the shawms to sound the alarm. A troop of Addis Ababa militia was ordered to reconnoiter in the direction from which the angry birds had come, and just before dawn they found Mikael's troops struggling through the fens, some of them hopelessly lost. As daylight began to filter in across the plain, they moved in to attack, slaughtering the horsemen as they staggered about in the mud.

Mikael's surprise attack had gone wrong, and when he moved in his cavalry from the front, Hapta Giorgis was waiting for him. But he had another tactic up his sleeve. He had detached the main body of his army in yet another flanking movement, putting this body of troops under the command of his well-trusted second-in-command, Ras Ali, a fierce young warrior of great bravery and dash. Ras Ali hurtled his troops on to the positions being held by Ras Kassa but they were beaten back by machine-gun fire. They re-formed and began to advance again, in line formation, shooting as they marched. The machine-guns mowed them down, but still they came on until they were up to and among Ras Kassa's men, and out came the spears and the curved Galla knives as the infighting began.

The noise of battle now rose over the plain of Sendafa: the rallying cries of the troop leaders, the shrieks of rage and pain, the neighing of the horses, and, from behind, the eerie high-pitched loolooing of the excited female camp-followers. It seemed at one time that Ras Ali and his men would sweep all before them; Tafari watching from behind could see the flash of their shields and the movement of their pennons as they battered forward, cleaving a passage through Ras Kassa's men. He girded his cavalry forward into the battle to seal up the gap in the Shoan Army's ranks.

In the center, Hapta Giorgis was having trouble of his own. His troops had begun to quail before repeated charges from the cavalry Mikael was battering against him. At one point the squire carrying the War Minister's green ceremonial umbrella fell to a sword slash; and Hapta Giorgis, knowing what happened when a troop of Ethiopian soldiers lost their rallying point, hastily snatched it up, wrapped it with his shamma and lion's mane to his back, and was back in battle—the umbrella bobbing like a talisman over his head.

For five hours the battle went on, and the skill and bravado of Mikael and Ras Ali was having its effect. The Shoan soldiers were showing signs of panic. And then suddenly something happened that turned the tide of battle, and it happened in such a way that Ras Mikael must have decided that the hand of fate was indeed against him. Once before, in the fight against the dervishes, he had seen what disasters can follow the loss of a leader. When King John had been killed, the Ethiopians, though they were winning, panicked and ran. And now Tafari and his cavalry had pressed the way into Ras Kassa's broken line and were pushing forward toward Ras Ali. For a moment the men around the Wollo general faltered and Tafari's horsemen were through. They surrounded Ras Ali and battered him to his knees, and he dropped his sword in submission. The battle was far from over and, until this moment, it had been going the way of Mikael's army; but seeing their general captured, the Wollo Gallas moaned in dismay and then turned and began to run. None of their officers could rally them.

It was at this moment that, on Hapta Giorgis's front, the tide also

began to ebb for Ras Mikael. It will be remembered that, to lull
him and delay him, Hapta Giorgis had sent him a gift of a mule-
train of ammunition. The cases of cartridges had been carefully
packed and anyone opening them and trying them would have found
them in firstclass condition—the top layers that is. But underneath
Hapta Giorgis had extracted the powder from the bullets (an old
Ethiopian trick) and substituted dummy powder.

It was with this dud ammunition that the enemy now began to
load, and as the fire grew more and more ragged Hapta Giorgis
tightened up his green umbrella and yelled for his men to charge.
Just before dusk, a great roar arose from one section of the front
and Hapta Giorgis saw through his glasses that Ras Mikael had been
surrounded by Shoan troops but was brandishing his sword and refusing to surrender. And then one of the Shoan generals, Ras Wasaw,
spurred forward on his horse and cried out: "Give in—and I guarantee
your safety!" Suddenly the shouts died down to a murmur and then
to a quiet so deep that Hapta Giorgis could hear the clink of metal
as Ras Mikael, his face and beard bloodied, tears streaming down his
cheeks, flung his shield to the ground and then his sword on top
of it.

It was all over. The Shoan Army had won, and the new régime
was safe.

On November 8, 1916, a victory parade of the Shoan Army took
place before Empress Zauditu on the Jan Meda, the racecourse of
Addis Ababa. It was a day of great rejoicing. First came Ras Tafari
and his Harar cavalry. Then Hapta Giorgis and his men, followed
by Ras Kassa.

Behind them, on foot, were the captives. Ras Mikael, stripped of
everything save his breeches and shamma, manacled at the ankles,
wrists and neck, was dragged past the jeering and shrieking crowd
by a chain attached to the arm of Ras Imru—back from the prison
cell in Harar into which Ras Mikael's son had flung him. The old
man stared defiantly at the hooting onlookers and, as Tafari afterwards said, "marched and looked like a king."

After him came Ras Ali and a few of the Wollo officers. But not
many prisoners. Those who had been able to do so had fled into the
swamps. The wounded and the captive had been dispatched in a
variety of ways, not least by mutilation. The Shoan soldier had not
changed much in the eighteen years since Gleichen wrote of him:
"His natural instincts are not humane ... the cruelties that distin-

Haile Selassie addressing the League of Nations, June 30, 1936

Haile Selassie with his two sons and daughter
in the gardens of 6 Prince's Gate in 1936

Haile Selassie with Brigadier D. A. Sandford and Colonel Wingate, April 15, 1941

Part of the procession that escorted Haile Selassie on his return to Addis Ababa after almost five years of exile

guished the soldier of fortune in the dark ages come natural to him . . . and (he) does not understand being checked for so doing."

For the next eight hours the victorious troops marched past the throne, soldiers and minstrels rushing forward from each troop to sing the Empress the songs of their battle exploits. After which the sheep and cattle were driven on to the Jan Meda and their throats cut, and the raw flesh sliced off and stuffed into ravenous mouths even as the animals were giving their last shudder.

"Blood is running in the capital tonight," the Italian Minister, Count Colli, reported, "and hands and faces are sticky from it. But not the blood of Ras Mikael's men any longer. It comes from the sacrificial sheep and oxen." He added: "Every woman in the city seems to have swarmed to the Jan Meda to greet the soldiers. Tafari has sent gifts of tej and talla. We shall have a shortage of meat, I doubt not, this summer and many more mouths to feed this winter."

Yes, it was all over. The great threat to the safety of the new régime had been smashed and Ras Mikael's teeth drawn for ever.[2] Ras Tafari could plan for the future now with only one cloud on his horizon. Lij Yasu was still at large. There were stories from some of Mikael's officers that he had come to join his father at Debra Berhan, but had left before the battle. Where he had gone and what he was planning no one for the moment knew.

The time would come when he would have to be reckoned with. But for the moment, Tafari could relax and think about the problems of Government. He sat, with controlled distaste, through the series of celebratory banquets at the palace, through the toasts and songs and boasting speeches. Then he and his wife went back to their home and their children.

The victory parade had been both a triumph and an ordeal for Waizero Menen. Triumph in the knowledge that her husband had been the architect of the great victory; and sadness at the pathetic incident at its finale.

For at the tail-end of the great procession had marched the remnants of Lul Seged's army, cut to ribbons by Ras Mikael before Ankober. There were about eighty of them, and the crowd fell silent at the sight of them. And then a low moan rose among the throng as they saw who it was who came last of all.

It was a young boy, about seven years old. He wore no covering

[2] He died in jail in 1918.

to his head and none of the silks that usually bedeck young Amharas. His dress was simply a lion's skin slung across his shoulders
and far too big for his thin frame. It was the lion skin of a great
warrior.

Waizero Menen watched as the boy, bare-footed, padded by. This
was the son of her ex-husband, Lul Seged, in public mourning for
his slain father.

part two

PATIENCE

chapter six

COUNTER-REVOLUTION

IN THE YEARS that followed the deposition of Lij Yasu and the capture of Ras Mikael a phrase keeps recurring in the dispatches of the European diplomatic missions in Addis Ababa: "Conditions could not possibly get worse than they are at the moment." But, of course, they could and did.

1916-1918 were lucky years for Ethiopia only to the extent that Germany, France, Italy and Great Britain were too embroiled in their own war to have time or troops to spare; otherwise there is little doubt that the land would have been occupied and its territories split up between the colonial powers. It was ripe for the picking. Thanks to the clumsy arrangement which had been made (quite deliberately) by the Council of Ministers, control of State affairs had been split among three quite different personalities who could not hope to agree on a concerted policy. The result was lack of central control and a general chaos which the rases knew only too well how to exploit.

Several of the provinces in the North, spurning Queen Zauditu as their Empress, erupted in a rash of small republics, short-lived only because powerful warlords like Ras Walda Giorgis and Hailu and Seyoum moved swiftly in to overcome them. They did so, they declared, in the name of the Empress, but this was lip-service to an authority in Shoa which they would only accept so long as it did not interfere with them. While the triumverate in Addis Ababa wrestled for supremacy, the rases ravened on the countryside like locusts. Walda Giorgis in six months drove 50,000 cattle out of Wollo into his own province and did not worry when two-thirds of them died of "horse disease." There were some spectacular exhibitions of bloody gluttony on the way, for he had ordained that all animals incapable of making the journey across country could be eaten on the spot by his soldiers, who did not hesitate to hamstring one steer out of four and carve it up into warm portions of their favorite "palpitating" flesh. Ras Hailu had embarked in a large way in the slave-trade and had begun to decimate villages across the Sudan border from his native Gojjam. He was said to have 3,000 personal slaves at his Gebbi in Debra Marcos, of whom more than half were small boys, small girls and young women reserved for his "personal attendance." But many of his slaves made their way, in caravans led by Moslem Ethiopians, to the Danakil country whence they were shipped across the Red Sea to Arabia.

In a land filled with slave-raiders, poachers and lawless bands of hungry soldiers—who have always lived by loot in Ethiopia—trade had practically petered out, crops were hoarded and famine and disease were blighting the countryside. For the moment, however, there was little that Ras Tafari could do about the anarchic conditions of his country, no matter how ambitious were the plans he had made after Mikael's defeat. For he knew only too well that the power he needed had eluded him. He was twenty-four years old, he had been named Regent and Heir to the Throne, but he was very conscious that the oligarchy of the rases had cheated him of the autocratic control he needed to put Ethiopia in order.

Had Lij Yasu been caught in Harar, Tafari's hands might have been freer to manipulate the new régime to his own liking. But the Emperor was still at large and rumors of his movements and intentions came in from all parts of the country, stirring unrest among the chiefs, inciting the Moslems, throwing a threatening shadow across the throne. As Tafari explained to Thesiger, who privately urged him to exert his influence; "Until the prince is caught, I dare not move. The Empress is already being menaced from another quarter."

As, indeed, she was. With the defeat of Mikael and the flight of Lij Yasu, old Queen Taitu had emerged from banishment, and the widow of Menelik had not lost her appetite for power. Nor had her antipathy to Tafari been in anyway dissipated by the years. She did not anticipate having much trouble in getting rid of him, for she had no reason to doubt that her influence over her step-daughter, the Empress, was still as strong as ever; and not only that. Was not her nephew, Ras Gugsa, now married to Empress Zauditu, who adored him? And did he not, in turn, adore his aunt? With these two puppets dancing on her strings, how could she fail to outwit and discredit Tafari?

Like many another Ethiopian (and many a European) before and since, she was deceived by Tafari's mild manner into underestimating his skill as an intriguer and his ruthless quiet strength as a political in-fighter. Her plan was simple. She would move into the palace with her step-daughter and her nephew, and they would bar the gates to Ras Tafari. Then, from the palace, and in alliance with Hapta Giorgis, they would take over the running of the kingdom and appoint the chiefs upon whose loyalty (and tribute) they could depend.

Some days after she came down the mountain from Entoto, Tafari gave a banquet in her honor to which the Empress and her husband were invited. Presently, when the feasting began to grow drunken and raucous, Taitu and Zauditu withdrew, leaving Ras Gugsa with Tafari. For once the heir to the throne seemed to be eating and drinking as heartily as any of them, and soon both he and Gugsa were drunk. It was then that the girls were brought in. The following morning Gugsa awakened in the arms of a Galla concubine in a dwelling on the other side of Addis Ababa. There was a message for him. He would, for the time being, be the guest of Ras Tafari, who would spare nothing to make him comfortable; but, with the guard around the compound, it was desirable that he should remain where he was for the time being. No harm would come to him— *unless he tried to go to the palace.*

The Empress had waited all night for Ras Gugsa to come to her. It took her some days to realize that her husband would never share her marital bed again.

A week later—a week in which Zauditu demanded, asked, pleaded and implored Tafari to return her husband—it was quietly made known that the Empress Zauditu had divorced her husband and would henceforth devote the whole of her time and energies to the cause of her country. She had a new husband—and his name was Ethiopia.

As for Queen Taitu, she was sent back to Entoto to meditate on the failure of her plot.

So the first threat to Tafari's position had been rebuffed and the danger of a palace revolt circumvented. In one week and without the loss of a life, the Empress had been deprived of her allies, and the Regent had made it cruelly clear that he would not brook any attempt to undermine his position at court. He had broken up a marriage to demonstrate the extent to which he was prepared to go to protect himself.

The Empress swallowed her pride and accepted the *fait accompli*. But she did not forget the pain and humiliation of it; nor did she cease to love her husband. For the next twelve years she always hoped that one day he would come back to her. As for Ras Gugsa, he tried, he tried.

On February 11, 1917, Zauditu was crowned Empress of Ethiopia in St. George's Cathedral, Addis Ababa, by the Abun Mattheos. Ras Gugsa was not there to see his former wife take her place on the Imperial throne; he had been fobbed off with a province in the north.

It was hardly an auspicious moment for an accession. "The coronation ceremonies were barely completed," reported Thesiger, "when the provinces of Semyen, Wolkait, Wojju and Wogan revolted. The Moslem Wollos, who were being persecuted by the Shoan Army, attacked Dessye, and, though defeated, went on to raid Arussi. The Moslem and pagan tribes from Pinor to Dolo have risen and there are rumblings from Tigre."

Amid the chaos and confusion, Thesiger went on, "Ras Tafari stands alone, shouldering the full responsibility but without real power and uncertain whom he can trust." The Empress, still smarting from the pain and humiliation Tafari had caused her, "is making tentative efforts to assert herself." (One of these efforts was to incite her old lover, Ras Abata, to form a party to unseat the Regent.) "The Council of Ministers are intriguing for their own gains. The soldiers are discontented, the lesser officers—summoned to Addis Ababa last September—are impoverished. The soldiers can only live by looting, and the peasantry are becoming desperate. They are rising out of sheer indignation against the lawlessness."

Thesiger's messages about this time, especially when they mention Tafari, are a series of written sighs of disappointment. He refers to Ras Walda Giorgis's wholesale spoliation of Wollo and groans that the Regent allows him to get away with it. "It is this weakness on Tafari's part and his apparent inability to take any firm decision in the face of difficulties that make one almost despair of any amelioration of the state of the country as a result of Lij Yasu's departure."

But in one important way Thesiger, and the British Government, are to blame for Tafari's lack of resolution. How could he confound his enemies and discipline his allies without demonstrating that might, as well as right, was on his side? For this he needed rifles and ammunition, and the embargo on the import of arms was still being maintained. (Officially, that is. Secretly, the French were doing a thriving trade in arms-smuggling to some of the rases, a fact of which the British Legation had, through its Intelligence service, documentary proof.) Tafari asked Thesiger to supply him with 30,000 rifles for the personal use of his own forces. The British Minister admitted that Tafari was not only the one reliable force in the country but was also a firm friend of Britain, solidly in sympathy with the British war effort; but his recommendation was only lukewarm and he suggested that the Government should ask for a *quid pro quo* which he might have known Tafari would not swallow. It was that, in return for arms, the Regent should immediately proclaim the Germans and Turks *persona non grata* and expel their legations from Ethiopia. This Tafari refused to do. It would play into the hands of the pro-Germans at court at a moment when he was in no position to suppress them; but more than that, it would humiliate him by displaying him not as a British friend but as a British lackey.

Was it not enough, he asked, that he had promised to curb German and Turkish intrigues? But on this occasion it was not enough. At a time when he was in dire need, the attitude of the British Government was rather like that of Marie-Antoinette toward the starving peasants. Instead of bullets, they shipped to Thesiger the insignia of the Grand Cross of St. Michael and St. George, which he was instructed to bestow on Tafari "at an appropriate moment." He hung it on the Regent's chest on April 13, 1917, not in recognition of any spectacular achievement but more, one feels, to bolster his morale, for it was a moment when he was feeling particularly downhearted. The Empress had snubbed him by nominating the first Negus, or King, of her régime. It had been expected that the appointment would go to Tafari, who would be crowned either Negus of Shoa or Harar. Instead, the crown went to one of the most profligate rases in the Empire, Walda Giorgis, though the Empress must have known only too well that the title was unlikely to strengthen that wily reprobate's adherence to the Shoans. Moreover, Tafari was only too conscious that new plots were being hatched against him and that the Queen was implicated.

The Regent did not lose too much sleep over the antagonisms which surrounded him, for he was supple and well-informed enough to emerge intact from the intrigues; but there were moments when he chafed at his isolation and feared for the securities of Harar and the pleasures of family life he knew he could find there.

"Tafari confesses his weaknesses and sense of impotence," wrote Thesiger. "He wishes to resign the Regency and return as Ras of Harar. One day he will have to choose between resignation and a *coup d'état* against the Council of Ministers. I asked him why he didn't dismiss them, but he said that until Lij Yasu's capture he could not."

For, of course, the wayward and pestilential ex-Emperor was still at large and—thanks to the stupidity of the Shoans—his potentiality for trouble had increased rather than diminished in the months since his deposition. After the capture of Ras Mikael there had been a moment when a gesture of magnanimity toward the Moslems from the new régime in Shoa might have soothed their fears and mended the religious rift with the Christians; but what ever Tafari might have wished, he was too weak to control the rases who swept in to engorge Mikael's territories. They were not interested in a rapprochement with the Moslems, for that would mean that they would have to respect their women, their lives and their property, which, particularly in the case of Walda Giorgis and Hailu, was too much to ask. The raping and ravaging began, and it was from sheer instinct for preservation that the Moslem chiefs reached out and clutched at Lij Yasu once more, man of straw though he might now be.

Ever since the defeat of his father, the young ex-Emperor had been wandering through the Danakil deserts, half mad with fear and frustration, racked by disease, a prey to frightening bouts of megalomania and pitiful nightmares. There had been one period of two months when he lay on the point of death in a hiding place only a few miles from a Shoan Army outpost, with only twenty men to guard him and the last of his Danakil brides to minister to his deliriums. But though news of his condition and an approximate location of his sanctuary eventually reached the Shoans, no one made any serious effort to seek him out until Tafari was informed—and by the time he had ordered the militia to move, he had gone again.

During the early months of 1917, Lij Yasu made contact with one of his father's old chiefs, Ras Imer, whose lands had been seized by the Shoan armies and his womenfolk sold into slavery. He had gathered around him a force of some 25,000 men and they were well armed with spears and rifles, though short of ammunition. Ras Imer rallied the ex-Emperor's flagging spirits and spurred his ambitions anew to lead a Moslem crusade against the infidel.

All through February and March, Ras Imer's forces ranged through Wollo picking up recruits and stocking up with supplies. It was decided to establish the headquarters of the rebels in the ancient fortress of Magdala, just north of Ras Mikael's old capital of Dessye. Both symbolically and physically, it was hard to think of a place more likely to stir the hearts of Ethiopians. It was here that Emperor Theodore, with Ras Mikael fighting bravely by his side, had defied the British armies led by General Napier and had been overwhelmed only by superior forces and modern armaments. Physically, Magdala was an all but impregnable fortress, perched on a mountain buttress with only five precipitous paths leading into it, all easily covered by the defenders above with rifle-fire, stones or even (as Lij Yasu and Imer contemplated at one time) boiling water. To Tafari, if not to the other chiefs, another parallel with Theodore's last stand at Magdala must have occurred: that Lij Yasu, like the Emperor before him, was mad. But mad to the point that he too, when the Shoan armies moved in, would kill himself?

Unfortunately, the Shoan troops were not of the same caliber as the British. Tafari was inclined to agree with Thesiger that "the Abyssinians are not good at scaling narrow mountain paths, or facing avalanches of rocks, and long-range fire." He could only hope, with the Minister, that "Lij Yasu's troops will desert—or Lij Yasu will, as usual, desert his troops and get out alone."

Meantime, he had a plan to bestir the reluctant Shoan besiegers. To ring Magdala he had dispatched armies under the command of Ras Demissie and Ras Abata, neither of whom was the most trustworthy commander for the task. Ras Demissie, it will be remembered, was related by marriage to Lij Yasu. Ras Abata was an old enemy of Tafari's—though it is true, in his case, that he was an even greater enemy of the Emperor, who had jailed and tortured him. Thesiger had urged Tafari to go himself and to take the War Minister, Fitaurari Ras Hapta Giorgis, with him. But the War Minister was consolidating his position in Addis Ababa, and so long as he stayed behind, the Regent must needs remain too, to keep his eye on him. The only other warlord with an army which might have been battered against the fortress belonged to Negus Walda Giorgis, but that old man was too busy digesting his spoils to come to the help of the Shoans.

So Tafari had no alternative but to make use of the forces available until reinforcements could be brought up. But he had an idea for putting spirit into the troops under Demissie and Abata and fear into the hearts of the Magdala defenders. So far the Regent had never left Ethiopia in his life, nor had he even seen an airplane. But he had read about them and he had heard of their exploits both on the Western front in France and in the skies above Kilimanjaro, where the British were using them increasingly in their war with the German commander, von Lettow-Vorbeck. He talked it over with Thesiger (who, in this instance, wholeheartedly supported him) and was encouraged to draw up a formal request that two British warplanes be sent to Ethiopia from Egypt, complete with pilots and observers. The idea was for the planes to bomb and strafe the fortress and sow such terror among the defenders that they would cut and run.

In backing the request, Thesiger cabled: "My Italian colleague and I agree that Magdala is the crux of the situation, and that Tafari must finish with Lij Yasu without delay. Magdala cannot be taken without the aid of aeroplanes and the matter is very urgent, as the rains are approaching. Tafari must be supported for if he falls general anarchy will follow."

The reaction of the Foreign Office was, after first swallowing hard, to agree that the proposition might be worth entertaining, and they cabled to say that the request had been passed on to the War Office (through which the planes would be supplied) for their comments. The War Office went purple in the face. Under no circumstances, they said, could they possibly send airplanes to a country where no one had ever flown before,[1] where the savages had barbarous methods of treating prisoners, and where they would be interfering in a civil war in a country which wasn't even one of our Allies. When Thesiger persisted, they replied that even if they could find the planes they could not possibly let them be armed with bombs or machine-guns, since it wasn't our war. (They knew so little about Ethiopia that they failed to produce the only excuse which would have been valid—that the planes of the time would not have been able to take off, because of the altitude of the Ethiopian uplands.) They were still arguing when the rains began to pelt down on Magdala and turned the plain around it into a quagmire, and then it was too late.

While these exchanges were taking place, Ras Demissie and Ras Abata sat around on the plain and made no effort to storm the fortress. They must, at times, have envied the beseiged, for it was they who were plentifully supplied with food and wine and women,

[1] Unless the Queen of Sheba essayed a flight with one of the gifts King Solomon made her when she left Jerusalem to return to Ethiopia. It was described as "a machine to ride in the air."

whereas the plains around had been picked clean. By night they could hear the sound of merriment and catch the glint of fires, and watchers who got close reported that they had even caught glimpses of Lij Yasu gesturing mockingly at them from the battlements.

It was not until June, when the rains were beginning to come down heavily, that reinforcements arrived. Hapta Giorgis had evidently convinced himself that Tafari had consolidated his position in Addis Ababa and that it was no use waiting on the Empress's schemes and plots to topple him—a contingency which he had been poised to exploit. He agreed to go north with his army and persuaded Ras Kassa to fight beside him once more, as he had against Ras Mikael. They arrived outside Magdala on June 6, 1917, and threw a cordon of troops around the fortress. But one reconnaissance was sufficient to dampen their fighting spirits and for them to declare the fortress impregnable. "It would be asking brave soldiers, who are prepared to perform the improbable to essay the impossible," he wrote to the Regent, and Ras Kassa agreed with him.

They decided instead to parley with Ras Imer, the commander of the garrison. An emissary was dispatched with a note offering him a full pardon and a substantial reward for him and his followers if they would surrender and deliver up Lij Yasu. "He is a royal prince and we are loyal soldiers of the Empress," Hapta Giorgis wrote. "He will come to no harm at our hands but will be delivered to the safety of his sister in the capital."

The answer was not long in coming. The body of the emissary, mutilated, was flung over the cliffside for the Shoans to find the following morning. The position could not be more difficult. The rain poured down. Food was scarce and conditions for the besiegers were miserable in the extreme. The troops had begun to kill and eat their donkeys, a sure sign of desperation. Those who had homes which could be reached along the slippery mule tracks had already begun to desert.

Toward the end of July, there was a break in the downpour and Hapta Giorgis and his generals used the break to send away scavenging parties for food and forage. It was a mistake. The watchers in the fortress reported to Ras Imer that the besiegers were thinning in numbers and that some routes down the cliffsides were not even being blocked. On July 31, Imer roused Lij Yasu and led him and a raiding party of about 1,500 men through the break in the Shoan lines. It was several days before Hapta Giorgis even learned that they had slipped through his hands, and by that time they were swarming over the country, gathering reinforcements. On August 8 they trapped a force of Ras Kassa's troops in the neighborhood of Dessye and scattered them, taking 300 prisoners, all of whom were mutilated and slaughtered. It was fortunate for the Shoans that they did not continue their advance into Dessye, for they could easily have taken the Wollo capital, which was almost completely undefended.

By this time Hapta Giorgis was sounding the tocsin as far south as Addis Ababa, urgently demanding reinforcements and arms. "The prince is loose again and his force is growing," the British Minister cabled. It was true. For Lij Yasu it was almost like old times. Recruits came flocking to him at every village. The intoxication of potential victory seemed to drive the rheums from his body and he was his old, arrogant, petulant self, haranguing his followers with promises of gold and women and land, flogging and torturing prisoners, guzzling over raw meat and tej and wenching with the girls whom the chiefs once more gladly gave him.

During August, while Lij Yasu celebrated and Ras Imer recruited, Tafari made urgent preparations to leave for the front. He had ordered recruits to go north from Harar and from Addis Ababa and commanded his officers to "give every man in every village a rifle and tell him to make for the Wollo country." He knew that there was a certain risk for himself if he left Addis Ababa. His agents informed him that there was tense anticipation at the German Legation, where all members had been issued with arms and told by the Minister, von Syburg, to stand by for "important events." German emissaries were said to be in communication with the Empress and with old Queen Taitu in her retirement palace on Mount Entoto. The Moslems in the capital were stirring, roused by rumors that a *jihad* was about to begin. There were stories that the Danakil, bribed by German infiltrators from Arabia, would soon rise and cut the railway from Jibouti. Most sinister of all, the new leader of the Council of Ministers, Bitwaded Igazu, after months of servilely licking Tafari's slippers, had begun to attack him openly, accusing him of turning the Empress into a puppet and a prisoner in her own palace. Of all the men in privileged positions in the Empire, there were few who had such low cunning or were so riddled with corruption as Igazu. Tafari once said of him: "He will sell his soul for money." He might have added, as Mirabeau did of Talleyrand, that for Igazu it would be a good bargain, since he would be getting gold for dung. The Regent realized that if this devious and decadent politician dared to speak out so forthrightly against him, the plot to unseat him must be strongly backed.

Nevertheless, he decided to go north with his troops to Wollo and join the War Minister in the clash with Lij Yasu now inevitably coming. He was about to depart from the capital when news from Hapta Giorgis reached him of a great battle which had been fought on August 27 on the plain between Dessye and Ankober. Ras Imer had decided to attack first before the Shoan Army could absorb its reinforcements, and he swept down upon the War Minister's troop concentrations with a horde of Moslem cavalry and spearmen estimated to number 40,000. But the wily Hapta Giorgis had brought both cannon and machine-guns with him to put backbone into his defenses; he had, moreover, provided himself through French sources with the first shrapnel shells to be used in Ethiopia. The result was a devastating slaughter. The Moslem soldiers were fanatically brave and made repeated charges, but only once succeeded in penetrating Hapta Giorgis's lines—and that was with his connivance. A portion of his front fell back and Ras Imer called upon his cavalry to follow him as he punched a way through it. The moment he was through, the Shoans closed around him and the massacre began.

"They are defeated with tremendous losses," reported Thesiger. "Ras Imer was killed, Fitaurari Serabenzu (his second in command) is seriously wounded. The casualties are great. I am told that there are 18,000 dead and wounded on the battlefield of whom two-thirds belong to the forces of Lij Yasu. Most of the prisoners taken have been mutilated, with the loss of a hand or a foot or worse—for having fought again after being previously pardoned for fighting with Ras Mikael."

And what of Lij Yasu?

The good tidings came to Addis Ababa that the ex-Emperor was among those who had been captured, but this quickly proved to be a false report. His *likamaquas*, or stooge, had been trapped while sporting his master's battle finery and had been borne in triumph to Hapta Giorgis, who had promised a large reward for Lij Yasu's apprehension, but the false prince had been handed back to his captors after the deception was discovered—and they took compensation for their disappointment in their own particularly Ethiopian ways.

Lij Yasu himself had escaped once more. He had been seen with a few followers on a patch of rising ground at the beginning of the battle, watching Ras Imer's first charge go in. But Moslem captives declared that he had decamped with the first news that the battle was not going well for them, and was making for the desert.

"Lij Yasu had a bad reception from the Danakil when he came among them," reported Thesiger, for the desert chiefs considered it proper for a chief to die with his defeated troops. "It is rumoured that he is trying to reach Arabia." In fact, he was to spend the next two years skulking ineffectually about the desert, sick in body and mind, no longer taken seriously even by the Moslems—and certainly not by Ras Tafari. When news came, in the early months of 1918, that Lij Yasu was lying seriously ill in a desert hamlet near Ankober, racked by incipient general paralysis of the insane, the Regent did not even bother to send out to bring him in. He rightly calculated that the discredited wreck of the former Emperor could do him less harm rotting in freedom than if he were brought in chains to the capital and, perhaps, turned into a martyr or a symbol by the Regent's enemies.

"He is finished," he said. "Let him be."

He was much too preoccupied with the plot against his own person which simmered on in Addis Ababa, despite the triumph of the Shoan armies in the north. Thesiger reported to the Foreign Office on September 21, 1917: "A counter-revolution against Ras Tafari is planned for the 27th of this month—which happens to be the first anniversary of the deposition of Lij Yasu—the object of which is his own arrest. The Empress is implicated but she is merely the tool of Igazu. The Mahel Safari (the former bodyguard of Emperor Menelik) form the nucleus of the conspirator's force. Tafari has sent for 2,000 of his own Harar troops, nominally to relieve his guard, but he has delayed demobbing them, so that he now has 4,000 troops."

Thesiger pointed out that though the revolt may have begun as a plot to coincide with Lij Yasu's attacks in the north, it was now boiling up into a *coup d'état* of its own, with the old Queen Taitu and the German Legation keeping the Empress and Bitwaded Igazu hot with a combination of bribes and exhortations.

"If Tafari wins against them," commented the British Minister, "he will be in a position to arrest Igazu and all the members of the old Council of Ministers, and the ground will then be free for reform." He did not add what might happen if Tafari lost, but then, he did not need to. It seems certain that the Regent had taken him into his confidence and that Thesiger had no doubt of the outcome.

On September 27, the Mahel Safari marched into the palace and

its commander, dressed in his most resplendent fighting dress and
hung with battle honors from Menelik's day, craved an audience of
the Empress. She was expecting him. He fell to his knees before her
and then crawled to her throne, where he kissed her feet and asked
permission to bring before her "a traitor who has been conspiring
against the best interests of Your Imperial Majesty and our country."

Empress Zauditu turned to Queen Taitu, who had come down
from the mountain for the occasion, and smiled.

"Bring in your traitor," she said.

There was a rattle of chains and the prisoner was marched into
the audience chamber, where he fell to the ground in sobbing prostra-
tion. The Empress and her stepmother stared at him in silent consternation. It was Bitwaded Igazu.

"Here is the plotter against Your Imperial Majesty," cried the
commander of the bodyguard. "What shall we do with him?"

The Empress paused, and then espied Tafari coming into the audience chamber. "Give him into the custody of our beloved Regent,
Ras Tafari," she said, smoothly. "In his great wisdom, he will know
best what to do."

Bitwaded Igazu languished in the dungeons for a month or so,
and then, as usual, he bought his freedom with a gift to the Treasury
of two chests of ill-gotten Maria Theresa dollars. Tafari could have
had him quietly put away but found him too contemptuous for such
treatment. But, shortly afterwards, in her palace on Mount Entoto,
Queen Taitu, Menelik's scheming widow, fortuitously died from a
heart attack. The Regent saw to it that she had a most resplendent
funeral, and the Abun Mattheos led the solemn dance of the priests
which preceded her departure into Menelik's mausoleum. "I rode
there with the staff of the Legation," wrote Sir Gerald Campbell,
the chargé d'affaires, "and was present at the funeral dance held before
the Empress, Tafari, the Ministers and the higher chiefs. . . . Her
death will be a relief to Tafari, as she was opposed to him and used
her powers to intrigue to his disadvantage. Her sentiments were pro-
German. She was 76."

It was certainly a relief to Tafari that the old lady was dead, for
she had indeed been a thorn in his side. But if he could now sleep
easier in his bed, he was not much nearer to his ambition. He still
lacked the authoritative power he needed to unify his country, to
inaugurate reforms, to put down tyranny and abolish the despotism
of the rases. Still standing in his way, a solid conservative phalanx,
were the Empress, the War Minister, the warlords and the Ministers,

all determined to thwart any plan he might make to ameliorate the lot of the people—for amelioration of the lot of the masses, they knew only too well, spelled danger to their feudal privileges.

For Ras Tafari, 1918 was a deflating and a dispiriting year. He followed the arrest of Igazu and the death of Queen Taitu with the dismissal of the Council of Ministers, and he got ready to gird himself for a struggle for supremacy with the Empress and the rases. But for this he needed arms for his private army and the British Government was still procrastinating over the 30,000 rifles for which he was asking, this time because the Italians feared that he might use them against Taitu's relatives—Ras Wollye and Ras Gugsa—in the North. (The Italians were in the process of buying the allegiance of the two warlords and thus ensuring a buffer state along the frontier with Eritrea, and they did not want to see them displaced.) True, toward the end of the year they changed their minds and decided that Wollye and Gugsa were, in Count Colli's words, "surly, arrogant and untrustworthy," and they withdrew their objections to Tafari's request. But by that time near disaster had struck him.

The great influenza epidemic of 1917, which swept over Europe and killed people by the thousand, somehow made its way to Africa. By 1918 it had reached Dar es Salaam, in German East Africa, and from there it made its way first to Jibouti and then to the Ethiopian uplands, where it was at first mistaken for an epidemic of typhoid. One of its victims was the Regent. He collapsed and was carried to his bed on September 2. The British and Italian Legations both sent doctors to attend him,[2] but between September 7-8 he was hovering between life and death. News quickly spread through Addis Ababa that he had died and the Empress summoned and reconstituted the Council of Ministers, while Hapta Giorgis announced that he was taking over the reins of Government from the Regent—"temporarily," he announced hastily, when a great wailing and moaning began in the city. "His threatened demise has brought home forcibly how much influence he has quietly acquired during the past one and one-half years," wrote Thesiger. "The Government is completely disorganized." So great, in fact, was the unrest among the people at his reported death that the Ministers, who had at first rejoiced at his prospective demise, grew alarmed and came to Tafari to plead with him to show himself. Though he was still far from recovered, he

[2] One of them, Doctor Chaiban, was later reported by Thesiger to "have contracted a chill from his tireless attentions and died on September 17."

walked to the balcony of the Empress's *elfin* during the Maskal celebrations and waved to an ecstatically happy crowd.

But it was several months before he was back at his desk again
and by that time the Council of Ministers had consolidated themselves and he would have to start the business of getting rid of them
all over again. "The only man who wishes his country well," sighed
Thesiger, "is Tafari. . . . Will he be obstinate and see the game
through? He wants so much to go back to the tranquility of Harar.
But he may win yet." And he added, ominously: "If he loses, the
time for European intervention in Ethiopia may be near."

Not, however, if Tafari could help it. For a week or two after
his recovery he went to Harar to convalesce and be nursed back to
health by his devoted and beloved Menen. He returned to Addis
Ababa in December and decided to say good-bye to a difficult and
unfruitful year with a flourish that would show everyone—Ethiopian
and foreigner alike—that he was still a force to be reckoned with
and would be pressing on with his plans. In Europe the Great War
was over, and on December 26, 1918, he chose the occasion of the
opening of the Versailles Conference to send a message to King
George V in London in which he made his sentiments clear.

"On behalf of Her Imperial Majesty Empress Zauditu," he cabled,
"I address to you on the occasion of the forthcoming Peace Conference our most hearty congratulations on the victory of the Allies.

"We thank God he has brought this murderous war to an end
and that he has granted victory to those who strove for the rights
of peoples. Thanksgiving services will be held in our churches to
celebrate this great event."

He went on, obviously for home consumption: "Our people are
all the happier in the knowledge of the victory of the Allies in
that they too have suffered since the beginning of the War from the
course our own political leaders have steered. This course was distasteful."

And he ended by stressing that, if he had his way, the days of
isolation would soon be over: "Desirous of entering into closer relations with other nations and cementing friendship with our neighbours, we intend shortly to send to Europe a special mission which
we hope will be favourably received by Your Majesty's Government."

It was his way of serving notice that his hand was back on the
steering wheel of Ethiopian affairs. Unfortunately, it was still a dual-
controlled pantechnicon that he was driving, and very much of a
bone-shaker at that.

chapter seven

ETHIOPIA
JOINS THE LEAGUE

FOR TWO YEARS after the defeat of his Wollo army, the ex-Emperor, Lij Yasu, had been a fugitive from the Shoans and for most of that time it was the fierce tribes of the Danakil Desert who gave him shelter. But in 1921 they grew tired of him and the manic tantrums of his diseased mind, and through one of their chiefs, Abubekr, they negotiated his sale to the Empress for a peace treaty and an annulment of unpaid back taxes.

Unfortunately for Tafari, he was in Harar when the royal fugitive was handed over, and there was not time for him to get his hands on him. Free, Lij Yasu was a menace of diminishing value, but in captivity he could well prove to be an embarrassment to Tafari's position as heir to the throne should he come into the hands of one of his enemies. The Regent therefore petitioned the Empress to deliver the ex-Emperor into his custody, promising to keep him in comfort and health and pay due regard to his former glories. Whether health as well as comfort was, in fact, what Zauditu desired for her half-brother is unlikely. Fond though she may at one time have been of him, she could not fail to be aware that his existence was a constant challenge to her as well as to Tafari, and that her best policy towards Lij Yasu was to see him in the hands of someone who would not kill him, "but needst not strive officiously to keep alive." But this thought also occurred to the War Minister, Hapta Giorgis, and to the Shoan ministers. They forced the Empress to promise that Tafari should be specifically "exempted from the responsibility" of acting as custodian of the captured prince. A squabble began as to who should get Lij Yasu's custody, and a seasoned schemer, Ras

Hailu of the Gojjam, tried to do some horse-trading. (In Hailu's hands, Lij Yasu could have proved a most useful pawn. Hailu's daughter, Waizero Sabela, was Lij Yasu's only recognized wife and mother of his daughter.) But if Tafari could not act as jailer himself, he was determined that Lij Yasu should pass into the control of someone who would neutralize him, and in this aim he succeeded. Lij Yasu, bound according to royal tradition in golden chains round the wrists and ankles, was handed over to Ras Kassa, who was now warlord of Tigre with his headquarters at Axum, the ancient capital of Ethiopian kings. Ras Kassa, one of the most steadfast and least ambitious of rases, pledged himself to give the royal captive his most respectful attentions.

This he did indeed. He had an Italian doctor brought down from Asmara, in Eritrea, to treat the royal patient's syphilis. He was "confined to quarters" rather than imprisoned in a cell, and was given all the food and comforts he desired. Once he had recovered his appetite, these comforts included a steady diet of female entertainment, and it was this liberal supply of women to his quarters which was to precipitate one of the great crises of Tafari's life.

But that was later. For eleven years, from 1921 to 1932, Lij Yasu became a pampered hostage and ceased to be a factor in Ethiopian affairs.

For a picture of what life was like in Ethiopia in the early years of the 1920's I would recommend readers to turn to the writings of C. F. Rey, who traveled extensively all over the country between 1922-26.[1] Rey has the ability to be quite ruthless in his descriptions of the savagery and backwardness of the land and people without ever appearing spiteful, or concealing that he is deeply fond of Ethiopia and all who live there.

These were the years when Ras Tafari was still fighting the Empress, Hapta Giorgis and the feudal rases in his efforts to get his programs for reform accepted, and, at least in foreign affairs, he had made some progress. In 1923 he had persuaded Queen Zauditu to allow an application to go forward to Geneva for Ethiopia's admission to the League of Nations. The application was at first resisted by a number of countries—Britain, Switzerland, Australia and Norway among them—on the grounds that Addis Ababa's control over

[1] His travel book, *In The Country Of The Blue Nile*, has a rather nostalgic preface from Major General Lord Edward Gleichen, who never got back to Ethiopia after his adventurous journey in 1897.

Ethiopia was uncertain and that the central Government had taken no adequate steps to control the widespread trade in slaves and arms.

Italy and France, both of whom had ambitions to increase their trade and influence in Ethiopia, supported the application and lobbied the other nations into agreeing. Ethiopia was unanimously elected a member, and although Hapta Giorgis grumbled that "we are now under the evil eye of the foreigner," it was to pay dividends for the country within two years. In this same year, Tafari had dared what no other Emperor or heir to the throne had ever dared before, and left the country. He traveled to Aden as the guest of the Governor and, to the alarm of his entourage, fulfilled a lifelong ambition by taking his first flight in a plane. He was also given an exhibition of bombing from the air, an experience which confirmed his long-held belief that airplanes could become useful handmaidens of Ethiopia, for peace and for war. But only in the right hands, his own; he issued an edict upon his return to Ethiopia prohibiting the import of airplanes into the country except with his special permission.

The visit to Aden whetted his appetite for foreign travel and in 1924 he accepted invitations from various foreign governments to visit Europe. Dare he go? Would his enemies unseat him while he was away? There was only one way to make sure that they would not, and that was to take them with him. He sailed from Jibouti in April, 1924, with an entourage which included Ras Hailu and Ras Seyoum, Waizero Menen, thirty attendants and six lions (two for King George V, two for the Paris Zoo, and two for President Millerand, who also got four zebras).[2] *The Times* saluted his arrival in London—he had visited Jerusalem, Cairo, Marseilles, Rome and Paris on the way—by writing on July 7, 1924: "The arrival of Prince Tafari Makonnen in London today is an historical event, for never in the history of the royal house of Ethiopia, which is descended by tradition from the issue of King Solomon and the Queen of Sheba, has an Abyssinian monarch or heir to the throne been known to quit his native mountains in the heart of Africa. The tremendous rupture with the past which his journey involves shows the boldness, the enlightenment and the resolution of the prince's character. A visit to London has long been his cherished ambition, planted in his youthful heart by the example of his father, Ras Makonnen, who was special envoy of the late Emperor Menelik at the Coronation

[2] He left Hapta Giorgis behind to look after the Empress and the other rases, and Ras Kassa to look after Hapta Giorgis.

of King Edward VII. He brought with him a gift of a processional Cross which still stands in the nave of Westminster Abbey, for the Abyssinians are among the very earliest of Christian peoples."

On the other hand, the London Evening News wrote: "The first thing one notices about Ras Tafari, the Prince Regent of Abyssinia, is his bowler hat. The next shock comes from the pair of elastic-sided boots peeping shyly from time to time from beneath his shamma, the native cloak that falls in graceful folds about his slight person. The reason for his billycock and jemina is that in his native country His Royal Highness is heavily swathed in a cloak of gold and a lion's mane, and the hard round hat which most of us have to wear he finds comfortable. The reason why he bought a hard round hat goes back to the beginning of time. An Abyssinian considers it a sign of deepest respect towards his host to alter the appearance of his head, and he chose the billycock in preference to a top hat as a gesture."

Ras Hailu went on a gay tour of the sights, and for him the favorite recollections of his visit were his evenings at a series of Paris night clubs, his appearance (with the Regent) at a dinner party at Buckingham Palace "when we ate off gold plate," and a vast shopping spree which subsequently filled his storehouses at Debra Marcos with cases of champagne and vintage wines, cigars, tinned goods, masses of suits, shirts and women's dresses, and a motorcar (which he had stripped at Addis Ababa and brought across country by mule train). Since he had always been one of Ethiopia's richest princes and Mr. Zaphiro, the Oriental Secretary of the British Legation in Addis Ababa, was prepared to vouch for his affluence, he had had no difficulty in obtaining a loan from the Bank of England to finance his extravagances. He loved to recount how Ras Seyoum, inspired by his example, hurried round to ask for similar accommodation, and on being asked for security replied that surely the fact that he was a prince was sufficient. The bank manager replied, coldly: "You look like a prince but you talk like a child," and turned him away empty-handed.

But for Ras Tafari such were not the highlights of his journey; he preferred schools and universities to night clubs (though he too spent considerable sums on wine and the purchase of two motorcars), and the newspapers were soon referring to him as "the thoughtful Prince." From France he had hoped to obtain an agreement which would give Ethiopia free port facilities at Jibouti (for it must be remembered that his country had no ports of its own), but he was fobbed off with vague promises. From Mussolini, the new premier of Fascist Italy, he got a hearty slap on the back and a verbal promise of financial aid. From the British he received the Crown of Theodore, which General Napier had taken back to England after his victory at Magdala; it was now returned to him by King George V and it was a gesture which deeply moved him.

Except for the sights, and the facts and figures which he stuffed into his mind during the journey, the Crown of Theodore was about the most tangible object he brought back from his visit to Europe, but it was enough to make him a popular hero when he returned to Addis Ababa. "He was given a really extraordinary welcome," wrote C. F. Rey, "being met at the station by no less a personage than the Abun himself and everyone else of note in the capital; salutes were fired, addresses of welcome read from the Government and others, and he was driven through the town in an eight-horsed carriage and welcomed in state by the Empress. This expression of feeling, together with the calm which had prevailed during his four and a half month's absence, formed a significant tribute to the growing strength of his position."

Rey added that it was unfortunate that Ras Tafari "was not able to point to any diplomatic triumphs as the result of the journey, and this fact, doubtless combined with the heavy cost of the tour, caused the appointment of a body of Ministers to check his activities later on, when the first enthusiasm aroused by the glamour of the tour had subsided." He was still being chivvied by the rases, though "whether this arose from fear of commitments which might be entered into by the Regent, or from jealousy on the part of the great chiefs who had been left behind . . . is not clear. Their power in the land is great. . . . Theirs is the class that placed the present rulers on the throne, and accordingly their views have to be treated with consideration, though unfortunately those views are not, as a general rule, of the most enlightened character."

In the next few months, Tafari was to put it much more strongly than that.

Nothing made clearer to him the abject condition of his country than the memories he had carried back with him from Europe. At one dinner party in London he had heard a guest refer to Addis Ababa as "an African shambles," and although he realized that the phrase was not meant to be taken literally, he resolved to wipe out the insult by wiping out some of the eyesores which had stimulated it. It would be no easy job, and C. F. Rey wryly recorded of this period that while Tafari might think of schools as a sign of progress, others had different ideas: "The main impressions made on the minds of Abyssinians who toured Europe seems to have been a desire for motor-cars, and so while three years ago the only cars in the place were one or two belonging to the Regent—which were hardly ever used owing to the absence of roads—now there must be at least a couple of hundred of various makes in Addis. . . . As they began to arrive, it was realized that roads must be made for them to run on, and so roads were rapidly constructed in the town, and now on the few kilometres of comparatively smooth track available Citroens and Fiats and Fords rush wildly about, to the manifest joy of the drivers and the equally manifest dismay of the horsemen, pedestrians, and herds of animals which always throng the city."

The Regent did succeed in getting one school built and sent to Europe for teachers to be brought out at his own expense. He encouraged those who could afford it to abandon their mud huts— the Ethiopians had never had a particularly intense sense of domesticity—and build stone erections of a more permanent character, and he also started propaganda in his own newspaper, *Light and Peace,* in favor of wearing boots.

But, as Rey pointed out, "the veneer of civilisation has not yet spread very far or penetrated very deeply. Murderers are executed in a little hut in the town, wherein they are tied to a post, rifles are trained on them through tubes fixed in the walls, and at a given signal the triggers are pulled by relatives of the murdered man. This is an advance on the system in force a year or two ago when the murdered was held down in an open field and shot gradually by members of the aggrieved clan. Some six years ago they were hanged on trees in the market place, and I have seen half a dozen at a time suspended there for several days."

Rey mentions that by 1924 Europeans were no longer admitted to the banquets at the palace "at which thousands of soldiers, priests and beggars (all the most worthless members of the community) are fed on immense quantities of raw meat," but they still went on and he had been smuggled into one at which 18,000 were fed in relays. The streets of Addis Ababa were filled with mendicants displaying sores, stumps for limbs, or proclaiming themselves sufferers from leprosy and smallpox. There was still no sanitation in the town, and scavenging was left to hyenas and jackals.

"The intermediate stages between the new and the old are no less interesting to observe," Rey wrote. "It has, for example, always been the practice of Abyssinians to be followed in all their outings, however short, by an armed party of soldiers or attendants or slaves, or a combination of all these. . . . This year I saw an Abyssinian who had succumbed to the attractions of a bicycle, and had obviously just learned to ride it, pedalling along the road in his flowing robes, while behind him toiled and panted his perspiring escort on foot. . . . On another occasion I was riding across the road near the Regent's palace when the guard stationed at the gates, seizing their rifles, indicated that the Prince approached. A motorcyclist soldier in khaki sped along in front, followed closely by H.I.H. seated in a motorcar painted longitudinally in the three colours of Ethiopia—green, yellow and red. Beside and behind the car galloped a wild-looking escort of Abyssinians in their native dress, armed with rifles, spears, swords or shields, and obviously enjoying their reckless dash through the town."

One of the sights of Addis Ababa at this period, when the capital was getting its first roads, was the Ceremony of the Stone Laying. For the opening of each new stretch of highway, the Regent appeared to lay the first stone. "Chiefs and ministers followed, and so on down through the hierarchy until thousands of individuals were to be seen toiling like ants along the whole stretch of road to be dealt with, while their feudal superiors watched the progress of the work from the nearest shady spot. . . . And every morning for a week the Regent surveyed the work until the road was ready; but—the modern touch—from his motorcar, while at the same time transacting business of state with his ministers and officials."

It has been mentioned that one of Tafari's first acts upon returning from his visit to Europe was to build a school at his own expense and to send to Europe for teachers to man it. It was a venture that not only involved him in expense but a certain amount of resentful opposition. There was already one school in Addis Ababa (the institution, founded by Menelik, which Tafari had attended for a time) but it was now directed entirely by priests and its educational standards were low. Its directors chose to regard Tafari's venture as a dangerous rival and went to the Empress and Hapta Giorgis to make dark charges that the school was a conspiracy to force Ethiopian children to abandon their religion and become Roman Catholics. The buildings were erected but lay fallow for two years, while Tafari fought the opposition. The school did not open its doors until 1926 when Rey saluted it as "the first real educational effort by the Abyssinians." He added: "If it succeeds and extends

[it] may affect profoundly the future of the country. It is of course for this reason that it was opposed by the reactionary elements."

When the school eventually did open there were places for 180 children, bringing the grand total of places available throughout the whole of Ethiopia to 291. At the opening ceremony, Tafari harangued the rather surly collection of rases who had been dragooned into attending. "The time has passed for mere lip-service to our country," he said. "The crying need of our people is education, without which we cannot maintain our independence. The proof of real patriotism is to recognize this fact and—in the case of those who possess the means—to found schools and to forward the cause of education in every way. I have built this school as a beginning and as an example, which I appeal to the wealthy among the people to follow."

But the appeal fell on shuttered ears. "The big chiefs do not want their sons to be educated," Rey commented. "And the sons themselves do not care much about learning either; they are least keen of all the boys at Ras Tafari's school. They like to learn English or French but beyond that they say they need to know nothing—they have their fathers' land to inherit, ample wealth at their disposal, and what more do they want? Whereas their less fortunately endowed brothers at the school, having more incentive acquire more."

He added, not without prescience: "When they grow up and realize that theirs is the knowledge but that the power is in the hands of others, less capable and more reactionary, one of two alternatives may well eventuate. Either a serious social upheaval will take place, with the attendant risk to Abyssinian independence of civil war, or reaction will so assert itself that a collision with the outside world becomes inevitable."

For the moment, however, a collision with the outside world seemed unlikely, and Ethiopia could thank Tafari for that. His success in persuading the League of Nations to accept Ethiopia as a member had earned him scant gratitude from the Empress or the rases when it was granted in 1923. But in 1925 they had cause to change their minds. In that year the British and Italian Governments, with that sublime arrogance which characterized the colonial powers of the day, decided to meet and make some arrangements about Ethiopia. After some weeks of discussion, there was an exchange of letters between the British Ambassador to Rome, Sir Ronald Graham, and Signor Mussolini, the Italian premier and Foreign Secretary, in which they agreed to approach the Ethiopian

Government and demand certain concessions and spheres of influence. The nature of the concessions can be summed up by quoting part of Mussolini's letter to Graham on December 20, 1925:

> I have, therefore, the honour to state to your Excellency that the Royal Government [of Italy] will support the British Government with the Ethiopian Government in order to obtain from the latter the concession to construct a barrage at Lake Tsana,[3] together with the right to construct and maintain a motor road for the passage of stores, personnel, etc. from the frontier of the Sudan to the barrage. The Royal Government take note, on the other hand, that the British Government will, in return, support the Italian Government in obtaining from the Abyssinian Government the concession to construct and operate a railway from the frontier of Eritrea to the frontier of Italian Somaliland, it remaining understood that this railway, together with all the necessary works for its construction and operation, shall have free transit across the motor road mentioned above.

It appears to have occurred to neither the British nor the Italians to consult the Ethiopians first before concerting their plans, and Tafari was incensed when he heard about it. To Mussolini he sent a frigid protest and to the British a pained reproof in which he said: "We should never have suspected that the British Government would come to an agreement with another Government regarding our Lake."

To the League of Nations itself the Regent then penned a note, which deserves quoting at some length, illuminating as it does Tafari's subtle use of pride and humility to impress the delegates of an international body in his country's favor.

"*To the State Members of the League of Nations.* Our Government has recently received from the British and Italian Governments identical notes informing us that these Governments have arrived at an agreement to support each other with a view to obtaining [the concessions mentioned above]. We have been profoundly moved by the conclusion of this agreement arrived at without our being consulted or informed, and by the action of the two Governments in sending us a joint notification. In the first place, on our admission to the League of Nations we were told that all nations were to be on a footing of equality within the League, and that their independence was to be universally respected, since the purpose of the

---

[3] Tsana, a vast lake in the Western highlands of Ethiopia, feeds the Blue Nile and provides the silt and the flood waters which irrigate the Nile Valley in the Sudan and Egypt.

League is to establish and maintain peace among men in accordance with the will of God.

"We were not told that certain members of the League might make a separate agreement to impose their views on another member even if the latter considered those views incompatible with its national interests. . . .

"We cannot help thinking, therefore, that in agreeing to support each other in these matters, and in giving us a joint notification of that agreement, the two Governments are endeavouring to exert pressure on us in order to induce us to comply with their demands prematurely, without leaving any time for reflection or consideration of our people's needs."

Here Tafari proceeded to enunciate the Ethiopian's suspicion of the foreigner which even he, the most enlightened of them, shared with his compatriots. "Throughout their history," he wrote, "they have seldom met with foreigners who did not desire to possess themselves of Abyssinian territory and to destroy their independence. With God's help, and thanks to the courage of our soldiers, we have always, come what might, stood proud and free on our native mountains."

He advanced this, in his note to the League, as the reason why he must tread prudently before allowing foreigners to establish themselves for ostensibly economic purposes which might turn out to conceal political aims.

And here he deftly mixed the humble with the proud: "Nor must it be forgotten that we have only recently been introduced to modern civilisation and that our history, glorious though it be, has not prepared us for ready adjustment to conditions which are quite often beyond the range of our experience. Nature herself has never gone forward by sudden bounds, and no country has been metamorphosed in a night. With our well-known eagerness for progress—given time and the friendly advice of countries whose geographical position has enabled them to outdistance us in the race—we shall be able to secure gradual but continual improvements which will make Abyssinia great in the future as she has been throughout the past. But if we try to go too fast accidents may happen."

He ended: "We should like to hear from members of the League whether they think it right that means of pressure should be exerted upon us which they themselves would doubtless never accept. We have the honour to bring to the notice of all States members of the League of Nations the correspondence we have received, in order that they may decide whether that correspondence is compatible with the independence of our country, inasmuch as it includes the stipulation that part of our Empire is to be allotted to the economic influence of a given Power. We cannot but realize that economic influence and political influence are very closely bound together; and it is our duty to protest most strongly against an agreement which, in our view, conflicts with the essential principles of the League of Nations.

"Addis Ababa, this 12th day of Senié, in the year of grace 1918 (June 19, 1926). Tafari Makonnen, Heir to the Throne of Abyssinia."

By the time they had read halfway through this small masterpiece, the British and Italian Governments were running for cover. With hands on hearts, they proclaimed the innocence of their intentions. This, however, was not what interested Tafari; he was more concerned to keep out of the corner into which the British and the Italians, between them, were trying to push him. The publicity enraged by his appeal to the League enabled him to do so. It was a long time before any foreign Government tried to put pressure on him again.

But so long as Ethiopia remained a land so arrogantly backward there would always be the risk of foreign intervention, and of this Ras Tafari was only too well aware. "It is bad enough to be ignorant, but it is wicked that some of our people should be proud of it," he said. "We even have some of them who persist in seeing a virtue in the enslaving of our people."

This, at the time it was made (1924), was a bold remark indeed, for the two powerful figures who, with him, formed the ruling triumvirate in Ethiopia, the Empress and Hapta Giorgis, were both known to be unabashed keepers and buyers of slaves. A year earlier, the Empress Zauditu, in a communication to the British Government, had condoned slavery in these words: "The reason why some men were declared slaves was that certain nations were at war with us, and this had caused money to be spent which those nations had to repay by their labour, and this also, that they might learn virtue by communication with Christians."

This might explain if not excuse the sale in Addis Ababa, Gondar and Harar of tens of thousands of captives at the end of Menelik's Galla wars, but it had no bearing on the slaving which had continued long after the wars were over. Fitaurari Hapta Giorgis did not even bother to explain his fondness for the slave system, preferring to boast of the boon he found it. On the broad estates he had acquired since the death of Menelik he had accumulated thousands of slaves of both sexes—to labor in his plantations, to cook and scrub, and to provide a steady but constantly changing supply of concubines.

Tafari had persuaded the Empress to accept certain conditions to which Ethiopia's membership of the League was made subject, and one of them was a promise that all efforts would be made "to secure the complete suppression of slavery in all its forms, and of the slave trade by land and sea." He had also persuaded her to issue an edict making the selling of slaves a crime punishable by death,[4] and by the heavy fining of the rases and chiefs in whose territory the trade went on. But so long as there were slaves working on the Empress's estates and in the households of Hapta Giorgis, it seemed unlikely that the rest of the country would emancipate their chattels. As Rey pointed out, domestic slavery was something "on which the whole social system of the country rests. Every household has its slaves, from the thousands owned by the great landed proprietors to the single slave of the comparatively poor man." He mentioned that in 1926 "slaves are owned by the servants of many European households in Addis Ababa, not excepting some of the foreign legations. Indeed, it is difficult to distinguish slaves from their owners; they are clothed, fed and housed in the same way as their masters."

There was no doubt in Rey's mind that Tafari was in earnest in his determination to end slavery in Ethiopia, and not just to appease the League of Nations, but there is more than a hint that he thought the Regent something of a mad liberal to attempt it. "A distinguished Abyssinian of advanced ideals, a cultured and broadminded man, recently freed his own slaves; they seemed mildly interested but refused firmly to depart from the precincts where they had lived quite happily for many years. They were consequently told they could remain, and were fed as usual, receiving also a small monthly wage. But they declined firmly to do any work except at such times as the spirit moved them, for, as they pointed out, what was the good of being free if they had to work?" The Regent, who genuinely abhorred the enslavement of his people, must have wondered sometimes whose side his so-called foreign friends were on. At a time when he was doing his best to persuade Ethiopians of the evils of slavery, bondage and serfdom, an Under-Secretary of State for Foreign Affairs stood up in the House of Commons and said: "There are forms of slavery and servitude which, however repugnant to our ideals, at all events are not susceptible of the description of being grossly oppressive, and I think that to a very large extent the slavery which undoubtedly exists in Abyssinia belongs to that comparatively mild type."

Simultaneously, Rey was writing: "To abolish the system of domes-

[4] Menelik did the same, without much effect.

tic slavery outright would be an impossibility: to attempt to do so would plunge the country into civil war and anarchy forthwith. Even to attempt to make a beginning by giving too drastic effect to the decree that children born of slaves should be free would be hotly resisted, for that would be to cut off all fresh supplies, now that slaves cannot be bought or sold and raiding has been reduced to very small proportions. Without their slaves Abyssinians, from the Empress downwards, would be deprived of their amenities—from the great State banquets at the palace, where thousands are fed on raw meat, to the everyday labour of fetching water for the smallest hut from the rivers and wells."

It was difficult enough to persuade the rases and the people that slave-owning was wrong, without having foreigners encouraging them to believe otherwise. Sometimes Tafari must have wondered what it was that the so-called civilized powers really wanted of Ethiopia.

There were moments in the early years of the 1920's when the bone-headed obstruction to his ideas with which the Empress and Hapta Giorgis confronted him must have brought him close to despair. But not for the first time it has been stressed in this story that Tafari Makonnen had the great virtue of patience. He knew how to wait. And when his frustrations seemed beyond bearing, he could always remind himself that time was on his side, because they were old and he was young. They would have to die one of these days.

Toward the end of 1926, word reached him from a friend in the old man's household that Fitaurari Hapta Giorgis was gravely ill. He took all precautions to see that the news went no further and made his plans. From Harar he called in the commanders of his armed units and gave them marching orders to various parts of the country where there were telegraph offices, and instructed them to encamp in their vicinity. He was the first to be told that the old war-horse was dead, and Tafari did not stop to mourn. He telegraphed the news to his commanders, and then, escorted by his personal guard, rode to the palace to tell the Empress.

Nor did she waste time in tears, for she realized only too well the significance of Hapta Giorgis's demise. The bulwark had been swept away. There was no one now to defend her against the oncoming tide of Tafari. Or was there? The moment Tafari took his departure, she sent out messages to all the rases telling of the old tory's death, and to Ras Kassa in particular—for she believed him a conservative like herself—she appealed for help. She hoped that in the scramble for Hapta Giorgis's rich legacy, the rases would mop up his land and his men—and keep them out of Tafari's hands.

She was, of course, too late. The telegrams had gone out to the Regent's troops, and they were in the process of carrying out their instructions. Some had moved in on Hapta Giorgis's estates; others had recruited his soldiers with bribes and promises of more to come; and still others had delivered the news to rases and chiefs known to be friendly to Tafari, telling them at the same time of promotions in their ranks, of gifts of land, and gubernatorial appointments in the places where the old War Minister had once held sway. As for Ras Kassa, Tafari had already taken care of him with a munificence which the Empress would not even have thought necessary (but the Regent could never forget that Kassa was the custodian of Lij Yasu). Kassa had already sworn his allegiance to Tafari, and he was one of the few among Ethiopia's warlords who, when he gave his word, kept it.

The Empress had lost the game even before she could make a move. The lands, the rich storehouses of arms, ammunition, grain, silver and gold were divided up; the slaves were offered their freedom (though most of them were taken over by their new masters); and Tafari had control of the Ethiopian Army, together with the money to clothe and feed it, and the armaments to keep it in readiness for action.

There was another death in 1926 that removed from the Ethiopian scene one other powerful reactionary who had always stood in Tafari's way. Abuna Mattheos, the Archbishop of the Ethiopian Church, was a tory for no venal reasons. Like his predecessors, and according to tradition, he was not Ethiopian himself but a Coptic priest appointed by the parent Church of Alexandria. He had arrived in what must have seemed to him a remote and savage mountain See well knowing that he might never be allowed to leave it again, and he had ruled according to his lights, pledging himself never to interfere with local politics. But that had meant he was a staunch defender of the *status quo*, that he opposed all change which he thought might weaken the hold of the Church on the people, and he had clashed with Tafari repeatedly. Now, after forty-nine years of holy exile in which he had crowned both Menelik and Zauditu, he was dead at the age of eighty-three.

Rey, who was in Addis Ababa at the time of his funeral, described it as an astonishing scene, for the mass of the people had held the Abun in superstitious and reverent awe. "The Regent, the *corps diplomatique* and thousands of chiefs, followers and slaves took part in the procession, the streets being thronged with dense masses of soldiers and people; the cortège was headed by the gilded chair of the Archbishop, in which was a large oil-painting of him shielded by a colourful ceremonial umbrella. The body, covered with an embroidered cloth, was carried by monks, hundreds of priests following in their striking robes, with embroidered umbrellas and long praying sticks. Although the route was only half a mile long, the procession took nearly four hours to cover it, so dense were the throngs and so elaborate the ceremonial; the Empress in person met the body at the church, where it was temporarily deposited pending formal interment in some suitable sanctuary."

As he walked in the wake of the old diehard's episcopal chair, Tafari must have thought hard about the character of the next head of the Church. He had always believed that the Ethiopian Church should be ruled by an Ethiopian bishop, but for the moment the tradition was too strong for him and he would not carry the people with him if he tried to meddle with the appointment. All he could do was indicate to the authorities in Cairo that a man was needed of enlightened views and modern ideas; and when he arrived, Tafari was determined to win him over to his reforms; for this new Abun would one day be the priest who would crown him Emperor of Ethiopia.

So in one year, the two most influential reactionaries in the Empire, and the closest allies of the Empress in her opposition to Tafari's ambitions, were removed from the scene. Hapta Giorgis had died, fittingly enough, on December 12, 1926, the anniversary of the death of his beloved old master, Emperor Menelik. Within a few days, the Abun had followed him.

Now the time of stalemate was over, and the tug of war between the Empress and the heir to the throne could begin.

chapter eight

NEGUS TAFARI

ETHIOPIA WAS, in 1926, a land of few roads. The railway connected the French Somaliland port of Jibouti with Dire Dawa and Addis Ababa. There were telegraph lines and telephone services to Harar, Gondar, Debra Marcos, Dessye, Axum and a few more provincial capitals. But to get from one capital to another *physically* was still a major undertaking involving mules and donkeys, armed guards and all the paraphernalia of a safari. In the dry season, that is; in the rainy season, no movement was possible in the South.

Any trade between Addis Ababa and its hinterland had perforce to be by pack animals, mules, donkeys, ponies, or, in the lowlands, by camel. And, as Rey found to his discomfort when he journeyed through the land at this time, "even this intercourse is cut off in the rainy season, for then the tracks become impassable, the rivers unfordable, and large tracts of the country turn into spongy mud, through which it is difficult, if not impossible, for laden pack-animals to plough their way." He cited the case of one caravan on its way from the capital to Lake Rudolph in the Southwest which had expected to take five months on its journey. Long enough. But the rains came early and it was fourteen months before the travelers sighted the lake. Rey discovered that on one main trade route out of Addis Ababa to the west donkeys were used "because it is known that nearly all pack-animals die on that bit of track, so bad is the going, and donkeys are cheaper than mules. . . . The sights and the smell along the track were too horrible to describe, the dead bodies of the unfortunate animals lying in every direction in all stages of decomposition, over quite an extensive area."

It was a state of affairs which must be remedied if the disparate parts of this far-flung Empire were to be stitched together, though how was not as easy as some foreigners seemed to imagine. "You must build roads," they said. But to build the sort of roads Ethiopia needed would cost an amount of money which would embarrass the budget of a European power, let alone one like Ethiopia, which in 1926 was exporting not much more than $9,000,000 worth of goods a year. To the west of the capital, where the roads were most badly needed, the landscape was a crazy succession of Grand Canyons in which, every few miles, the tableland plunged from temperate to tropical climates, from seven or eight thousand feet down by precipitate gorges, to rushing torrents three or four thousand feet below. Roads would have to be hewn out of solid rock, tunnels blasted, galleries gouged out of the cliffside, bridges built. How could it be done without calling in the aid of foreign powers who—such was the mood of the time—might turn an economic trade agreement into something more dangerously political?

There were times when Tafari must have chafed at the difficulties of keeping contact with and control over the barons who were now under his aegis. After the first resentments and confusions, it was surprising how quickly most of the warlords had hastened to recognize that the Regent was now paramount in the Empire. As was usual in a feudal state such as this, Tafari had summoned the rases to the capital to give personal confirmation of the fact that they recognized the new situation, and in they came with their lavish tributes and declarations of loyalty. Even the Empress Zauditu's ex-husband, Ras Gugsa, thought it politic to journey south from his province of Begemeder and bow in fief to the Regent. (He was allowed to see the Empress alone as a reward, but it seems unlikely that the Regent remained ignorant of what took place between them.)

There was, in fact, only one recalcitrant among the more powerful of the provincial governors, and he was a florid and temperamental exhibitionist—Dejazmach Balcha of Sidamo. He too had received the summons to the capital, and he was quite well aware of the reason for it. He ignored it. It may be that he had had enough of Ras Tafari's rises in the world, for he had suffered from them before. He had made no secret, especially when in his cups, of his contempt for "the shy one." If there had been an Amharic word for "milksop" he would have used it to describe Tafari. Why should he bow the knee to such a mannikin?

The weeks passed and the Regent waited. Was Balcha on his way? Could it be the atrocious state of the routes from the south which was delaying him? When it became apparent that the reason was contempt rather than road conditions, Tafari ordered Balcha to come at once, and this the Dejazmach decided to obey—but in his own fashion. His imminent arrival in Addis Ababa was reported to the Regent a month later together with the information that he was by no means unescorted; he had brought with him an army of at least 10,000 men. Most of the more powerful Ethiopian chiefs had their own headquarters in or around Addis Ababa, and Balcha's was a compound in the hills some three miles south of the capital. Here he established himself and encamped his army, and here he stayed.

Emissaries of the Regent arrived bearing greetings and extending an invitation to a banquet Tafari planned to give in his honor. Balcha was too old a hand at Ethiopian guile to be gulled by the flowery cordiality of the greetings and he replied that he would be honored to grace the Regent's table, but he would be insulting the stature of his host if he came humbly with only a few retainers. Could he, therefore, bring his personal bodyguard with him—or at least part of it? Tafari sent back a messenger to inquire how many that would be. Only, replied Balcha, a mere six hundred men. He was making it quite clear that if Tafari had any intention of detaining him, or disciplining him, there would be a fight for it.

To his astonishment, the Regent's reply was honey sweet; but of course the guard would be welcome and would be treated as distinguished guests. Balcha, however, was taking no chances and he warned every member of his entourage before they rode into the capital the following day that any man who ate or drank himself into a stupor would be whipped.

It was a memorable banquet, for more than one reason. The food was lavish and the tej and wine flowed, and Tafari was at his most persuasive and charming. Without retreating an inch from his avowed policy of modernization and reform for Ethiopia, he took great pains to solicit Dejazmach Balcha's cooperation "as one of the elder statesmen of our country and a valued adviser on the welfare of our people." These overtures were received with ill-concealed scorn by the Dejazmach and, as the wine began to ferment in his head, he grew increasingly belligerent. He made it clear that not only would Tafari not win him to his side by argument or flattery but he would also fail to do so by force. Waving his hand to the ravening warriors hacking at the carcasses in the body of the hall, he pointed out that they had brought their rifles as well as their swords to the feast and they were ready to fight at a signal. Not only that. If they and their master were not back at his compound by nightfall, the rest of his considerable army had instructions to march on the capital.

Tafari looked at him with those winsome dark brown eyes and asked him, sorrowfully, why he was so distrustful? He was an honored guest. How could he possibly think that harm was being planned for him?

The feasting and drinking went on, and then the singing, boasting and speechmaking. Balcha's bodyguard, in the Ethiopian tradition, sang their extemporaneous songs which hymned the might of their chief and chortled over the dire destinies of all, no matter how self-important, who might threaten him. Tafari's men stirred and some rose to reply in song, but the Regent ordered them to be silent—unless they had praise to sing about their guest? No? Then it was better not to sing at all. The expression of triumph on Balcha's face as he stilled the voices of his retinue was, observers say, wonderful to see. Visions were obviously passing through his mind of glories to come. He had overawed and frightened the little man on the dais beside him. All it took was a demonstration of strength and a few covert threats, and Tafari was cowed almost to the point of abjection. After this he would not dare to initiate reforms to which the rases objected, and after this it would be Dejazmach Balcha who called the tune at court.

That afternoon, with a salute of guns from the Regent to send him on his way, Dejazmach Balcha rode back at the head of his bodyguard to his compound south of the town, and for most of the way it resembled the progress of a conqueror. The route lay along a river valley between rolling hills until, a mile or so out, the hills fell away and the valley broadened out into a vast plain. It was here, in a canvas city of many-colored tents, that Balcha's army had encamped around his compound, so many of them that they almost filled the landscape. But where were they now? The plain was empty except for the smoke from doused and dying fires.

While Balcha had sat and feasted and boasted, an army under Tafari's ally, Ras Kassa, had moved out of the capital by a devious route through the hills and infiltrated his camp. It was an army that came bearing gifts—and threats. There were chests of Maria Theresa dollars for those who would sell their rifles, and generous bonuses for those who would promise to go back to their homes without fuss or bother. For the recalcitrants, of whom there were few, the whipping stocks were put up, but Ras Kassa reported later that it was necessary to lash only half a dozen before the rest of the army recognized the vital necessity of quitting Shoa and hurrying south, dollars jingling in their pockets, for Sidamo. One of the chroniclers of the day's events reported that "Dejazmach Balcha recognized the adroitness of the manoeuvre which had outwitted him, and though he sought sanctuary for a few days in a neighbouring church, he was persuaded to give himself up." This is something of a simplification. Balcha, after the first moments of panic, tried to reorganize his columns and march south to Sidamo, but runners advised him that Ras Kassa was waiting for him down the road. He then decided to make a commando-like dash into the capital itself, hoping to storm his way to the palace and solicit the aid of the Empress. Tafari had anticipated this and his troops blocked the route.

It was only then that Balcha recognized that he had been checkmated by a master and paid off his bodyguard, telling them to make their own way south. With the aid of the Itchege he was smuggled into St. Raguel's Church on Mount Entoto, which was promptly surrounded by Tafari's troops. From Tafari's point of view, the choice of sanctuary and the patron of it could not have been better, because, before the arrival of the new Abun, the Regent was anxious to clip the wings of his theological subordinate, whom he considered too political, too ambitious and too reactionary. The fact that the Itchege had advised and helped Balcha was an excuse it would have been difficult to invent, and he exploited it. Not only did he surround the church but he surrounded the Itchege's residence, too, and put his squads through a night-and-day routine of drill and rifle practice which proved so crashingly effective that the cleric decided to give way. The Itchege promised to behave and was forgiven. Dejazmach Balcha was shown the door of the church, promised to behave, and was also forgiven—so long as he entered a monastery to repent his sins of pride, ambition and greed.[1] His final words, before the doors were locked behind him, were: "Do not underestimate the power of Tafari. He creeps like a mouse but he has jaws like a lion."

That was in 1927. Less than two years later, a small group of ministers, alarmed by the rapidity with which they believed Tafari was opening up the country to the hated foreigner, persuaded the

[1] He did not emerge again until the war against Italy, when he fought for his country and was killed just before the Italians occupied Addis Ababa.

Empress to involve herself in yet another plot to remove the Regent.
It was a conspiracy of such ineptness that one almost suspects Tafari
himself of engineering it to tempt Zauditu into placing herself completely in his power. Certainly, though he pretended ignorance of
the cabal until the last moment, it seems more than likely that he
knew what was supposed to happen to him almost as soon as the
intriguers themselves.

One of the eye-witnesses of the plot was a sterling British character
named Daniel Sandford (of whom more will be heard in this story),
a British officer who had been seconded to the Legation in Addis
Ababa in 1914 and—except for war service—had been there ever
since. By 1928, when these events were taking place, he had settled
down to farm outside the Ethiopian capital and he and his cheerfully
indefatigable wife, Christine, had produced a family for themselves
and examples of fertility in other fields that were even more impressive to the Ethiopians.

Mrs. Christine Sandford, in her biography of the Emperor, *The
Lion of Judah Hath Prevailed*,[2] writes of the 1928 plot: "The reactionary party realized that their position was fast becoming untenable and . . . a conspiracy was formed to depose the Regent from
his trusted position. . . . The Regent had gone down, as was his almost
daily habit, from his own house—the little Gebbi—to the palace in
which state affairs were conducted—the big Gebbi. Hardly had he
set foot within the hall when the gates of the palace were closed
behind him, and held closed by troops within. Machine guns, posted
in the roof of the Menelik mausoleum, which stands within the wall
of the palace enclosure, were trained on the entrances. Within, the
Empress was questioning the Regent on rumours reported to her
that he was aiming at supreme power. Disposing scornfully of such
allegations of disloyalty, Ras Tafari maintained complete self-pos-
session in the face of threatening soldiers of the palace guard. Ordering the great doors of the Gebbi to be thrown open he passed out and
down the steps of the assembly hall. The force of his personality held
the crowd. Outside the main gates there had already arrived retainers
from his own palace who had been hastily armed with any weapons
which his wife, Waizero Menen, who had been apprised of the situation, could lay hands on."

The gates were opened at the Regent's command and his troops
raced inside. "In the silence of surprise Ras Tafari mounted his mule

2 Cassell and Co. Ltd.

and rode slowly towards his own house; his calm and confidence had won the day."

But much more than the day. That evening the palace guard was rounded up and its commander, Dejazmach Abanko, chained and flung into jail. Tafari had a short, sharp and crisply businesslike interview with the Empress. The following day, when the Ministers met at the Old Palace, one would never have guessed that they were ever opposed to the Regent either as a man or as a ruler. Was it the faint chink of chains behind the doors that made them so eager to hail him as a patriotic leader and themselves as his eager apostles of reform? Without a murmur of dissent, they passed and signed a petition to the Empress asking her to offer preferment to one of her rases of a nature which Tafari had always persuaded her to oppose until now. Only once during her reign had she made one of her rases a King, or Negus, and that was old Walda Giorgis, long since dead, whom she had elevated to spite Tafari. Thereafter, the Regent had grown powerful enough to forbid her any more such preferments. Ethiopia, he said, must centralize around the Empress in Addis Ababa—and the populace must look to her, and not some petty local king, as the catalyst of their existence.

Now the Council of State asked the Empress—"in the teeth of my advice," the Regent murmured—to raise Tafari to the status of Negus. There was little that the Empress could do except to sign the ordinance, knowing as she signed that she was putting the last ounce of power into Tafari's hands and opting, perhaps for all time, out of the control of events in Ethiopia.

"The ceremony which took place a day or two later," [3] writes Mrs. Sandford, "was symbolic of this change. A silken tent had been pitched in the palace grounds over against the old Church of the Trinity. Here, at an early hour, assembled the participants: the Empress Zauditu and her officers of state, Tafari with his own personal officers, the Itchege or chief of the monks, who was acting head of the Church in the absence of an Abun. There were present the *corps diplomatique* and one or two privileged spectators—the author's husband being one. After some intoning by the priests Tafari rose and, descending from the throne erected for him, advanced slowly towards the Empress and knelt at her feet. Silk hangings were draped around the pair as the crown was placed on his head. Then the hangings fell apart and as Tafari—the king—rose to his feet there was a

[3] October 7, 1928.

startling zip as swords whizzed from their sheaths and were waved on high. His officers thronging round him seemed almost to carry him back to his throne."

There followed "a dramatic pause" and then the mass of well-wishers bore Tafari off in triumph to a nearby church, where he was to receive the acclamation of the people. The Empress remained behind "alone—a forlorn figure in the almost deserted tent."

chapter nine

NEGUSA NAGAST

WHEN THE TIME comes for an epitaph to be written for Emperor Haile Selassie, I can think of none more appropriate than: "He shaped rather than waited upon events." His great patience, his remarkable capacity for biding his time, had never meant that he stood idly by; and at no time were his shaping fingers and subtle mind more actively engaged than in the eighteen months which followed his coronation as Negus Tafari Makonnen in October, 1928.

It would have been easy for him to believe that all the obstacles blocking him from supreme power had now been removed. There was, indeed, a heady temptation to assume that the opposition had been routed and that he had won personal security for himself at last, plus the freedom that went with it to proceed with his plans for Ethiopia's future in the world. For who could challenge him now? The Empress was no more than a sad, acquiescent, impotent old lady, immured in the palace. The Old Guard of feudalistic diehards had been overawed. True, Ethiopia's new Abun had been, against Tafari's will, once more appointed from the mother church of Alexandria, but the new primate, Monsignor Kyril, had indicated at once that he would refrain from interfering in local political affairs except—and he stressed this—if he first consulted with the Regent. Moreover, he brought from Cairo a *fiat* permitting him to inaugurate five new bishops of Ethiopian nationality, the names of whom he was willing to receive from Tafari.

On the international front, matters were going well now that the powers in Europe accepted him as having emerged supreme. Signor Mussolini, swallowing the snub administered to him by Tafari over the Anglo-Italian Agreement, had decided to woo the Regent and sent a suitor of great persuasive charm, a new Minister named Giuliano Cora, to solicit his friendship. The result was the signing in 1928 of a Treaty of Friendship and Arbitration which was to last twenty years and pledged that neither the Italian nor the Ethiopian Government, *under any pretext* (and this, of course, was subsequently to prove ironical) would "take any action that may prejudice or damage the independence of the other" and agreed to submit all disputes not susceptible of solution by diplomatic procedures to processes of conciliation or arbitration.

He pressed on with his encouragement of foreign enterprise and investment in Ethiopia, but in this direction his success was a mixed one. A Belgian group of financiers took over the alcohol monopoly and, at least from the point of view of health, this seemed not before time; until their advent, the so-called whiskies, rums, gins and brandies sold in Ethiopia came from Greek distilleries which, it was said, concocted all of them in the same germ-ridden still and merely added different synthetic flavorings. Their effect upon liver, kidneys, eyesight and sobriety was considerable. The Belgians compensated the Greeks for loss of business but speedily discovered that the local drinkers preferred the potent old hooch to their smoother and less jolting liquors. The Greeks began to produce their poteens illegally (and therefore paid no tax), and the Belgians faced bankruptcy, particularly since they were not allowed under their mandate to manufacture the two staple drinks of the country, tej and talla, both regarded as home industries.

Tafari had awarded cotton monopolies in Harar to the French and the Belgians, coffee plantations to the Belgians in Arussi, timber concessions to the Swiss and the Italians in the forests on the mountain slopes outside Addis Ababa, an oil-pressing monopoly to the Greeks, and a young man who was subsequently to become his son-in-law, Fitaurari Desta, had even started to produce a commodity for which 99 percent of the population had hitherto shown the most considerable disinterest—soap.[1] There were rumors that Tafari took commissions in return for these privileges, but if that was so, the words that the British Minister, Wilfred Thesiger, had used on the occasion of similar accusations in 1918 were still true: "He may take private commissions, but what he takes greedily with one hand he hands on to the people with the other."

What he needed particularly urgently before he could expect

[1] They used other cleaning agents.

foreign business firms (rather than acquisitive governments) to invest in Ethiopia was some sort of confidence in the stability of the country. Financially, how did he stand? He persuaded the French to send him a financial adviser to look into the monetary system of the country, but he unfortunately could diagnose Ethiopia's disease without recommending a particularly easy cure. So far as banking was concerned, the situation had not changed since Rey wrote, in 1927: "The oldest undertaking is the Bank of Abyssinia, which, established by charter from Menelik in the latter years of his reign,[2] started its career by making no profits for twelve years, and then, since 1918, has paid dividends varying from three to five percent, with a non-dividend-paying interval of three years, 1921-23. It is indicative of the backward state of the country that the bank has achieved so little success, for it has a banking monopoly of fifty years, and many other favourable and exclusive privileges, such as *inter alia* the right to issue banknotes, to mint coinage and to take charge of Government deposits."

Rey added, wryly: "It is only fair to say, however, that all these obligations have not always been observed by the Government, and that for many years the Abyssinians suffered from the curious delusion that the bank had been established solely for the purpose of lending them money on comfortable terms whenever they needed it and for as long as they liked; the shattering of this dream led to a certain amount of peevishness."

For all the monopoly enjoyed by the Bank of Abyssinia, an attempt was made some time before Tafari became Negus to establish a purely Ethiopian bank. "After a year's working they announced a dividend of nearly 100 percent, an event which caused some excitement and a distribution of largesse among the staff. How this somewhat dramatic success was arrived at, and whether a certain amount of confusion between depositors' accounts and profits may not have contributed to the results, has not transpired. But there has been no news of any further dividends."

The trouble with Ethiopia's currency system was that no one trusted it—not, that is, the notes issued by the Bank of Abyssinia. Even two stations down the line from Addis Ababa, at Dire Dawa, the Bank itself cashed them at a rebate of three percent. The only money of any value anywhere in the Empire were round, heavy Maria Theresa dollars, silver coins the size of old English crowns or

[2] As a subsidiary of the British-controlled Bank of Egypt.

American silver dollars,[3] which were minted first by the Austrians and then the Italians. They were cumbersome and inconvenient—especially in bandit-infested country—but the traveler who wished to buy supplies or mules needed to carry sacksful with him on his travels.

Tafari's French economic expert told him his currency would never be stable until his country's political situation was stable, that foreign business would not be prepared to invest in monopolies if the contracts signed in Addis Ababa were repudiated or ignored in Gondar, Debra Marcos or Debra Tabor. How far did his writ run? Was he *really* master of his country? For all the flattering attentions which governments and their envoys were now beginning to lavish upon him, Tafari knew that his mandate to rule would never be accepted implicitly by the rases until he was recognized by them as the supreme arbiter—and that would never be so long as he was heir to the throne and not the occupant of it. While the Empress lived, they would continue to regard Tafari as something of an upstart, and a dangerous one, and themselves as potential rivals with him for the succession. His position was ironically equivocal; he had made himself head of the State and won the right to rule, but he needed the title that went with it before the rases would willingly bend their knees.

Meanwhile, all he could do was shape events as they presented themselves and wait until the time came when he could exploit them. To consolidate his own personal authority, he took steps to modernize his Army. He had won to his side an old lieutenant of the Emperor Menelik, a doughty warrior named Dejazmach Mulugeta, and he gave him the position once held by Fitaurari Hapta Giorgis of Minister of War. He persuaded the Belgian Government to send him an Army Mission, half from Brussels and half from the Congo, to train his troops and equip them with modern weapons—up-to-date rifles, machine-guns, armored cars and some light tanks and artillery. He repatriated from Kenya a number of Ethiopians who had served in the King's African Rifles and installed them as officers or under-officers, and he recruited hundreds of freed slaves as the nucleus of his battalions. But perhaps his most important investment, so far as his armed forces were concerned, was in the air.

Ever since his first ride in an airplane in 1921 in Aden, Tafari

---

[3] Coins of the same size, minted by Menelik with his own head on them, were never accepted by the normally xenophobic Ethiopians, even though they contained more silver than the Maria Theresa dollars.

had become a fervent believer in the future of aircraft, and he had followed their postwar developments with the sharpest interest. Once it became apparent that they were now capable of flying high enough to overcome Ethiopia's altitude and reliable enough to cruise safely over her rugged terrain, he made up his mind. He had long since issued an edict forbidding any private person or organization in the Empire—and that included both rases and foreigners—to own an aircraft and he also forbade foreign airlines to fly into or over Ethiopian territory. This was not because he did not believe in flying machines but because he realized only too well how damaging they could be if placed in the wrong hands. The possession of airplanes would be his own private monopoly—on behalf of the State.

In 1929 he arranged the purchase, through France, of four modern (for those days) biplanes equipped with machine-guns and capable of carrying bombs. He hired a French pilot named Maillet to run this nucleus of an air force, and Maillet was shortly afterwards joined by another French pilot, Corriger. Soon the natives on the plains outside Addis Ababa began to talk with awe of the "bird from the skies" which roared low over their huts and looped, sideslipped and banked around the Entoto Mountains. Not that the aircraft flew too frequently; Tafari did not wish his people to become too accustomed to the sight of them. But he did use Maillet to fly between Addis Ababa and the North as his personal courier, and this was to prove important.

Now that he had tuned up his military machine to what was, for Ethiopia, humming condition, the Regent turned his attention to the question of allies. Of the powerful rases who ruled the provinces beyond Shoa, whom did he most mistrust? With Balcha confined to a monastery and a pro-Tafari governor installed in his place in Sidamo, he could rely almost implicitly on the loyalty of the warlords to the South. In the East, Harar was, of course, his own bailiwick. In the North was Ras Kassa, custodian of Lij Yasu, a religious and unambitious chief, content to govern and follow his religious preoccupations. But in the West? Here he could not be sure.

At his capital at Debra Marcos was the richest warlord in Ethiopia, Ras Hailu, a blustering, ebullient and ambitious show-off whose claim to the throne, by blood, at least, was as valid as Tafari's. Ras Hailu was supposed, according to a coarse Ethiopian joke, never to emerge from his tent in the morning until he had urinated through the flap—to see which way the wind was blowing. He was a famous fence-sitter in any emergency. But there were rumors reaching

Tafari that he had been growing restless lately and grumbling at efforts to control him from Shoa.

In Wollo there were two other powerful chiefs, Ras Seyoum and Sultan Abu Jaffar, both with large private armies and both said to be chafing. Could it be that they, like Hailu, were being incited by the chieftain from whom Tafari believed he had most to fear? This was Ras Gugsa.

It will be remembered that with the elevation to the throne of Zauditu as Empress of Ethiopia in 1917, Tafari had resisted the attempts of the Queen to install her husband, Ras Gugsa, as her consort in the palace. He had insisted that Zauditu first divorce Gugsa and then pledge herself to a celibate reign (he did not want any child of hers to come between him and the throne), and this she had done under protest. But the marriage between Zauditu and Gugsa had, in fact, been one which had rather more emotional ties than the usual dynastic union of Ethiopian aristocracy. The Empress was heartbroken at her enforced separation from her husband and she never forgave Tafari for insisting on it. Ras Gugsa was rather more skilled at dissembling, and after a period under the surveillance of the Regent's troops he had been considered "safe" and allowed to go back to his native North, where he was given the governorship of the province of Begemeder. For years he successfully convinced everyone, including the Regent—though probably not Zauditu— that he had forgotten his wife, accepted the divorce, and was no longer a danger to the succession. The late Major R. E. Cheesman, who was British Consul in Northwest Ethiopia from 1925-34—during which time he plotted the course of the Blue Nile from its source near Lake Tsana—described an encounter he had with Ras Gugsa in 1927 in his fascinating book, *Lake Tana and The Blue Nile*. He calls him "fat and sixty" and "pompous, a monk at heart, but hospitable and human, with a sense of humour and a scarcely veiled dislike of the foreigner, in spite of which he gave me a smiling welcome." Gugsa in his years of enforced separation had apparently acquired a passion for building new churches. "He spent all his spare time and money building them round Debra Tabor" and he insisted on taking Cheesman to the top of the tower of his latest—by a rickety ladder made of two trees lashed together with creepers. "His somewhat rotund figure did not lend itself to such acrobatic feats, but quite undaunted he began to climb without a moment's hesitation. I had no opportunity now of backing out and the chances of escaping a nasty fall looked no brighter for either of us when fifty servants sprang after him, swinging like monkeys themselves and holding his hands and guiding his feet to the safest timbers. I then discovered he was wearing a pair of European-made shoes, the shiny soles of which rendered them the last thing to wear when climbing."

The scaffolding at which they were aiming was extremely precarious and Gugsa "was gasping when it came to scrambling from the ladder to the platform. I felt certain he would slip and roll to the bottom, fifty feet below, sweeping all his officers and me off the ladder in his descent, but we got up and looked out of the circular hole in the tower, where the big round metal-covered top was being lashed ready to fix in position. There certainly was a fine view of the country all about, and in returning to earth I delayed until the Ras had started, thinking that if we were going to fall I should be the last one to arrive and should have a soft cushion of humanity to land on."

Cheesman considered that Ras Gugsa was building too many new churches and that his resources "would have been better expended on the many old churches in Begemeder that were badly in need of repair." But the Ras had his reasons, and one of them was to convince the people of his deep religiousness and to ingratiate himself with the priests, for this was one of the most devout areas of Ethiopia.

Was it possible that this pious, paunchy, ageing chieftain still cherished hatred and resentment toward Tafari and still dreamed of winning back his wife? If the Regent's spies were to be believed, he was already conniving with Ras Hailu and soliciting support from Seyoum and Sultan Abu Jaffar. There had even been a devious approach to Ras Kassa, it was rumored, suggesting that he would be well rewarded if he relaxed the vigilance of his guards one evening and allowed the imprisoned ex-Emperor, Lij Yasu, to escape into Ras Gugsa's possession.

The Regent decided that the only way to tempt a leopard into the open is to offer it some live bait, and he had the very thing not far away from Ras Gugsa's borders. In parts of Wollo near Dessye, the Azebu Gallas, a notoriously restless and recalcitrant tribe, had been causing trouble since the beginning of 1929, and so far none of the chiefs had been able to persuade them to pay taxes or quell their subsequent outbursts of robbery, burning and pillage. Now Tafari addressed a message to "our beloved Empress's willing servant," ordering him to take his troops and march into Tigre to suppress the rampaging tribesmen. This Gugsa promised (in a message meant for Zauditu) he would proceed to do but in his own fashion.

It was not long before Addis Ababa heard, with a quickening of tension, exactly what fashion Gugsa had chosen. Far from fighting the Azebu Gallas, he sent his emissaries among them to seek their friendship and alliance against one whom he dubbed "the treacherous cause of all Ethiopia's troubles" and "the betrayer of our Church." Negus Tafari Makonnen, Gugsa declared, was in the process of destroying the nation and delivering its God-fearing subjects to the tyranny of a foreign Church. He was in league with the Jesuits, had been a secret Roman Catholic for years, and would soon organize a campaign to force honest Ethiopian Christians to declare their allegiance to Rome, or face torture from the rack, boiling oil, thumbscrews and all the other terrible paraphernalia of that well-known branch of the Roman Church, the Inquisition.

It was a shrewdly thought-up sham upon which to base a campaign against the Regent. He would not be able to deny that he had been brought up by Roman Catholic priests in Harar during his childhood. It was he who had opened the Tafari Makonnen School in Addis Ababa, over the protests of the Ethiopian Church, and staffed it with French teachers. And was he not constantly and continually inviting advisers into the country, most of them French, Belgian and Swiss, ostensibly for business reasons, but really to prepare the country for his act of apostasy?

Among the superstitious and avid Copts of the North it was a campaign that made considerable headway, and there must have been moments when Tafari regretted ever having given Gugsa the opportunity to launch it. News reaching the capital reported that the atmosphere in the country along the borders of Begemeder and Tigre was rapidly reaching that in which a crusade could be launched; hundreds of Gallas were swarming towards Debra Tabor and pledging themselves to fight for the Church against the machinations of the Shoan traitor. "I have no hesitation in describing it as a situation fraught with the most dire consequences for the régime in Shoa should it be allowed to mature," wrote Signor Cora to Rome. He might have added that some of the Italians in Eritrea were not exactly helping the situation by surreptitiously breaking the Arms Agreement and shipping rifles and munitions to Gugsa.

By the beginning of 1930 . . . the most alarmist rumors were current in Addis Ababa of an imminent revolt against Tafari led by Ras Gugsa from the North. The whole of Tigre, Wollo, Begemeder and Gojjam were said to be in a ferment, and not only was Ras Gugsa's army saddled, armed and ready for a campaign, but those of Hailu and Seyoum were said to be standing by. Among the legations in Addis Ababa there was little doubt that the rebellion, when it came, would be of such proportions and supported by so many troops from the North that nothing Tafari could do would stem it.

Not, it was noticed, that the Regent seemed particularly troubled by the portents from the North. He showed no sign of moving out of the capital. He continued to appear at diplomatic functions and road-opening ceremonies and Church dedications. It took some time for the observers in the capital to realize that if Tafari was not moving his armies certainly were. From Harar, from Sidamo and from other provinces in the South they poured through Shoa on their way toward Begemeder and they took their guns and tracked vehicles with them. Moreover, Ras Mulugeta, the Minister of War, had disappeared from the capital. He turned up at the beginning of March at the head of the Ethiopian army on the plains of Anchim, to the south of the Begemeder border, and there he encamped.

It was just about this time that Maillet brought news from Dessye by plane that Ras Gugsa had made up his mind. He would march south with his army and his flock of perfervid religious crusaders to rid Ethiopia of the Roman traitor in the capital. He told his cheering followers that soon the threat to the Church would be ended in bloodshed, and power restored to the God-fearing Empress whom Tafari had kept in thraldom for thirteen long years. Gugsa added that he had rallied the other chiefs of the North and West to his banner and that they would appear when the time came to call them in; but for the moment they were not needed. Why, Tafari was so afraid that he had not even dared to stir from the capital.

In fact the Regent had no intention of leaving Addis Ababa for he had much to do there. Thanks to his air courier he was closely in touch. He had given Ras Mulugeta his instructions and relied upon that cunning old soldier to carry them out. He had other things to do. One of them, of course, was to keep an eye on the Empress Zauditu and her cronies, for news that her ex-husband was about to start a revolt was almost certain to stir old aches in her bones. Not that he had much to fear, he believed, in that direction. Eager though the Empress might be to help Ras Gugsa, she was hardly in a fit mental or physical state to do anything about it, for she had been indisposed for some time. She spent most of her time in church, in prayer, and (though fasting rigidly) was a fat and forlorn figure clad in an ensemble of black robes and bonnet which made her look extraordinarily like a saffron-colored half-sister of Queen Victoria.

The Regent was more concerned to obtain the cooperation of the Ethiopian Church in the rebuttal of Ras Gugsa's charges of heresy. It was now that his cultivation of Abuna Kyril and the fact that six of the most powerful bishops in the Empire owed their preferment to him began to pay its dividends. The Abun willingly signed a document proclaiming Negus Tafari Makonnen a devout son of the Church and excommunicating all those who dared to traduce him. The six bishops sent out encyclicals to their flocks hailing Tafari as a truly Christian king. These documents the Regent took away to his private printing press where he had them reproduced as leaflets, thousand upon thousand of which he printed.

On March 28, 1930, Ras Gugsa moved with a force of some 35,000 tribesmen across the borders of Begemeder along the route leading south into Shoa. He had told his perfervidly excited armies that the crusade had begun and that the other chieftains of the North and West merely awaited the word to join them. Soon the Roman heretic, Tafari, would be driven from Addis Ababa and Shoa would be once more in the hands of true Christians.

Now came the third reason why the Regent had remained behind in Addis Ababa. He had his "air force" to get ready for operations. It so happened that on March 27 a foreign plane had suddenly appeared and landed, against all the laws, on a field just outside the capital where Tafari kept his planes. Out of it stepped a Frenchman, the Comte de Sibour, and his wife, the daughter of Gordon Selfridge, the owner of a famous Oxford Street, London, department store. They explained to the angry Ethiopians on the ground that they were on an air safari across Africa and had taken a chance about flying over Ethiopia. Their plane was impounded and they were placed under arrest—until the Regent heard about them. He sent for them at once and told them that he would release their plane and give them their freedom on one condition: that they fly northwards the following day and scatter leaflets over some recalcitrant tribesmen who were in rebellion. At dawn the next day they took off with two biplanes piloted by Maillet and Corriger and made for the Anchim plain, where de Sibour swooped low over the gawking Ethiopians while his wife ladled loads of leaflets on the soldiers below.

Some of the leaflets contained the declaration from the Abun hailing Tafari as a true son of the Church. Others announced the excommunication of Ras Gugsa as a traitor to his Empress, his Regent and his religion. Yet a third batch warned the tribesmen that if they did not desert, the birds in the sky now circling above would return and deal death to them.

Next day the de Sibours were allowed to go into Addis Ababa while arrangements were made for them to proceed on their way south to Kenya.[4] Maillet took up his plane again and this time carefully noted the position of Ras Gugsa's forces, after which he landed on a grassy strip outside the headquarters of Ras Mulugeta, the Minister of War. He reported that many of Gugsa's troops had already begun to desert, and that numbers of troop concentrations away to the West—probably belonging to Ras Hailu—were dispersing. That night Mulugeta moved his troops into position in a ring overlooking Ras Gugsa's encampment. It was evident that the significance of the planes overhead, apart from their potentiality as leaflet- or bomb-droppers, had not occurred to the warlord from Begemeder; neither he nor his men seemed to realize that their positions had been discovered and they were surrounded.

The battle began on the morning of March 31, 1930, and it did not last long. At 9 A.M. the two planes from Tafari's air force roared out of the sky upon Ras Gugsa's encampment, dropping small bombs among the milling, terrified soldiery. They made six runs, until their supply of bombs ran out, and then Maillet returned and scattered hand grenades, from which he pulled the pins with his teeth. There was more noise and flame than actual damage, but the attack achieved its object in creating terror and chaos. Without waiting to pack their tents, the Gugsa Army began to make southwards—or, at least, part of it, for a considerable number of soldiers had had enough and were decamping the way they had come.

It was then that Ras Mulugeta and the Shoan Army fell upon the rebels in their disarray. First they were pinned down by artillery and machine-gun fire, after which the Shoans advanced. The slaughter lasted for two hours, after which the survivors fled. All, that is, except Ras Gugsa and his personal bodyguard. They formed themselves into a ring of about one hundred men and they went on fighting long after the rest of their forces had deserted them. Repeated challenges to Ras Gugsa to surrender were scornfully rejected. Finally a bullet caught him in the throat, at which his bodyguard

[4] They left without their plane, which the Regent forced them to sell to him—but at a profitable price. De Sibour returned to Ethiopia in 1941 and was part of the force which helped Haile Selassie to return to his kingdom.

fell back in dismay; and a Shoan tribesman rushed in with his sword and dispatched the warlord of the North.

The embittered ex-husband, the pious rebel, was dead.

So, two days later, was his wife. Maillet flew back from the battlefield to bring the glad tidings to Tafari (it would have taken days to reach him by land), and he rode to the palace to give the Empress the news of his victory—and her defeat. She had already guessed, for she could hear the booming of the victory drums and the firing of artillery salutes. For her, too, it was the end of the struggle. She had been ill for some time but had insisted on following a rigid bread-and-water fast for Lent, and confirmation that Ras Gugsa was dead was too much for her in her weakened condition. It could be said that she died there and then of a broken heart. It was perhaps just as well. The future for the Empress after these tragic events could hardly have been comfortable.

For twenty-four hours after the Empress died, Addis Ababa throbbed with all kinds of rumors, for there had as yet been no announcement of her demise. How had Ras Gugsa been defeated so easily? What had happened to the aid he had been promised (or so it was said) from Hailu and Seyoum and Kassa? (It would be some time before the populace would learn the truth about that—of how Tafari, shaping events with his accustomed skill, had bought them off long before with promises of aggrandizement, but pledged them to conceal from Gugsa the fact they were no longer in his crusade.)

So at long last the ambition Tafari had cherished in Harar at the age of seven had come to pass, and the throne of the Empire of Ethiopia was his for the taking. On Megabit 25, 1922, by the Ethiopian calendar (or April 3, 1930, by ours), he issued the following message to the people of the Empire:

"Proclamation in the name of the Crown Prince and Regent Plenipotentiary of the Ethiopian Realm, His Majesty King Tafari Makonnen, on his ascending the Imperial Throne with the name of His Majesty Haile Selassie the First, King of Kings (Negusa Nagast) of Ethiopia. PROCLAMATION. In accordance with the Proclamation which our Creator abiding in His people, and electing us, did cause to be made, we have lived without breach of our Covenant as mother and son. Now, in that by law and commandment of God, none that is human may avoid return to earth, Her Majesty the Empress, after a few days of sickness, has departed this life. The passing of Her Majesty the Empress is grievous for myself and for the whole of the Empire. Since it is the long-standing custom that when a King, the Shepherd of his people, shall die, a King replaces him, I being upon the seat of David to which I was betrothed, will, by God's charity, watch over you.

"Trader, trade! Farmer, plough! I shall govern you by the law and ordinance that has come to me, handed down from my fathers."

He was Emperor of Ethiopia and thirty-seven years old.

part three
FRUSTRATION

chapter ten

LIJ YASU AGAIN

THOUGH THE EMPRESS ZAUDITU died on April 2, 1930, and Tafari
Makonnen succeeded her on the following day, it was not until
November 2 that he was crowned as His Imperial Majesty Haile
Selassie I,[1] Conquering Lion of the Tribe of Judah, Elect of God,
Emperor of Ethiopia. There were several reasons why an immediate
coronation was impossible, not least of them the fact that forty
days must be set aside for formal mourning of the Empress's death.
Then there was the supervention of the rainy season which would
turn the country into a quagmire until the end of September, preventing the chiefs from traveling to the capital for the ceremonials.
But above all, there were two things to be done: to persuade the
great European powers that the coming coronation was something
of much more moment than the mere elevation of an African king,
so that their presence at the festivities would need more than a per-
functory representation; and to make the capital—if possible, the
country too—at least superficially worthy of an influx of distinguished visitors from abroad.

Addis Ababa in 1930 rather resembled a shanty town with wedding
cake trimmings. Over the rolling hills, right up to the edge of the
palace, tumbled a mass of milk-chocolate colored mud huts, half of
them thatched, half of them covered in the garish, glinting new
strips of corrugated iron which had begun to be so fashionable.
There were still only one or two buildings of more than one story,
and the only ornate structures were religious edifices such as St.
George's Cathedral or the mausoleum of the Emperor Menelik. The
shops were run by Armenians whose giggling, pretty daughters
seemed manacled to them by invisible chains; the night club was

[1] Haile and Selassie were his two baptismal names.

operated by a Greek, staffed by a pliant mixture of Hungarian, Rumanian, Czech and White Russian cabaret girls (who danced for the customers for their suppers but preferred to sleep with the customers for their breakfasts), and memorable for the foulness of its whisky and the sweetness of its champagne; the hotel was called the Imperial but fell far short of its name, except in the lavishness of its fleas and lizards; the bumpy, rutted streets were pungent from open drains and plangent with the honk of motor horns and donkeys, both of which were apt to be carrying dignitaries sporting colored umbrellas above their august heads—except when it was raining; and every third hut was a tej-beit or mead-saloon whose door was guarded by an imperious mamma but whose interior provided tastes of fermented honey in the front room and seductive glimpses of dusky, pomegranate-sized breasts from the back. All of these were in the process of being refurbished for the Coronation.

A new fence was put around the palace, still a sprawling jumble of nondescript buildings, and Ethiopia had its first whiff of the smell of pitch, when the road leading from it to the Cathedral and on into the town was covered with asphalt. The town policemen, who until now had identified themselves by a thump from their staves, were given brand new uniforms and instructed (temporarily, at least) to reverse their usual procedure of beating a suspect first and asking questions afterwards. The city's estimated population of 20,000 prostitutes and tej-beit girls besieged Armenian venereal disease quacks and chemists to get themselves in healthy trim, and hired Greek specialists in languages to pick up a few words of English, French and Italian in time for the foreign customers they anticipated.

Haile Selassie had arranged that the official guests for the Coronation should be delivered to the capital by a series of special trains from Jibouti. France was represented by one of her marshals, Franchet d'Esperet, and Italy by the heir to the throne, the Prince of Savoy, but it was the British who had decided to send the most distinguished delegation. From all the surrounding colonies came governors, army and fleet commanders—from Somaliland, Aden, Kenya and the Sudan—and, as representative of King George V there was Prince Henry, Duke of Gloucester.[2] On the evening be-

---

[2] One of the English guests was not a member of the official delegation but had been invited personally by the Emperor. He was a young undergraduate from Oxford named Wilfred Thesiger. Haile Selassie had asked him as an affectionate gesture to Thesiger's father, the late British Minister.

fore the Coronation the road-mending, the erection of flags and triumphal arches, was still going on, and Major Cheesman, the British Consul in Northwest Ethiopia, who had come in from Dangila for the ceremonials, recalls in his diary that he was asked by the British Minister, Sir Sidney Barton, to take a message to one of the Ethiopian Ministers. He went to his office where "I found him out, but he was said to be in a certain street. Here I saw a little group of men in the twilight in the middle of the road. I got out of the car and walked towards them, and someone said in a subdued tone: 'Janhoi!' (Majesty!) There he was with a handful of men, within a few hours of his Coronation, inspecting a patch on the road which was being mended with a steam roller."

Shortly after dawn on the morning of November 2, before the world Press, the foreign guests and a great concourse of rases in their lions' manes and most resplendent robes, Abuna Kyril anointed the head of Haile Selassie and placed on it the triple crown of Ethiopia. Simultaneously, the rases put on their coronets, then made their obeisances to him, after which the celebratory shooting, shouting, loolooing, feasting, dancing and drinking broke out all over the city. As the Emperor and Empress left to begin their parade beneath the triumphal arches, officials moved among the distinguished foreign guests with trays of Coronation medallions and asked them to take one each as a memento of the great occasion. Major Cheesman records that the wife of one of the foreign delegates took a handful, and then, seeing that she was observed, murmured weakly, *"Pour les enfants!"*

For ten days the capital gave itself over to feasting and dancing. The city was full of licentious soldiery roistering and wenching in the tej-beits. The night club had to send urgently to Jibouti for reinforcements of sweet champagne, while the Greek bootleggers desperately tried to keep up with the demands for hooch. Meat prices rose and buyers roamed the surrounding countryside buying up cattle (though the Emperor saw to it that the traditional raw meat banquets were held out of sight of his foreign guests). It was a barbarous African equivalent of Glasgow Cross at Hogmanay and Mr. Evelyn Waugh was not the only foreign correspondent who viewed the goings-on with a distasteful eye. *The Times* wrote: "There were two main objects behind the hospitality and pageantry of the Coronation. First the Emperor wished to impress on his own countrymen, and particularly the rases, that he was accepted by the royal families of Europe, and in this he succeeded. Second, he wished to impress his European guests with the fact that Ethiopia was an up-to-date, civilized nation. In this he was only partially successful, for the Abyssinians are still backward in culture and progress, and the true state of affairs inevitably appeared from time to time. Enormous efforts had been made in Addis Ababa for the European visitors, and if some of the improvements excited amusement there was more to admire in the degree of success with which the authorities were able temporarily to disguise the nature of the people. Many of the visitors were able, however, to see a little more of the country than was officially prepared for them. These realized that the gold braid, brass bands and fine motor cars of Addis Ababa, the caviare and the sweet champagne, were a very superficial introduction to the national life."

After this sour and patronizing opening, the writer continued: "It is absurd to pretend that Ethiopia is a civilized nation in any Western sense of the word. Communications are hopelessly bad. A few miles outside Addis Ababa there is not a single motor road. The country's only railway does not pass through a single town with the exception of Dire Dawa, which sprang up on the line at the time of its construction. Harar, an important provincial centre, can only be reached by two days' mule ride up the circuitous mountain caravan route. Cities of the north can only be reached by organizing a caravan and trekking to them. Abyssinian officials have yet to discover anything derogatory to their dignity in taking presents of money from perfect strangers. The finance of the country is rudimentary.... Crimes of violence are common in the countryside. Though punishment by mutilation has been abolished from the penal system, the conditions of the prisons are grossly unhealthy. Deaths from typhus frequently follow imprisonment for trifling debts. Slaving is universal though many modifications have been made in the trade."

Having delivered himself of this indictment, the correspondent reined in his charger, but only a little: "One could prolong the list of barbarities to much greater length, but the object of this report is not to show up Abyssinia but to restore a correct balance of opinion. Europeans misled by the descriptions of the travel agents will be disappointed. Another generation of public officials will have to grow up before the country will be suitable for development on European lines. It is full of adventurers and frauds of every kind. Meanwhile the Emperor's more frantic admirers are probably highly delighted to find the country is so unmarked by tourists and speculators. The archaeology and anthropology of the country are practically unknown, and it seems most likely that in these directions Ethiopia will excite most European attention during the next decade."

The last sentence could hardly have been more wildly incorrect, of course; but it was the tone of the article rather than its indictments—all of them true enough—which hurt the new Emperor. He was only too well aware of the backwardness of his country and the weaknesses and rapacities with which the régime was riddled. But he regarded *The Times* as the spokesman of a people and a Government which regarded him with goodwill. Surely the start of a new reign was no time for a great newspaper to sneer at his people and refuse to believe there was any possibility of improvement in their condition? The article read more like the first underhand blow by the Italians to undermine him rather than the sage advice he had expected from the British.

In fact, the moment the Coronation ceremonials were completed and the foreign guests sent on their way, Haile Selassie began implementing the plans for reform and reconstruction which he had been drawing up ever since his accession the previous April. The rases were right when they suspected that Haile Selassie, once in power, would threaten their security with his new-fangled ideas, for the intention of his whole program of reformation was to frustrate the corrupt designs of the provincial warlords and draw the country together into a centrally controlled administration. For this reason he had risked offending the three powerful rases, Hailu, Seyoum and Kassa, who had helped him by holding aloof while he dealt with Ras Gugsa. For their non-intervention on the rebels' side they expected to be rewarded, as they would have been in the olden days, with crowns of their own—that they would be made kings when Haile Selassie was made King of Kings. But this was just what the Emperor did not wish to see in the new Ethiopia that he was envisaging; he wanted an end and not an increase to the system of petty kingdoms proliferating over the face of the land. "So long as the feudal system continues," he wrote about this time, "no real stability or social progress can be looked for." But before it could be ended a decision must be made as to what should take its place.

Six months after the coronation, Haile Selassie did something which no Emperor of Ethiopia had ever done before. He changed the status of his people from chattels of the rases into subjects of the State. And, more important, he offered them a written Constitution. As Edward Ullendorff writes in his authoritative book, *The Ethiopians*: [3] "This was an entirely voluntary act for which there was no public clamour in the country, but it has always been the Emperor's particular strength to judge the right moment and to grant the right measure of advance."

The 1931 Constitution was far from being a revolutionary measure, for it intended, as the Emperor put it, initially to mark "the transformation of Ethiopia to a limited monarchy" and to "establish a Constitution whereby the whole people may be made to share our labours in accomplishing the heavy task of Government at which former Emperors laboured alone." [4] The measure introduced two deliberative chambers—a Senate, appointed by the Emperor, and a Chamber of Deputies, chosen by dignitaries and chiefs—which could do little more than advise the Emperor. It was in fact a rehearsal or "dry-run" for a democracy to come, in which, as he said himself, "it is necessary for the modern Ethiopian to accustom himself to take part in the direction of all departments of the State."

He added: "Therefore, on this principle, in order that all suitable persons may become participants in the task, we have established two Houses of Parliament. The members who will consult together in these chambers will come from various provinces, chosen under the authority of the Emperor, until such time as the people have reached a degree of education and experience enabling them to make the choice themselves. Their decisions will be by a majority vote, and if the Emperor approves them they will be put into effect. Decisions taken in the Parliament and approved by the Emperor will be executed for the whole of Ethiopia and by the Ministers, who will be responsible in the matter and will see that the requirements of Government and people are duly fulfilled."

There were plenty in Western Europe (ignoring Mussolini's much more rigorous régime in Italy) who sneered at Haile Selassie's measures as "window dressing" to impress the foreigner. In fact, it was a brave first step from feudalism to paternalism and it took place rather more smoothly than other African countries have moved in the opposite direction more than 30 years later.

Haile Selassie realized that a salutary centralization of the Ethiopian Government meant the establishment of departments to which only lip-service had been paid so far, even by Menelik. Personnel must be trained to form the nucleus of a Civil Service. Ministers and de-

[3] E. Ullendorff, *The Ethiopians* (Oxford).
[4] Speech by the Emperor when signing the 1931 Constitution.

partment heads must be appointed. There must be built up, as Ullen-dorff pointed out, a system for the recruitment of a "reliable cadre of educated men" to organize the security forces, the financial administration and customs services, and all the paraphernalia of modern government. There was also a desperate need of money. The new Emperor was a reformer but he was not too idealistic to realize that his reforms would have to be paid for.

"Nobody can be unaware," he once said, "that in any part of the world whatsoever the vital principal of a government consists in money. As it is the soul that keeps the body alive, so it is money that keeps a government alive through all its difficulties. Well, a man, whoever he may be, does not cease from the utmost thought and effort to prevent his soul—that is, his life—being separated from his body—that is, to prevent his dying—until such time as God has determined it for him. And similarly a government, so long as it preserves the name, must exert the utmost thought and activity to prevent the Treasury becoming empty of money and full of difficulties arising over payments."

To stimulate the economy the Emperor realized that he would have need of expert help, and for this—lacking an educated class of his own—he turned inevitably to foreign countries. He chose carefully so that his scales should not be overloaded with too much influence from a particular nation. His adviser on foreign affairs was one not likely to be partial on big power questions: he chose a Swede, de Virgin. His legal adviser, Auberson, was Swiss. His adviser on interior affairs, particularly slavery, was an Englishman named de Halpert.[5] But perhaps the most important appointment was that of an American, Colson, to the Ministry of Finance. He had been seconded from the State Department in Washington and he was so much an ideal man for the job that he soon became the Emperor's principal adviser on all affairs. Of him, G. L. Steer writes, in his moving book, *Caesar in Abyssinia*:[6] "In strength of purpose and steadiness of aim he stood head and shoulders above Virgin, the Swede, and Auberson, the Swiss. He was combatively anti-Imperialist. He distrusted the limitrophe powers in the following order: Italy, France and Great Britain. But in his personal dealings with their representatives he behaved perfectly; he made friends of many."

Colson won his way into Haile Selassie's trust because he never

---

[5] He resigned in 1933 on the grounds that anti-slavery measures were not being vigorously enough enforced.

[6] G. L. Steer, *Caesar in Abyssinia* (Hodder & Stoughton).

tried to flatter him or "butter up" the Ethiopians. "Colson saw the weaknesses of Ethiopian national character quite clearly. He knew that there was a lot of graft; that much time was wasted on discussion; that they were over-suspicious and made unnecessary enemies; that they could not say no; that their conceit was phenomenal."

He did not hesitate to tell the officials whom he was supposed to advise that they were acting like fools. But "he served the Ethiopians loyally but frankly. That was why they liked him and depended on him."

It was the task of these experts to organize the new Ministries, recruit a staff for each of them, and advise the officials appointed at their head "tactfully" how to run them.[7] They also, under Colson, drew up a scheme for operating provinces under central control rather than through the rases on the spot, and three provinces in which Haile Selassie's own compliant nominees were incumbents were chosen as "models" for an experiment in government from Addis Ababa.

All these were developments not likely to allay the suspicions of the provincial warlords, but to bring them around to accepting his modernizing ideas the Emperor adopted a very old Ethiopian stratagem. His new Constitution had been announced in July, 1931. He sent messages to all the rases to tell them that it would be formally signed in November of the same year; and that their presence, therefore, was required in Addis Ababa to witness the signing of the historic document and also to take their place in the new Houses of Parliament as the first Senators of the Empire. They were told to bring their robes and coronets with them.

It was an invitation to a celebration, which any Ethiopian finds it hard to resist, and only two of the rases did so—Ras Kassa because he was engaged in a religious penance, and Ras Hailu because he was still sullen over the Emperor's failure to make him a king. He stayed sulking, fuming and plotting, in Debra Marcos.

The signing of the new Constitution was almost as spectacular an event as the Coronation itself. After the official ceremony the rases, clad in all their finery, marched from the palace to a tent half a mile away, which had been erected beside some tentative foundations. This was as far as the Emperor had got with the new Houses of Parliament; but to those who grumbled there were compensations, including a

[7] Haile Selassie took over the Ministry of Education for himself, to emphasize education's importance in Ethiopia's future, and he has held the job ever since. He still quizzes scholarship students personally who have returned from abroad.

series of great banquets and lavish entertainments at which, for once, the Emperor went out of his way to show himself an enthusiastic host. The festivities went on for several days and it was some time before the rases, sated with wine, food and various extravagant romps,[8] decided it was time to make their way back to their provinces. They discovered that many of their troops had been paid off and that the Emperor had expressed a wish, which he was sure they would obey, that they remain in the capital to give him their guidance as senators of the new régime. Despite their grumbles, he kept them in Addis Ababa until the beginning of 1932. In the meantime, under the direction of the quadrumvirate of foreign advisers, administrators were moving into their provinces and setting up in business as advisers, tax collectors and consultants.

It was the first move by the Emperor to attack the rases on their own ground and break up their feudal powers. Its initial success was impressive.

Unfortunately, however, Ras Hailu was not one of the warlords who had been sequestrated. He remained in his luxurious redoubt in Debra Marcos, the capital of the vast kingdom of Gojjam, safe from the infiltrations and interferences of the reformer in the capital. But if Haile Selassie could not tempt Ras Hailu to Addis Ababa, at least he could bind him to the new régime by an ancient method—a dynastic marriage. He sent an emissary with friendly greetings to Ras Hailu and sought the hand of one of his younger daughters for his eldest son, the Crown Prince. The Emperor calculated that such an alliance would stifle any hostility which Hailu felt toward him. In this he was wrong. The ruler of the Gojjam accepted the Emperor's offer "with great joy" and the marriage was arranged for the end of the year.

But in fact the engagement did nothing to still Ras Hailu's suspicions of the Emperor and hatred of his reforming zeal. Besides, he had a scheme that would make him not just the helpless father-in-law of a Crown Prince but the all-powerful father-in-law of an Emperor.

It was many years later than the events now being recounted that the author first met Ras Hailu, and by that time he was an old man in a position which should have been parlous and abject, as will

---

[8] One of them "married" a Polish-Jewish cabaret girl named Rachel Brauer and gave her a dowry of $15,000 to send off to her father living in the Polish Corridor, to whom she announced that she was now "the wife of the King of Abyssinia." She appears to have got her rases confused with her Neguses.

become apparent later in this story. But even then he was a flamboyant and, in many ways, ingratiating character. In 1931-32 he was at the height of his power, rich as Croesus, arrogant and capricious. Major Cheesman visited him frequently at Debra Marcos while he was stationed there as British Consul for Western Ethiopia and undoubtedly found him a formidable and resplendent character with a tremendous pride in his rank and importance.

"I was shown to the chair on his right and he sat on the throne," Cheesman wrote of one visit. "He was wearing the dark official cloak of Ethiopia, with an extensive display of medals and foreign decorations, among which I recognized the KBE. His legs were clothed in tight-fitting white breeches and he wore European shoes."

There were ceremonial processions led by massed brass bands, a church service conducted by Ras Hailu's own bishop, and a vast banquet for 2,000 guests. As Cheesman and his host approached the palace from the church on their richly caparisoned mules, "I noticed a large pile of rocks heaped on the turf nearby. It appeared that the Ras was building yet another house and had taken the opportunity of the banquet to get the rocks carried up the hill to the site. Each of the 2,000 guests was invited to shoulder one of the rocks, and we waited to see them load up. The pile diminished rapidly." There was some delay at the entrance to the banqueting hall, "much pushing and shoving and it looked as if a free fight might break out. The guards seemed to have conflicting orders. They may have been separating those with invitations to lunch from those who were trying to pass in uninvited, but they seemed to be using canes on all and sundry. The Ras and I had to wait until the crowd dispersed and a way was cleared for us." Then down they sat to a meal (of sixteen courses for Cheesman, of vegetarian dishes for Hailu, who was fasting), washed down with tej, talla, and (again for Cheesman) white and red wines, champagne, brandy, whisky, crème de menthe, cointreau and peppermint, all of which he was urged by his host to drink. Of the tej which Hailu drank, "each steward poured a little from his bottle on to the palm of his own hand and drank it before filling it for his master, as a precaution against poison."

All this time the court jester was singing songs and making jokes, and two tiny black dwarfs, Ras Hailu's mascots, were prancing around the room, turning handsprings, pouring beer over the head of some unfortunate guest, and even playfully tweaking the hair of their master, as if to suggest that part of it was a wig (as indeed it was).

After the Ras and his guests had finished eating, the stewards who had served them came forth and sat down and ate before their master. "He called to the head steward to come close, and after requesting me to watch, made him throw back his head and open his mouth wide. Then grasping a large wad of food in his hand he thrust it into his servant's mouth, completely filling it.[9] Two men holding brass candelabra with lighted candles had stood on each side of the Ras's table throughout the meal."

Yes, Ras Hailu lived and looked like a medieval king, even if he did not have the title of Negus. To demonstrate the skill of his fighting men, he organized for Cheesman a day of equestrian sports in which the principal event was a tournament between rival teams of riders. The teams were mounted on horses rather than the more normal Ethiopian mules "and were armed with long straight canes which they threw as spears." They carried shields and each side advanced in turn, the attackers "galloping after the others with horses fully extended, each one taking a man and trying to throw the shaft to hit him." The leading group tried to ward off the missiles with their spears or by wheeling their horses but "some men were decidedly skilful and got hits when the horses were a hundred yards apart, and one realized that their spears would do great execution in the ranks of a flying enemy."

The arrogant possessor of so much territory, treasure and troops was hardly likely to view with equanimity any schemes by the Emperor to diminish him, and the planned marriage of his daughter to the Crown Prince was an insufficient bribe to secure his cooperation. Besides, he had another daughter who might well prove much more valuable. She could help him with a plan which, if it succeeded, would not only circumvent the Emperor's intentions but would also bring him the title he so hungrily desired and an influence that would extend far beyond the confines of Gojjam.

It will be remembered that Ras Hailu's eldest daughter, Waizero Sabela Wangel, had once been married to Lij Yasu and had been sent back to her father when he acquired his taste for small boys and Danakil virgins. She brought back with her the only child of

[9] Major Cheesman may be said to have paid Ras Hailu back in his own coin when he gave him a return dinner a few days later. "Abyssinians pride themselves that they can eat hotter foods flavoured with red pepper than most other people, and after warning Ras Hailu of the potency of Tabasco sauce I offered him some. He helped himself bravely and as bravely praised it with tears streaming from his eyes. He then asked if he might try it on one of his old officials, who licked up enough to make him choke, after which the patriarch muttered: 'Ah, I can truly say that this is the Mother of Heat.' "

the marriage, a daughter.[10] Major Cheesman was one of the few people outside Ras Hailu's own circle to have seen Waizero Sabela after her divorce. He had lunch with her in the separate house and *ménage* she maintained in Debra Marcos, his first meeting with her being in a dark room where, "as my eyes got accustomed to the gloom, I saw a little dark woman reclining between two cushions on the floor, her figure draped in clothes in such abundance that her form could hardly be distinguished." Cheesman described her as being "not plain and not beautiful, and both complexion and eyes were dark." He added: "The picture of this woman and her child, who through no fault of their own were destined for a life of loneliness and obscurity was pathetic. Had her royal husband ruled more wisely and retained the loyalty of his subjects, she would instead have been in the Palace in Addis Ababa, surrounded by pomp and circumstance, and the child would have been heiress to the throne of Ethiopia."

It had occurred to Ras Hailu that she still could be, if Lij Yasu were to escape from his bondage, if Haile Selassie and his reformers could be defeated, and if the ex-Emperor could be brought back in triumph to Addis Ababa to claim the triple crown.

Lij Yasu had been a prisoner of Ras Kassa for eleven years now. He had seen an Italian doctor in Axum who had treated him with the drug 606 for his syphilis, and from this he appears to have improved in health; and there were reports that he had recently abandoned his fervor for Islam and taken confession from an Ethiopian priest. Eleven years of confinement had scarcely improved his appearance or his manner, and if he had been a lean and arrogant dictator before, he was a fat and flabby tyrant now, given to fits of ungovernable rage, apt to collapse into tearful tantrums, and pathetically grateful to Ras Kassa for salving his pride by treating him as a hostage worthy of certain imperial privileges.

These included his own quarters in a castle at Fiche in Shoa (midway between Addis Ababa and Debra Marcos), where he had been installed after an attempt to escape within a few weeks of his initial incarceration. He had an entourage which included a personal valet, a cook and a staff of squires, and a minstrel. His captor, Ras Kassa, was a God-fearing and church-going chieftain but was not inclined, such being Ethiopian broad-mindedness, to see any conflict between his own religiousness and the satisfying of the sexual needs which his hostage soon indicated were clamant. After the first few months

10 Not a son, as some record books have it. A son of the ex-Emperor would have put a much more powerful weapon in Hailu's hands than he in fact possessed.

of imprisonment, and in between Yasu's bouts of illness, Kassa kept him plentifully supplied with female comforts. Lij Yasu was now thirty-four years old and had established the fact with his jailers that his appetites were too enfeebled by physical weakness, or jaded by too much experience, to be satisfied with an occasional virgin to share his couch. Three or four women were admitted at a time to the royal quarters and there were banquets of a kind at which the women danced or performed their peculiar specialities, and at which, when drunk and stripped of his clothes, Lij Yasu was apt to make long and boastful speeches to his bored or impatient auditors. At one time, Ras Kassa reported, Lij Yasu conceived a passion for young mothers and Kassa's men dutifully scoured the district bribing brides attractive enought to tempt him and willing to leave their babies behind while they acted as wet-nurses to the wayward hostage. There was an incipient international scandal in 1929 when an Addis Ababa cabaret girl turned up in Jibouti and complained that she had been raped by two of his entourage and whipped by "an Ethiopian prince" who was being held prisoner "outside Addis Ababa," but the girl withdrew her statement forty-eight hours later and departed, first class, in a mail steamer for Marseilles.

Years of sequestration had, if anything, stimulated rather than doused Lij Yasu's dreams of being an Emperor, and his hatred of his cousin, Haile Selassie, who ruled in his place, was psychotic. He yearned to see the present Emperor grovelling in chains at his mercy, and this was sufficient incentive to make him willing to listen to any scheme which might provoke a successful rebellion against the present régime and procure his own restitution. From the spies Ras Hailu had infiltrated into Fiche, he was sure Lij Yasu would welcome and cooperate in any escape plot which had a reasonable chance of succeeding.

In April, 1932, the ruler of Gojjam managed to smuggle an emissary into Yasu's quarters and broke the news to the excited captive that plans were afoot for his release. There would be no danger if he carried out the instructions which Ras Hailu had sent him. All he had to do was to ask Ras Kassa (as he had several times in the past) to be allowed to give a feast for himself and his entourage. The party would be for a date some weeks hence and a number of women would be required. The rest could safely be left to Ras Hailu. He would arrange for the escape and he would have an escort ready to convey Lij Yasu into Gojjam. There Hailu's army would be awaiting him, ready to march against the Shoans, and, with the help of other rases, topple Haile Selassie from his throne. The price that Ras Hailu asked in return was, in the circumstances, a small one: merely the crowning of himself as Negus of Gojjam and Begemeder, plus a place beside Lij Yasu on his throne—if not in his bed—for Sabela. This the ex-Emperor eagerly promised to do.

To implement his plot, however, Ras Hailu needed the cooperation of some of his fellow rases from the North—or at least he thought he did—and this is where he made his mistake. He sent messages to certain warlords telling them nothing of his plan to engineer Lij Yasu's escape but calling upon them to support him in the fight to preserve their feudal privileges against the reforms the Emperor had begun to initiate. But the fact that he had to send certain of the messages to Addis Ababa, where the rases were cooling their heels, rather than to the provinces, inevitably meant talk. No Ethiopian can resist gossip. Inevitably, rumors of Ras Hailu's intrigues reached the Emperor.

At first Haile Selassie refused to believe that Ras Hailu was conspiring against him. He was all for doing nothing. But as talk became feverish in the capital his friend, Ras Imru, and his old ally, Ras Kassa—who knew nothing of his prisoner's involvement in the plot—urged him to take precautions. It was finally decided that Ras Kassa should write a letter to Ras Hailu expressing treasonable sentiments against Haile Selassie's régime and suggesting a conference between the two warlords. The Emperor promised that he would take action if Hailu's reply revealed his willingness to enter into a conspiracy.

The reply, in fact, showed Hailu feverishly eager to meet Ras Kassa and discuss insurrection, and Kassa responded with a summons to a rendezvous close to the Gojjam frontier with Shoa, not far from Fiche. Haile Selassie sent Ras Mulugeta and the Shoan Army north to infiltrate into the hills, and when Hailu turned up with his bodyguard for the meeting, they swept down to surround him. He was brought secretly to Addis Ababa and confined to a barracks outside the capital. But still no hint came through that his plotting was connected with the escape of Lij Yasu and Hailu did not enlighten his captors.

In the second week of June, 1932, while Ras Kassa was in Addis Ababa, Lij Yasu held his long-promised feast and there was much singing, dancing and roistering. Many of the guards were invited to join the revellers. In the early hours of the morning, when most of them were dead drunk and the only others on duty were clinking their Maria Theresa dollars and looking the other way, Lij Yasu slipped out of the bed in which he had been lying with one of the women. She had hidden her clothes at the foot of the bed—the usual four-poster which appears in every Ethiopian audience chamber— and the prince squeezed his corpulent body into her silk shamma, sandals and headshawl. Dressed as a woman, he made his way into the courtyard and through the compound to a gap in the walls where mules and an escort awaited him. Now for the first time he was told of Ras Hailu's arrest, and his inclination was to go back at once to his prison quarters; he was terrified of being killed. His rescuers, how- ever, urged him to accompany them and reassured him. Though in jail, Hailu's writ still ran through Gojjam. Once the party had crossed the frontier into Gojjam country they would be in safe territory; and once in Debra Marcos, there was an army waiting to be sent into action.

It was not until twenty-four hours after Lij Yasu's escape that the Emperor learned of it, and he at once declared a state of national emergency. Telegraph wires and telephones were cut. Frontiers were closed. The so-called "express train" to Jibouti from Addis Ababa (on which, it so happened, Sir Sydney Barton, the British Minister, was traveling home on leave) was halted and its passengers held incommunicado by the army. A curfew was declared in Addis Ababa. Ras Mulugeta and his troops were ordered to scour the Gojjam fron- tier regions for trace of the fugitive.

Luck was on the Emperor's side. It had been dry for several days in Gojjam, even though the "little rains" had started, but now a fierce downpour hosed the hills and filled the dry or merely muddy river-beds with flash floods. One of these effectively blocked the prog- ress of the escaping prince, and his entourage was sighted from the air by Maillet. As soon as they realized the hopelessness of their posi- tion, his escort began one by one to desert. He was captured four days after his escape, covered with mud, half-mad with hunger, frus- tration and fever. He still wore a woman's shamma, clasped to his fat shoulders by a jewelled brooch, and his eyes were heavily painted with kohl.

The golden chain was looped around his neck once more, and he was taken in an old Chevrolet bus to Addis Ababa—and thence to his final place of imprisonment.

For his part in the plot, Ras Hailu was fined 300,000 Maria Theresa dollars—about $150,000 at the then rate of exchange. The engagement between his daughter and the Crown Prince was broken off, and he was taken from the capital to a safe jail in the Shoan hinterland. Since he was of royal blood, he had invoked the law that he could not be executed, so that Haile Selassie had perforce to spare him, though not necessarily in royal comfort and definitely without female compensations. The next few years would be difficult for him, but he was an irrepressible old scamp and it would be a long time before he ceased to be one of the spices in the Ethiopian stewpot.

His rich province of Gojjam was given to Haile Selassie's faithful friend from boyhood, Ras Imru.

For Lij Yasu, it was the end of the royal road, though not yet the end of his life. He too, of course, was saved from execution by Menelik's embargo, but this time Haile Selassie determined that only captors under his direct command should guard the royal prisoner. Not that there seemed much to worry about; the abortive escape seemed to have broken Lij Yasu completely, and he had become a pathetic and blubbering wreck in which there no longer struggled the handsome, imperious prince of a few years back. There would obviously be no more escapes. To make sure, however, the Emperor had him transported into his own province of Harar and incarcerated him in a high-walled stone house, shaped not unlike a church, in the village of Grawa, tucked into the Garamalutta Mountains. For reasons which need not be gone into here the author, during his stays in Harar, was unable to visit Grawa but another writer, David Buxton, was there in the years following the last war, and in his book, *Travels in Ethiopia*, he writes: "It is distressing how some writers on Ethiopia, not content apparently with genuine thrills and wonders (of which the country surely offers plenty) must needs conjure up sensational falsities from their own imagination. One has read, for instance, of Lij Yasu languishing behind the bars of a huge iron cage, etc. I saw no sign of anything so extraordinary. From a distance the prison, which crowns the hill above the village, was surrounded by three high concentric walls, with heavily barred gates. Within the church-like prison building itself were two very high rooms with small windows near the top of the walls, perhaps eighteen feet above the ground. A smaller chamber, apparently the royal prisoner's bathroom, adjoined. The whole place was certainly impregnable and well designed for its purpose."

Here the willful boy who had once been Emperor of Ethiopia languished, tethered like the lions in the palace in Addis Ababa by a light, long chain (though his was royally gold). On November

22, 1935, he died at the age of 37, from general paralysis of the insane.

It was just as well that he died when he did. The war with Italy was on, and six months later the Italians were in Harar. Flabby ruin though he was, Lij Yasu could have made a useful puppet for the Fascist régime in Ethiopia.

chapter eleven
MISPLACED FAITH

IT IS PERHAPS hardly necessary to emphasize that the accession of Emperor Haile Selassie did not bring overnight, or even overyear, improvements and reforms in Ethiopia. It was still a primitive and backward land, full of poverty and disease, corruption and cruelty. Those who visited it for the first time in the 1930's could not believe that it could ever have been worse—which it certainly had been —and friendly though they might be in their inclinations, they were only too often shocked by what they found.

As it turned out, Ethiopia probably had no better friend than a young doctor-missionary named John Melly, who risked his life for the Ethiopians and was eventually killed by one of them; but when he first arrived in Addis Ababa in 1934 he was horrified.

"Conditions here are appalling," he wrote. "The country is way back in the fifteenth century—ruled over by feudal lords—with sanitation unheard of. This is the capital, Addis Ababa, which outstrips the rest of the country by 500 years. Yet there are neither drains, water supply or electric light. [There was, in fact, an electric generating station.] Anyone who wants these things must arrange their own. The country is about the size of France and Germany together—with an estimated population approaching that of Canada. To serve this there are 400 Hospital beds—practically all Missionary Hospitals and practically all in this town. And the whole country is positively ridden with disease. The things that meet the eye at every step are infantile paralysis, T.B. and leprosy. And I understand that typhus, smallpox and venereal disease (90 percent of the population) are rife." [1]

But at least Melly had been invited out because it was hoped that

[1] *John Melly of Ethiopia*, edited by Kathleen Nelson and Alan Sullivan (Faber & Faber).

he would help to operate a new, 300-bed hospital, and there were many other foreigners in Addis Ababa—not counting the rogues, the adventurers, the cabaret girls and the journalists—who were in the process of planning the development of the country. The blueprints were on the table even if the roads and buildings they were meant for were still unstarted. In 1932 the Anti-Slavery and Aborigines Protection Society sent Lord Noel Buxton to Addis Ababa to report on the abolition of slavery, and he asked at once to be taken to the Slave School (so-called), the existence of which had been reported to him in London. Major Cheesman and George Heroui, son of the Ethiopian Minister of Foreign Affairs, had the task of taking Lord Buxton on his tour, and they searched high and low for the Slave School, though neither had ever heard of it.

But they tried. "The party started off full of hope," wrote Cheesman in his diary. "It happens that the Amharic language is not rich in terms and to the ordinary Ethiopian the word *Shankalla* covers not only a *slave* but any person of colour. They found a private house and knocked, to be confronted by a very surprised dark South American woman and her husband, who were running a successful jazz band in the town. Apologies and a hasty retreat followed. The only actual release of a captive that I heard of was that of a caged Bateleur eagle, which the Commission bought from a native at a station on the railway. It was taken outside the town and given its liberty."

In fact, Haile Selassie provided Lord Noel Buxton with details of more than three thousand slaves who had been released and the records of nearly seven hundred slave traders who had been convicted and punished. Noel Buxton departed in a somewhat disillusioned condition; he should have been around in the 1920's.

What Haile Selassie needed after 1932, when the last of his overt enemies was annihilated, were ten years to clear up the mess in which he knew only too well his country had relapsed, from years of uncertainty, corruption and lack of central direction. He had already invested most of his own personal fortune in Ethiopian developments (land, factories, building projects) which would be worthless if he lost out on his reforms. He had put his money on development, and had a vested interest in letting it develop. But he needed time, and time was not something Europe intended to allow him.

Even before Italy had signed the Treaty of Friendship with Ethiopia in 1928, most of the world, particularly Britain and France, had come to regard Italy as the country with presumptive rights in

Ethiopia, and the fact that Haile Selassie did not agree with this interpretation of what he considered a simple treaty of friendship was laughed off by the powers as African naïveté. So long as Britain's rights in Lake Tsana, controlling the flood waters of the Blue Nile into the Sudan and Egypt, were remembered, the Tory Cabinet did not particularly mind if Ethiopia came completely under Italy's sway. Jones and Monroe put it this way in their *A History of Ethiopia*,[2] which was written in 1935 but reprinted in a new edition as late as 1960 with this comment unchanged: "No reasonable person can quarrel with the case for Italian expansion; it is excellent and pressing. Italy is a virile nation needing raw materials for her growing industries and an outlet for her surplus population. She came too late into the nineteenth century scramble for colonies, and, owing to an inefficient government, was poorly treated at the Peace Conference. Adjustments are clearly called for."

At first, as they had done before Adowa, forty years earlier, the Italians believed that they would achieve their aims by sheer superiority in guileful politics, infiltrating through the rases, bribing Ministers, and gradually gaining a hold over the whole country. They got their first shock after the signing of the 1928 Treaty of Friendship. This, among other things, contained a clause agreeing to Ethiopia's use of the Italo-Eritrean port of Assab and the building of a road to connect it with Ethiopia, the project to be jointly financed. But here things went wrong. The Ethiopians wanted the road to stretch from Assab to Dessye in East-Central Ethiopia and then continue along the crude highway south to the capital, Addis Ababa. The Italians would agree only that it should go as far as Dessye, and demanded a wide swath of country under Italian control the whole length of the highway from the Ethiopian frontier to Dessye. The Ethiopians, by this time alarmed that the road might become an Italian arrow in the heart of Ethiopia, demurred. They announced instead that their section of the road would be built by the Dutch, and that it would still proceed south to Addis Ababa. No, said the Italians. So that part of the Treaty never came to fulfillment (though the Italians built their section of the road).

This was indeed disillusioning for Italy, and particularly for Mussolini, who had long since decided that Haile Selassie was an attractive puppet who would soon be dangling from his knee, mouthing the flattering adjectives of a Fascist satrap. From the world, however, and

[2] Oxford University Press, 1935.

from Addis Ababa, he succeeded in concealing his irritation with the Emperor, and as late as September 1934, he reaffirmed Italy's faith in the Treaty of Friendship. Earlier that year he had told the Assembly of Fascists in Rome that "there must be no misunderstanding of the centuries-old task that I assign to this and future generations of Italians. There is no question of territorial conquests—this must be understood by all both far and near—but of a natural expansion which ought to lead to a collaboration between Italy and the peoples of Africa, between Italy and the nations of the Near and Middle East."

In the meantime, however, he ordered his controlled Press to step up attacks upon Ethiopians as a backward, cruel and slave-trading people who were badly in need of control by a "civilizing" power; and earlier he sent one of his principal marshals, de Bono, to Eritrea to look over the situation for what—and this was 1932—he had decided would be war. De Bono afterwards wrote in his *Anno XIII: The Conquest of an Empire:* [3] "It should be noted at the outset that we had not yet experienced any beneficial results from the famous treaty of friendship of 1928. On our own side we had scrupulously observed its provisions, and Abyssinia, in different ways and under various circumstances, had taken advantage of it. Nevertheless, we continued to note, and to suffer from, a hostility which continued to increase, greatly to our disadvantage. In 1932 nothing had been as yet settled as regards the character and method of a possible campaign against the probable enemy, nor in respect of the force which might have to be employed."

That year he persuaded Mussolini to send the King of Italy on a visit to Eritrea to stir up enthusiasm among the colonizers—and, of course, to draw attention in Italy to East Africa. "I felt it incumbent upon me," de Bono wrote, "to accompany His Majesty on this visit, which gave me an opportunity of revising on the spot my knowledge of certain matters which would help me to shape the details of the decisions which would have to be taken." The following year, 1933, he wrote: "The Duce had spoken to no one of the coming operations in East Africa; *only he and I knew* [de Bono's italics] what was going to happen and no indiscretion occurred by which the news could reach the public."

This was in the period when Mussolini was still professing warm friendship for Ethiopia and high regard for the Emperor. But it was

[3] The Cresset Press.

also the period when de Bono submitted to the Duce the following memorandum:

The political conditions in Abyssinia are deplorable; it should not be a very difficult task to effect the disintegration of the Empire if we work at it well on political lines, and it could be regarded as certain after a military victory on our part. The unruliness of the Rases, some of whom are open malcontents, may lead to a movement which will induce one or another of the stronger of them—even without the Emperor's wish—to rebel against the Emperor and give us an opportunity to intervene. But, on the other hand, the possibility must not be excluded that those chieftains who are on our frontier may attempt to attack us, counting on our present weakness. This being so, it is incumbent on us to prepare ourselves, so that we could withstand the shock of the whole Abyssinian force in our present positions and then pass to the counter-attack, and go right in with the intention of making a complete job of it, once and for all.

The Duce replied that a war against Ethiopia must be envisaged as beginning not later than 1936 (it began in 1935). De Bono sent a note: "Money will be needed, chief, lots of money." Mussolini answered: "There will be no lack of money."

There is no need to rehearse here the melancholy chain of events which culminated in the Italian invasion of Ethiopia. For an account of the sad and shuffling role played in the sorry tale by Great Britain under Baldwin and the shifty and sordid maneuvers of France under Laval, I would recommend a study of the second volume of Lord Avon's memoirs, *Facing the Dictators*,[4] in which he confirms with official documentation the shady trickery that went on at the time. It was the Wal Wal Incident which first brought Italian intentions to the notice of the world and gave the Emperor his first hint (which he refused at the time to recognize) that the European powers would not be prepared to stand by Ethiopia in the event of a clash.

Wal Wal was an important well, used equally by nomadic British, Italian and Ethiopian Somalis, which lay deep inside the deserts of Ethiopian Ogaden, at least 60 miles from the frontiers of Italian Somaliland. In 1930 the well was occupied by a troop of Italian Somalis, though they did not interfere with the tribes who came from all directions to water their camels and themselves. The Emperor, who had always been sensitive about Ethiopian rights to the Ogaden, even when he was a young Governor of Harar—and even today—

4 *The Eden Memoirs*, Vol. 2 (Cassell and Co., 1962).

celebrated his accession to the throne by ordering the man he had appointed as governor in his place, Dejazmach Gabre Mariam, to clear the territory of these Italian-sponsored intruders. So in 1931 Gabre Mariam took a force of some 15,000 men into the desert on a sweeping expedition against the so-called *dubats* or semi-official soldiers. For some reason, however, he seems to have missed Wal Wal. The Italian Somalis stayed on and their masters presumably decided that their occupation of the well had been recognized as a *fait accompli*. From then on, in their view, Wal Wal was part of Italian Somaliland; and when the build-up of troops began in Eritrea and Somaliland for the invasion of Ethiopia, a white Italian officer took soldiers to Wal Wal and erected there a fort on the foundations of one of the old bastions left behind by the Mad Mullah.

In fact, however, no one had recognized Italian rights to Wal Wal except the Italians themselves. Britain certainly went on accepting that Wal Wal was Ethiopian and, toward the end of November 1934, its members joined the mixed Anglo-Ethiopian Grazing and Boundary Commission on a tour which was to include an inspection of Wal Wal. They were accompanied by a bodyguard of 600 Ethiopian troops to protect them from the marauders who were not infrequent in these parts. They arrived at the well on November 23, 1934, and were surprised to find that it had been turned into an Italian encampment. The Italian officer in charge, moreover, strongly objected to the appearance of the Commission and was "unconciliatory and disobliging." Some hours after a difficult interview with him, the Commission's camp was "buzzed" by Italian warplanes and there was, for a time, a near-panic at the prospect that they were about to be bombed. The British decided to withdraw and take the Ethiopian members of the Commission with them, and to this the Ethiopians consented only so long as the bodyguard was left behind to indicate that there was no Ethiopian acceptance of Italian occupation.

On December 5, after all neutral witnesses had departed, the atmosphere of anger, antipathy and suspicion flared up into a military clash. Who fired the first shot will never be known, but one of the first to die was Fitaurari Alemayu, the commander of the Ethiopian bodyguard, who was shot down as he was leaving his tent. His second-in-command hurriedly retreated, leaving his troops to face the Italians and their armored cars; and when they at last withdrew they left behind a hundred casualties of their own, and some scores of the Italians.

Italy at once demanded compensation. Count Vinci, the Italian Minister to Addis Ababa, saw the Foreign Minister and read his instructions from Mussolini in Rome, which were to insist on the immediate payment of £20,000 by Ethiopia to Italy and, to rub salt in the wound, the attendance at Wal Wal of an official Ethiopian delegation which would salute the Italian flag there. Mussolini, who was well aware of the arrogance of the Ethiopians, can hardly have expected the Emperor to swallow such an insult, particularly since it concerned a portion of his native province; but Haile Selassie, aware that the situation was fraught with danger for him, resisted the temptation to meet a gesture of contempt with a slap in the face and, instead, invoked the 1928 Treaty of Friendship with Italy which had bound both sides to take such disputes to arbitration. Arbitration was, however, the last thing Mussolini now desired; all he wanted was either to humiliate Ethiopia into submitting to his domination, or to provoke her into the retaliation that would give him the excuse to attack.

But Haile Selassie had another card to play if arbitration failed, and this was the League of Nations. He had retained a great and touching faith in its effectiveness—much more so than its European members—ever since an appeal to it had crushed Anglo-Italian interference in 1925. What it had done then it should be able to do for him again, not only in settling the Wal Wal incident but also in checking the aggressive build-up of the Italian armies and air forces along his frontiers. He decided to refer the matter to the League.

When rumors of his intention first became known in Addis Ababa, the British Minister, Sir Sidney Barton, immediately informed the Foreign Office in London, where the thud of chins dropping could be heard all over Whitehall. Sir Sidney, who was to prove himself a good friend of Ethiopia, was instructed to hasten to the palace and dissuade the Emperor from involving the League; the last thing the Foreign Office wanted was to be mixed up in a dispute between a bunch of arrogant, upstart and bloodthirsty Africans and a European nation whose cooperation Britain was already beginning to seek in restraining the Germany of Hitler and National Socialism. The Orders from the Permanent Under-Secretary at the Foreign Office, Sir Robert Vansittart, who would have sacrificed his own grandmother to keep Italy sweet, pro-British and anti-Hitler, were "Head the little man off!"

Haile Selassie had no intention of being deflected and his application was forwarded to the League of Nations. Jones and Monroe, in *A History of Ethiopia,* summarize what followed: "For some months the dispute did not assume threatening dimensions. Owing, no doubt, to anxiety to settle it as unobtrusively as possible, it was not discussed by the League Council of January, 1935, nor at the meeting of the British, French and Italian premiers at Stresa in the following April. This silence later proved to have been a great mistake, for the Italian Government took it to mean that the European powers would turn a blind eye to their doings in Africa. This impression was heightened by an agreement which they signed with the French on January 7, 1935, establishing a joint front in Europe and adjusting certain territorial claims in Africa owed by France to Italy since the Great War. By one clause, France handed over to Italy 2,500 of her 34,000 shares in the Jibouti-Addis Ababa Railway. A further secret clause referred to Abyssinia in ambiguous terms which the French interpreted as a warning, the Italians as an intimation that they might go ahead." [5]

The Emperor's insistence that the League should mediate resulted in the formation of a conciliation committee but it never had a chance of reaching a proper decision, being composed of two Italians, one Frenchman and one American. (Later it was reconstituted with a fifth arbitrator but with its terms of reference confined strictly to the Wal Wal Incident—a clash which, it decided when it was too late to matter, was the fault of neither side.) Meantime, Britain, France and Italy met in Paris on August 16, 1935, as signatories of the 1906 Tripartite Agreement on Ethiopia, to discuss their attitude to that country—but without, such being the mood and manner of these colonial times, consulting Ethiopia herself. Shortly afterwards Britain and France, once more without consulting Ethiopia, proposed the so-called Zeila Agreement which, as Jones and Monroe state, was "comprehensive and most advantageous to Italy. It covered development and reorganization with the collective assistance of the three powers over all fields of Abyssinian national life: economic, financial, commercial, constructional, foreign concessions and settlement, modernization of the administration, anti-slavery measures, and police services. It suggested 'particular account being taken of the special interests of Italy'; it did not exclude the possibility of territorial adjustments. The one proviso was that these reforms should be freely assented to by Abyssinia in the fullness of her sovereignty."

[5] Oxford University Press.

Sir Sidney Barton was told to persuade the Emperor to accept the proposals, and after some hesitation he agreed to receive them as a basis for negotiation. But not the Italians. By this time "the desire for possession was burning too high in Italy," write Jones and Monroe. "The answer was a blank refusal. It was logical and honest [?] that the Italian delegate at the League Council meeting on September 4, 1935, should make what was, in all but name, a declaration of war. Abyssinian policy, he said, had forced Italy to the conclusion that she had to do with a permanent enemy; all possibility of peaceful collaboration had failed, and it was now beneath the dignity of the Italian Government to treat with Abyssinia on a footing of equality before the tribunal of the League of Nations." [6]

Throughout the shoddy maneuvers of 1935, the Emperor had been trying to build up the strength and firepower of his armed forces. He had dug deep into his own pocket to pay for contracts for arms which he had signed with Czechoslovakia and Belgium, and he had also ordered heavily from Britain and France. But at the height of the crisis—at the moment when the British Foreign Secretary, Sir Samuel Hoare, was promising the full weight of his country against aggression—the British announced that they were instituting an arms embargo against both sides in the dispute. This was blatant hypocrisy. Italy could supply her own arms and was pouring them into Eritrea and Somaliland (including squadrons of planes, batteries of guns and supplies of poison gas) through the Suez Canal, still at that time under the control of the British. All it meant was that at the most vital moment of her preparations to defend herself Ethiopia was starved of arms; the embargo was not waived until August and September, when it was too late to get the rifles and machine-guns through the mountain passes to the Ethiopian defenders along the Eritrean frontier. (In any case, the French procrastinated about loading armaments on to the trains from Jibouti to Addis Ababa, saying that the Ialians had threatened to bomb their bridges if they carried them; the Italians were, of course, now shareholders in the Ethiopian Railway through the Italo-French secret agreement, of which the Emperor, the other principal shareholder, remained ignorant.)

[6] I find it remarkable that the authors of this short history should still, in a new edition issued in 1960, allow these words to be printed without any other comment about Italy than: "Unfortunately she played her hand badly. . . . She baffled those who tried to understand her by perpetually shifting the grounds. There were many good points in the Italian case." In fact there were no points of any kind in favor of Italy's tactics, strategy or actual aggression. They merely sabotaged the Emperor's attempts to improve his country.

Mussolini's preparations continued apace. "The war towards which events were thus impelling us," wrote Marshal Badoglio in *The War in Abyssinia*,[7] "must therefore be swiftly begun, and must have as its object the utter destruction of the Abyssinian armed forces and the complete conquest of Ethiopia. . . . It would therefore be a war on a large scale . . . a war which forced us, in order to secure the crushing superiority that was necessary, to employ large forces and make abundant use of the most modern methods."

Ethiopia's own armed forces had not yet been mobilized, though the old Minister of War, Ras Mulugeta—confident that he could finish off the Italians—was angrily demanding their call-up. The Emperor was still hoping that Britain and France, through the League of Nations, would bring the Italians to heel and refused to credit rumors that all the Europeans were interested in were face-saving measures that would bring Ethiopia into the Fascist orbit—but gently. He took at its face-value Sir Samuel Hoare's famous speech of September 4, 1935, in which the British Foreign Minister pledged that "the League stands, and my country stands with it, for the collective maintenance of the Covenant in its entirety, and particularly steady and collective resistance to all acts of unprovoked aggression. The attitude of the British nation in the past few weeks has clearly demonstrated the fact that this is no variable and unreliable sentiment, but a principle of international conduct to which they and their Government hold with firm, enduring and universal persistence."

What else could it mean than that Britain would come to Ethiopia's aid should she be attacked? Just about this time Haile Selassie gave a great banquet to his warriors in the Palace in Addis Ababa at which raw meat was eaten and much tej drunk in the old style, and to his cheering soldiery he promised that though a fight might yet come, he was still putting his faith in the support of England and France. Then he added: "But if the efforts of other nations and our own fail, and devilish violence takes the opportunity to open war, sowing misfortune, shame and misery with the world as its field, Ethiopia will rise up, the Emperor at her head, and follow him in her hundred thousands with the valour and staunchness famous for a thousand years. Leaning on the Divine arm, she will resist the invader to the last drop of her blood, fighting from the natural fortresses of mountain and desert that the Lord has given her."

The Hoare-Laval Agreement, which would have eventually turned Ethiopia into an Italian dependency, shattered Haile Selassie's illusions

[7] Methuen and Co. Ltd., 1937.

about British or French good faith. Mr. Anthony Eden (now Lord Avon) was at Geneva when the Council of the League received a telegram from the Emperor. He had previously informed the League that he had ordered his Imperial troops to remain at least thirty kilometers from any Italian frontier so as to avoid any incident which might give Mussolini a pretext for aggression. His message went on: "We remind you of our previous request for the dispatch of impartial observers to establish the facts in regard to any aggression or other incident that might occur in order to fix the responsibility therefore. We further ask that the Council should take any other precautions it may think necessary."

Eden sounded out opinion among the League members and found that most of them were inclined to favor Haile Selassie's proposal. Eden himself was fully sympathetic with it. He was well aware that the rainy season in Ethiopia was almost over, and that campaigning time was near. He asked his assistant, Robin Hankey, to telephone the Foreign Office and advise them to support the request for observers. But by this time Mussolini's huffing and bluffing had thoroughly scared Baldwin and the British Cabinet, and they were all for backing down. Not only were they against sending observers to see fair play for Ethiopia but, if the League should decide to appoint them, they insisted that none of them be British.

"Could we not have called Musso's bluff and at least postponed this war?" asked Winston Churchill later. "The answer I am sure is yes. We built Musso into a great power." [8]

But this was a Government of craven and rather stupid men of few principles and little vision.

Lord Avon, one of the few who did have both, writes: "During the evening of September 28 [1935] the Abyssinian Minister came to tell me that the Emperor could no longer delay the general mobilization of his forces, which he was ordering forthwith. The Emperor's telegram to the Council drew its most serious attention to the increasing gravity of the threat of Italian aggression. The Abyssinian mobilization would not affect his previous orders to his troops to remain thirty kilometers from the frontier, nor his resolution to co-operate closely with the League of Nations in all circumstances."

Avon adds: "The long, tortured period of diplomacy was now over and we faced the arbitrament of war, upon which we now

[8] Quoted in *Facing the Dictators.*

know that Mussolini had decided in principle in January 1933, when he sent his representative to Addis Ababa to deceive the Abyssinians with fair words."

On October 2, 1935, the Italians attacked, and in the war that followed the Ethiopians never had a chance. The European powers had seen to that.

chapter twelve

CIVILIZING MISSION

TWENTY-ONE YEARS before the Italo-Ethiopian War began the
British Chargé d'Affaires in Addis Ababa, Major C. H. M. Doughty-
Wylie, sent a dispatch to the Foreign Office in which he used these
words (in a successful effort to dissuade the British from taking
punitive action against Ethiopian elephant-poachers):

> The Abyssinians are avaricious, it is true. But before this last tour of duty
> I over-stated the effect of their avarice. They have a stronger passion still, a
> fierce patriotism and distrust of all foreigners. They are disunited, corrupt, bad
> governors, but they have seen in recent years the many conquests of white
> men, and foreign aggression would unite them all.

It was not quite true in 1935. In the North, where Italian money
had been spent freely in the preceding years, there was at least one
important figure who put greed before his country. His name was
Haile Selassie Gugsa.[1] Haile Selassie Gugsa was the natural son of
a ruthless old warlord from Tigre, Ras Gugsa Araya, who had named
him his heir just before he died of syphilis in 1932. It did not follow
(as has been seen in his own case) that the Emperor would confirm
this deathbed nomination; he called the boy to Addis Ababa first to
look him over. He was a hard-drinking, hectoring youth whose
plump face beneath its gollywog wig of hair was almost always
scowling, and Haile Selassie must have been strongly tempted by his
coarse manners and truculent mien to disinherit him. Instead, on
the grounds that he was too young and inexperienced to deserve
more, he was given a small province in Tigre with his headquarters
at Makalle; the rest of the province was handed over, as a reward
for loyalty, to Ras Seyoum. But to soothe Haile Selassie Gugsa's

[1] No kin either to the Emperor or the Ras Gugsa killed in battle in 1930.

resentments, the Emperor gave him the title of Dejazmach and something else—the gift of his youngest daughter in marriage. (It was a dynastic union that would cause him deep personal regrets, for the princess—aged 13—had a brutal time of it, beaten, bullied and humiliated by her drunken husband, before she died less than two years later.) At the same time, Haile Selassie arranged that his own eldest son, Asfa Wossen, the Crown Prince,[2] should marry Ras Seyoum's daughter, another piece of dynastic calculation which took no consideration of the prince's feelings—or, of course, of Seyoum's daughter. The idea was to bind the whole of Tigre closer to the Emperor and to Shoa.

Haile Selassie Gugsa came several times to Addis Ababa between 1932 and 1935, and found it more convenient and comfortable to make the journey northwards by way of Eritrea rather than southwards over Ethiopian territory. From the Eritrean frontier the Italian Consul in Makalle arranged for him to be met by car and chauffeured to Asmara, where he was treated as an honored guest, thence taken by rail to Massawa and by steamer to Jibouti, where he boarded the train for Addis Ababa. In 1934, unhappy at his small-fry status at Court compared with the big fish the Italians made him seem, he asked the Emperor for an increase in his rank and possessions in Tigre and was tartly told that he had proved a bad enough governor of what he already held, and must learn to rule before he could expand his horizons.

From the moment of his refusal, Haile Selassie Gugsa went over to the Italians. Marshal de Bono wrote of him: "Gugsa was the son-in-law of the Emperor, but he was a malcontent. The Emperor . . . had deprived Gugsa of a good part of his territories in order to increase the power of Ras Seyoum; hence there was little sympathy between the two chiefs of Tigre; indeed there was positive if not manifest enmity. Our intelligence agents and the whole personnel of the Consulate at Adowa wisely took advantage of this state of affairs to win Gugsa to our side."

Shortly after his arrival in Asmara to take over the Fascist Command, de Bono began receiving letters from Haile Selassie Gugsa complaining of his lowly position in the Ethiopian ranks and "asking me for instructions as to his mode of conduct." Until the attack against Ethiopia actually began de Bono "had to discourage any impulsive act, any premature move, which would have broken the eggs before we were ready to make the omelette. I therefore recom-

[2] Who had once been betrothed to Ras Hailu's daughter.

mended Gugsa to keep quiet; to show himself apparently obedient and reconciled; for the day would soon come when I would give him categorical instructions."

Two weeks before the Italian invasion, Wodaju Ali, the Ethiopian Consul in Asmara, visited Makalle and from there flew to Addis Ababa in a royal courier plane. He reported to the Emperor that Haile Selassie Gugsa was in the pay of the Italians and was preparing to betray him. The Emperor asked him for proof and Wodaju Ali produced bank receipts for deposits made by the Italians into the Dejazmach's account. Still the Emperor would not believe that one of his chiefs was planning treachery. "Most of my rases take money from the Italians," he said. "It is bribery without corruption. They pocket Italian money and remain steadfast to Ethiopia."

He refused to replace the Dejazmach or to alter the military plan he had worked out in the North when the Italian invasion began—a plan by which Haile Selassie Gugsa and his army of 10,000 men would hold Makalle while the army of Ras Seyoum, further north, would gradually fall back and join them, so that they could fight together. For the most part, the Emperor Haile Selassie was a shrewd judge of men, but there were moments when he was both stubborn and foolish. He had once decided that Haile Selassie Gugsa was good enough to be made a Dejazmach and marry his daughter, and therefore he could not possibly be a traitor; to think otherwise would be to cast doubts on his own judgment. Later on, he was to acquire the suppleness and flexibility to escape from these rigid attitudes, but in this case he preferred to live with the omnipresent threat of treachery rather than be thought to have given preferment to the wrong man.

On the night of October 5, 1935, Haile Selassie Gugsa betrayed him. The Italians had meant him to stay in Makalle until the actual battle for the town began, by which time he would have been joined by Seyoum's army and his betrayal would have spread chaos, collapse and dismay along the whole of the Ethiopian front. But Haile Selassie Gugsa had learned of Wodaju Ali's visit to the Emperor and he believed that his number was up. He waited until the Italians had begun their attack and then he marched his army northwards to join them, destroying the telephone line—the only communication between Ras Seyoum and Addis Ababa—as he marched.

The effect of Haile Selassie Gugsa's treachery was to leave a vacuum behind Ras Seyoum into which he was sucked. He fell back without seriously blunting the Italian probes across the River Mareb, and gave Mussolini the first two big propaganda victories (practically bloodless) for which he was waiting. Adowa was entered and the shame of 1896 revenged. Next came Axum, ancient capital and religious fount of Ethiopian Christianity, where in the past the King of Kings had been crowned. In Adowa, Tigrean minstrels gave the Fascist salute and then sang songs of Italian valor. In Axum, Ethiopian priests said prayers for Italian victory and the Italians took one of the giant, ageless, mystic steles and shipped the lofty stone needle to Rome (where it still stands) as a propaganda totem.

It was another month before they actually reached Makalle, but they need not have hesitated. The way was open. Haile Selassie Gugsa had prepared it for them. Their procrastination to a large extent nullified the effect of Haile Selassie Gugsa's treachery—except as propaganda for the rest of the world—but he did provide them with one tangible and invaluable item. He brought with him the Swiss engineer who had been working in his area at the time of the Italian invasion, and this technician went with him into Italian hands. He had helped to plan and carry through the road which the Emperor had built from Addis Ababa to Dessye, and was in the process of planning an extension. The road was not on any map and the Italians were unaware of which way some of its uncompleted portions would run. The Swiss engineer had surveyed the whole route and brought maps with him—and these were the maps that the Italians used for the rest of the war.

To go into any detail about the course of the Italo-Ethiopian War would be an exercise in frustration, despair and tragi-comedy. In Addis Ababa few people seemed to behave as if there was a war on, with the possible exception of the legations and the foreign population. The diplomatic corps met, stared apprehensively at the skies, and then sent a message to Rome pointing out that there were six thousand non-Ethiopians in the capital and would he please not bomb them. (Mussolini promised to respect the integrity of their pink skins, but some skeptical Greeks and Levantines took to walking around with blue or white crosses sewn into their straw hats.) The Italian Minister, Vinci, staged a sit-in strike at his Legation and refused to be thrown out, but was finally persuaded to go when the embarrassed Ethiopians offered him a special train to Jibouti.

It was not until October 17, fifteen days after the invasion, that the Minister of War, Ras Mulugeta, was ready to move north against the enemy. "His force, the Yamahal Sarawit, or Army of the Middle, was numbered at 80,000," George Steer wrote in *Caesar in Abyssinia*.[3] He paraded his troops before the Emperor and "himself passed the throne about noon, preceded by hornblowers dressed in European clothes, their gigantic antlers lifted high." The grizzled old warlord drew his sword and advanced to the Emperor and saluted. His "chest blazed with decorations from his European journeys" and "typical of Abyssinian's intemperate old age he set his sword to earth and proceeded to give words of blunt advice."

He said: "Your Imperial Majesty, do not interest yourself too much in politics. Your weakness is that you trust the foreigner too much: kick him out. What are all these fools of the Press doing here? I am ready to die for my country, and you are too. War is now the thing and to conduct it you had better remain in the city of Addis Ababa. Send all the foreigners packing. I swear undying loyalty to you."

Steer wrote: "Mulugeta's army drifted off. We watched the curious procession pass the British Legation gates by twos and threes. What could they do? They thought that they could do everything. Barefooted, in their ragged dirty jodphurs, their swords sticking far away behind them, they moved along with a steady stride." Most took their wives and some had mules. "The men went ahead carrying the tent-poles, from the ends of which dangled sandals and a few pouches and calabashes: more pouches, holding food, hung around their persons. The woman leaning forward in her long broad skirts to haul the mule, brought up in the rear the tent and sacks of mashila and dried peas."

The Minister for War followed five days behind his straggling army. He had ordered his troops to Dessye and "in spite of his age (he was well over seventy) and his confirmed alcoholism, he proved himself an indefatigable marcher. Leaving at dawn, he would do twenty-five miles a day until four o'clock, when he encamped. Behind him followed his seven secretaries and their servants. . . . His military adviser was a Cuban machine-gunner, Delvalle, educated in Texas, and for some time a member of ABC, the secret Cuban revolutionary organization."

The Emperor, aware that the world was watching now, had given orders that harvest fields should be respected by the soldiery, village granaries preserved from seizure, women safe from rape; but Mulugeta was a dragon of the old school and no matter how gently he

[3] *Op. cit.*

pretended to breathe, the fire from his nostrils scorched everyone who came in his path. "When they saw a field of beans, corn or maize," wrote Steer, "they were down on it like a troop of monkeys; it was stripped and eaten raw." He arrived in Wollo, where the Crown Prince was trying to organize an army in the face of passive resistance from the notoriously anti-Shoan Azebu Gallas. A few floggings and hangings soon cured that.

On went the Minister for War and his armies, but oh, so slowly. He was afraid of air attack, so he sent couriers with horns ahead to the mountain passes, from which they were to blow alarms across the valleys if they saw aircraft approaching. In the area where Haile Selassie Gugsa had ruled, he halted to exact revenge from the populace, forcing all the men he needed to join the army and flogging and killing the rest.

Moving in small parties, hiding by day from Italian reconnaissance planes, it took Mulugeta two months to get his army to the Tigre. By that time (since Ethiopian soldiers serve only for two months at a time) his men were beginning to slip away; he had to bribe them with dollars—unheard-of thing—to stay. In the meantime the army of Ras Kassa was making similarly painful progress.

"Mulugeta had no field radio," reported Steer. "All his messages to commanders were taken by runners. Scattered over a large area for fear of planes, it was long before they could receive or respond to an order. They did not know, when they moved along, where their other parties were. They were never in the villages—that would be to expose themselves to bombardment. To keep together they lay near the road, mile after mile, or along the mountain tracks which ran east and west of it."

Steer added: "At no time had order been a quality of Ethiopian armies, but now even the mass movement which had carried them along vanished before the planes."

The commanders sent a message back to the Emperor about the planes complaining: "They chain us up like prisoners." But so far they had only had a taste of what was to come.

All this time Haile Selassie had remained in Addis Ababa while his rases lumbered forward to meet the invaders. He had much to do. He was still hoping against hope that the League of Nations—or, failing that, Britain and possibly France—would come to his aid, out of sheer self-interest, for surely they realized by now that Italy's aggression in Africa was merely a rehearsal for aggressions to come?

The announcement of the Hoare-Laval Plan dashed any possibility of direct aid. Perhaps, then, he would be allowed the arms that had been embargoed and loans to buy them? The British demurred, for they were now anxious to grovel their way back into Mussolini's affections; and when the Emperor tried to raise money by selling his oil rights (the Ricketts Deal), they consulted on how to quash it. The U.S. Secretary of State, Cordell Hull, saved them the trouble by quashing it for them. (Standard Oil of New Jersey was behind Ricketts.) Meanwhile, the French were still making difficulties about allowing arms to move along the railway from Jibouti.

According to the Italian estimates, which the Ethiopians encouraged them to exaggerate, the Ethiopian Army consisted of 300,000 regular and irregular troops, divided two-thirds to the north and one-third to the south, armed with 200 small cannon of various calibers and 3,500 machine-guns. There were also 15 airplanes, 8 of them in flying condition, 3 of them capable of combat. There was enough fuel for eight months' flying and enough shells for 300 rounds apiece for each cannon.[4]

With these puny weapons the Ethiopian warlords were convinced— with the skeptical exception of the Emperor himself—that they could easily drive Italy out of Ethiopia and out of Eritrea too, as they had done in 1896. "The two worst faults of my people," Haile Selassie once said, "are overweening bravery and superlative arrogance." He spent a good deal of his time counselling his troops not to meet the enemy head on, not to expose themselves to bombing, not to dress up but to dress down for battle. Even he was ignorant of what strides had been made in the tactics and weapons of modern war, and he had read a great deal, but his rases—shielded by their mountain kingdom from the Great War, out of touch and disinterested—knew nothing and cared less about modern cannons, tanks, armored cars, airplanes, machine-gunning and bombing from the air—and poison gas. They began by treating them with contempt, with far too little fear, and they ended by retreating from them in too much panic.

In Addis Ababa the Emperor had begun by wooing the international Press in the hope that the war correspondents, assembled now in vulture swarms, would influence world opinion to his side. He did not realize that though they could touch the hearts of their readers they had no power to stiffen the backbones of their governments. "We have come to the realization," the Emperor said to one war

[4] The Italians had four Corps of well-armed and motorized troops (120,000 in all), 100,000 irregulars and 350 airplanes.

correspondent, "that Ethiopia is now completely alone—with no friends to help her." It was not quite true. She still had friends, and some of them were influential. One of them was the British Minister. Sir Sidney Barton was, in the words of Chapman-Andrews, who once worked under him, "a member of the English bar and a real stickler for proper conduct. He had been brought up very strictly. Himself an Ulsterman, there was no compromise on matters which he regarded as of principle. He had a quick temper, which was not altogether a bad thing at times, though he did his best to keep it under control. During the Italian-Ethiopian war his complete devotion to the Ethiopian cause earned him not only the gratitude but the implicit trust of all Ethiopians."

He telegraphed repeatedly to London demanding that the arms embargo be lifted, and in November informed Mr. Anthony Eden that "while there was no sign of any collapse of the Abyssinian defence, the real danger lay in the lack of arms and the eventual lack of food." Sir Sidney added that "only positive assistance, such as the loans already asked for and refused at Geneva, could save Abyssinian independence."

Lord Avon wrote later (in *The Eden Memoirs*, Cassell and Co., 1962): "In the sorry pass to which all of us, but especially the Abyssinians, were now being reduced, His Majesty's Government had a mordant responsibility for the refusal to supply arms to Abyssinia. The Treaty of 1930, signed by Great Britain, France, Italy and Abyssinia, enabled the Emperor to 'obtain all the arms and munitions necessary for the defence of his territories from external aggression and for the preservation of internal order therein.' . . . As early as May, 1935, Messrs Vickers had approached the Foreign Office to ask whether a licence to supply arms to Abyssinia would be granted. I had then recorded my view that it was impossible to refuse. However, my opinion did not prevail."

Barton bombarded the Foreign Office, insisting that the arms should come "on legal and moral grounds," but thanks to the opposition from Vansittart, they did not. Eden minuted on November 29, 1935: "I confess that the Abyssinians seem to me to have had a consistently raw deal from us in the matter of arms. For many months we maintained an arms embargo which had no justification in equity, but seriously handicapped the Abyssinians and has, according to the War Office, made it almost impossible for Abyssinia to win a victory. In addition to this, we are now refusing to allow them to buy from Soley Arms (an armaments company) though I believe that anyone else in the world, except Italy, can do so. Finally, we are to tell the Abyssinians that they cannot buy six airplanes from surplus Government stocks."

Now the Treasury in Addis Ababa was depleted and there would be no money to pay for any considerable quantity of arms even should the embargo be lifted at last. There must have been a strong temptation in the Emperor's heart at this time to show his contempt, if not his anger, toward the foreigners who had so badly let him down. But he remained unfailingly polite and listened patiently to everything they had to tell him. Only in his attitude toward his own people, which became increasingly flamboyant, did he make fewer attempts to conform to a European image of a monarch. A flock of war correspondents flew after him when he visited the Ogaden front in the South, where things had gone wrong in the desert war against the Italians under Graziani. The Ethiopian chief of the Ogaden operations had ordered that three of the senior officers of his army be shot for cowardice. The Emperor commuted the sentences. "He's just trying to show us how civilized he is," said the correspondents. But they swallowed their words when they saw what happened instead to those who had fled before the enemy. Each ordinary soldier who had retreated was publicly flogged, thirty lashes across the back. The officers were stripped and flogged across the stomach. Haile Selassie turned with a small grim smile and gave a courtly and delicate salute to the official flogger, but otherwise displayed no expression as he left the groaning victims and the green-faced correspondents.

It was brutal, but it stopped the rot in the Ogaden, and it also stopped the world Press from inferring that the Emperor was effete and pseudo-European.

And yet, when the Emperor finally moved to the Northern front toward the end of November, 1935, and established his headquarters at Dessye, there was something of Edwardian England about his arrangements. "At his table four courses of well-cooked European food are served," reported *The Times*, "and a cellar is laid on." George Steer, who wrote that sentence, added later: "In the front hall lay a selection of solar topees, and, in a corner, a series of walking sticks for going to church, which the Emperor attended daily, for visiting in the town, for walking on the mountains, for inspecting the troops and the Red Cross hospitals. His best Arabs were brought up to Dessye."

Steer went on: "In the house he worked day and night, organizing the last detail in the construction of the two northward roads, that

Haile Selassie and Sir Winston Churchill outside of No. 10 Downing Street, October 22, 1954

Haile Selassie and Queen Elizabeth driving from Victoria Station at the beginning of the Emperor's state visit to Britain, October 10, 1954

The Emperor presenting Christmas gifts to children at an orphanage

to Korem and the branch road to Lalibela. Seeing that the food caravans went through Dessye regularly. Negotiating with troublesome
chiefs. Writing to his wife and his Council in Addis about his League
policy . . . air raid precautions . . . the decent treatment of Europeans.
Codifying and improving his regulations for the Ethiopian tactics
against Western arms—all except the spraying mustard gas, which
he did not foresee."

The Emperor had, as Steer so gently put it, "the gift of appearing
at all times, even in the middle of war, completely detached and
poised above the mêlée, pursuing his quiet, rather delicate and well-
dressed life without noting overmuch the noise that surrounded him."

And shortly after reaching Dessye, that noise increased quickly to
a crescendo.

Marshal de Bono had got his armies as far south as Adowa, Axum
and Makalle but there he had halted "to bring up supplies" and "to
improve his lines of communication." The premature surrender by
Haile Selassie Gugsa and the evacuation of Makalle had taken him
and his planners by surprise; they had got there rather too quickly;
they were amazed at the difficulty of movement in such a rugged
country; and now they urgently needed to regroup.

De Bono was, for his time and considering the régime, a civilized
and decent man, and he firmly believed that he and his fellow Italians
had come into Ethiopia not just as conquerors but as civilizers. One
of the first things he did when he entered Makalle was to issue a
proclamation ending slavery and making it illegal to possess slaves.[5]
He sent his officers—and his puppet, Haile Selassie Gugsa—far and
wide over Tigre spreading the news that life would be better for everyone under the Italians. Maybe these people were black, de Bono
reasoned, but they were also human and should be so treated. He
hoped news of his benevolence would spread across the land and turn
the rest of Ethiopia against its despot Emperor. Why fight, and
why kill these savages, he reasoned, if he could civilize them into
surrender?

In the midst of this heady, ideological dream he was aroused by
an urgent cable from Mussolini asking him what the hell was holding
him up. Why was he not pushing south from Makalle? He sent off
his explanations. But the Duce was in a hurry. The European powers

[5] Like many another Italian, he does not appear to have realized that Eritrea also had
its slave system.

had instituted sanctions against him through the League of Nations and he at least—though no one else, including those who had instituted them—believed in them and the harm they might do to the Italian war effort. Why the British might even close the Suez Canal and cut off Italy from the colonies. So he desperately needed to get Ethiopia in his hands before the League's plans could take effect. He could accept no excuses for delay.

On November 28, 1935, he recalled de Bono and replaced him as Commander-in-Chief of East Africa with Marshal Pietro Badoglio. From this moment the character of the war changed. So far the Italian Air Force had confined its missions to reconnaissance, to harrying moving troops, to bombing military headquarters. Badoglio changed the orders. From this moment everything Ethiopian was to be bombed —open towns, encampments, roads, hospitals and even those hospitals plainly indicated by the Red Cross and the flags of the European nations running them. From bombing civilians and wounded, Badoglio next armed his planes with a weapon he knew could not possibly provoke retaliation in kind and was most likely to create panic and chaos among the Ethiopians: they were fitted with bombs containing mustard gas.

In historical fact, these malevolent tactics had rather less to do with the outcome of the Italo-Ethiopian War than the Ethiopians' desperate lack of arms with which to fight back, plus sheer ignorance of how to wage a modern war. The gassing and the bombing were merely the twirled moustaches which Badoglio assumed to identify himself as the villain and strike atrophy and terror into the enemy; but it was sheer firepower against spears and swords, and up-to-date tactics against outmoded battle charges, that won him the war. That and the too eager bravery of the Ethiopians, and their determination to take the offensive.

"The first battle of Tembien had been fought by the Abyssinians with courage and determination," Badoglio wrote. "Against our attacks, methodically carried out and accompanied by heavy machine-gun and artillery fire, their troops had stood firm, then had engaged in furious hand-to-hand fighting; or they had moved boldly to counter-attack, regardless of the avalanche of fire that had immediately fallen on them. Against the organized fire of our defending troops, their soldiers—many of them armed only with cold steel— attacked again and again, in compact phalanxes, pushing right up to our wire entanglements, which they tried to beat down with their curved scimitars."

He added: "But, in contrast to so much valour, the Abyssinian command showed itself to be incompetent."

Badoglio did not exempt the Emperor himself from that contemptuous summation, and it is true that Haile Selassie's oft-repeated remark: "I am no soldier," seemed to be borne out by his activities as supreme commander. One of his first actions upon arriving at Dessye had been to replace Ras Mulugeta, the Minister of War, as Commander-in-Chief of the Northern Armies. Mulugeta had established himself with his army of 50,000 men on what was, in Ethiopian eyes, an impregnable stronghold, the mountain plateau of Amba Aradam, and there he received a message from the Emperor to tell him that he would, in the future, come under the command of Ras Kassa. Mulugeta was enraged, and rightly, for, as Badoglio commented with satisfaction, "the Negus has exchanged a warrior for a churchman." Haile Selassie must have been fully aware that though his Minister of War lacked subtlety and skill, he had prodigious valor and capacity for leadership, whereas Kassa was totally ignorant of the arts of war. He chose him for dynastic reasons. Kassa was a senior statesman of royal blood, and therefore he must lead.

Badoglio could have asked for nothing better. On January 21, 1936, he intercepted a radio message from Kassa to the Emperor announcing that his attack had failed, his ammunition was exhausted, that he was in danger of being surrounded, and desperately needed reinforcements.[6] The Italian commander commented: "But no function of command did [Kassa] exercise; no gleam of an idea of manoeuvre flashed upon him; not even that of employing his personal troops, the best and best armed. As in the past, so now the Abyssinian chiefs, fearing the friend behind them no less than the foe in front, could not make up their minds to throw the whole of their forces into the struggle, preferring to keep them intact so that their retreat might not be too actively opposed by a race always hostile to the defeated."

Ras Kassa had asked Mulugeta to supply him with reinforcements, but the Minister of War pretended not to get the message. Ras Imru, in Gondar, also stayed deaf to appeals, pleading that he had to put down an incipient rebellion in the province. But the real reason that both of them failed to respond was, sadly enough, probably due to

[6] Badoglio's interception services were expertly manned and they monitored all the radios —which were few—used by the Ethiopians. The Italians, of course, were in possession of the Ethiopian codes.

their antipathy to Kassa and their desire to see him be defeated, and thus diminished in the eyes of the Emperor.

"Such was the Abyssinian Command!" commented Badoglio, and on January 31 he gave orders that the first phase of what he called "the battle of annihilation" should begin. It would be directed against Ras Mulugeta on Amba Aradam, and Badoglio remarked in a telegram to Mussolini: "Ras Mulugeta will either accept battle or will have to retire southwards, thus uncovering Ras Kassa's lines of communication and abandoning his strong position on Mount Aradam. I hope he will decide to fight, in which case it will be an important battle."

It was, in fact, the vital battle of the war, and there was never any doubt of Mulugeta's eagerness to fight it.

Amba Aradam was a flat-topped mountain, five miles long from east to west, two miles wide from north to south, and approximately 9,000 feet above sea level. It lay athwart the road south from Makalle, and its tableland, covered with scrub and riddled with caves, could be approached by seven mule tracks. Otherwise it was (or seemed) incapable of being breached, for its sides were vertical cliffs except to the south and west, where it sloped rather more gently.

Badoglio had no illusions about the fighting quality of the Ethiopian troops who held Amba Aradam nor of the belligerent nature of the ill-tempered old man who commanded them. Until this mountain redoubt was swept aside, his advance into the heart of Ethiopia could not go on, and he knew not only from his observations since taking command of the Italian Army but also from his memories of 1896, when he had fought at Adowa as a cadet, that the Ethiopians would use their fortress well and fight bravely against all who came against them.

From the front, that is. Badoglio guessed that Mulugeta, as a commander of the old school, would not have prepared his defenses for an assault from behind rather than from the front and flanks. He also calculated that bombing, gassing and strafing from planes, plus heavy artillery fire, would force the Ethiopians to keep their heads down and prevent them from discovering—especially since Mulugeta had no radio communication—what was going on around them.

"For the execution of the operation, the last of which was particularly delicate, I relied above all on the aggressive qualities of our troops," reported Badoglio, dutifully, and then more realistically, "On the employment in manoeuvre of the powerful body of artillery at my disposal, and on the continuous activity of aircraft, in successive waves, with bombing and machine-gun fire from a low altitude." [7]

On the morning of February 11, 1936, Ras Mulugeta was, wrote George Steer, "pulling on his boots and wondering how long the Galla would stand these air bombardments, when the whole mountain thundered about his ears. He retired deeper into his cave. Amba Aradam from one end to the other was a cloud of dust. Again, the infernal explosions. Every human being on the mountain ran to his peculiar funkhole, obedient to the Emperor's orders and to four-month-old Ethiopian practice. Shells from two hundred guns fell neatly all over the mountain. The Ethiopians, who had never conceived such a weight of artillery, took them for bombs from the Italian planes which were spotting for the guns. Not a shot was fired from the tremendous Amba. Not a man remained on sentinel. They lay, wrapped head and body in their grey shammas, like immobilised pools of mercury in every hole and depression."

Badoglio put his First Corps into a frontal attack and, with relief, the Minister of War rallied his troops and sallied out to meet it. They were beaten back with tremendous losses, but they held the attack. In bravery they were supreme, but in tactics they were babes.

"In substance," reported Badoglio, "I intended to meet the violence of the Ethiopian mass attacks, and such numerical superiority as the enemy might be able to display, with a superiority both in tactical method and in the use of fire, in the certainty that these two factors, reinforced by the effect of surprise, would produce successful results against the enemy."

They did indeed. While his First Corps attacked from the front and his planes and artillery plastered the plateau, Badoglio sent his nimble Alpini troops around to the rear to climb the cliffs which the old War Minister considered unscalable. (Ethiopians don't like climbing cliffs, and if they don't climb cliffs how can anyone else?) They burst in upon the Ethiopian troops.

"Mulugeta raised a terrible din," wrote George Steer. "All his horn blowers blew and the War Minister himself drew his sword from his side. Messengers ran here and there to set the points of dirty mercury unrolling. Throughout the Amba the Ethiopians jumped to their feet, too late, for the first defences were taken. There was no barbed wire for the Italians to pass. After the first trenches there were no second trenches. . . . It was child's play for the machine-gun

[7] In five days the plateau was raided 546 times during which 396 tons of explosive and 30,000 rounds of ammunition were expended.

which rattled merrily into knots of black men, just awakened, and for the hand grenade, which cleaned the caves."

As dusk came down on the evening of February 19, 1936, the Italians raised their flag on Amba Aradam, and Ras Mulugeta, "abandoning all his equipment, his uniforms, medals, books, papers, his ceremonial dress," fled down into the valley. He and the remnants of his Army were pursued by planes and artillery, rounded up and shot. Not least of their troubles was the harrying which they had to bear from the human hyenas who lurked in the hills to attack them as they retreated. The Azeby Gallas had been paid by the Italians for just this kind of operation, but it was a scavenging job that these savage and sullen people would have willingly done for nothing; at least for one season every Azebu bride would find a dead man's testicles included in her bride-price. Mulugeta, fleeing south with a bodyguard and a British Red Cross officer, Burgoyne, discovered that his beloved son was missing in the retreat and sent messengers out to find him. One of them returned to announce: "Master, your son has been murdered and mutilated by the Galla on the edge of the mountain."

At this the old warhorse called to his bodyguard to halt and turned upon the ravening hordes, and it was while he was doing so that an Italian warplane spotted his khaki uniform and came down and machine-gunned the mêlée, Shoans and Gallas alike. So, braying out his last defiance, Ras Mulugeta died and the Battle of Amba Aradam was over. Neither Ras Kassa nor Ras Imru had come to the War Minister's aid, for they were unaware that a battle had even begun. The Italians, outflanking Kassa, got ready to deal with him too.

"Our casualties in the battle," reported Badoglio, "including dead and wounded, were 36 officers, 621 Italians, and 145 natives. The enemy's losses were enormous: they may be reckoned as amounting in all to about 20,000 men. These losses were due in a large measure to the heavy concentration of artillery fire, and, as we were able to prove later, to the relentless action of the air arm in pursuit. The determined guerrilla warfare waged by the local inhabitants against the fugitives during the whole of their retreat also contributed very materially to their casualties."

Badoglio was too much of an expert at Ethiopian fighting habits to miss the strategical value of his victory. "An Abyssinian army, whose organization and discipline are normally very feeble and slow-working," he wrote after Amba Aradam, "when once it has been beaten and put to flight, melts away. Each chief, with such fighting men as he has been able to gather around him, and each individual soldier, thinks only of getting back—each for himself and as quickly as possible—to his own village and his own house, in the hope of saving what can be saved."

He was sure that "this kind of army can never be reunited and used again." In this condition Ras Mulugeta's army now found itself, and it therefore no longer counted as an element to be reckoned with in future operations.

Badoglio regrouped his forces to envelop Ras Kassa's army and that of Ras Seyoum, which had now crossed to join him, and moved in to attack. But Seyoum, who had never had the stomach for fighting, and Kassa, who did not possess the skill, simply retired. They withdrew in haste with, as a White Russian officer, Colonel Konavoloff, who was with them, later wrote, "an absence on [Kassa's] own part or on the part of his chiefs, of the slightest initiative or any display of forethought or decision. They knew nothing about modern warfare, nothing at all."

The retreating army was such a rable of ragged men, women, children and slaves, of the wounded and sick, of starving, overburdened pack animals, that to Konavoloff it looked "more like the emigration of a whole people." The soldiers had begun to sell off their ammunition to buy food and were getting their bullets shot back at them from the Galla shiftas (bandits) to whom they had sold them.

"Long periods of inactivity, their own disorderly manoeuvres, the continual menace of the airplane, checks in the field, and finally the great retreat had demoralised these fighting men. They were far from thinking of battles or of victory. Our movement towards the south gave them hopes of reaching Shoa, where many of them were born, and where they could at last forget the weariness of the long forced marches, the horror of the bombardment from the air, the mortal danger of the machine-guns; the lack of hospitality among their neighbours whom they found actively hostile ... where they could, in a word, renew their old everyday life."

That they would not be out of danger even in Shoa, "that the enemy was advancing more and more, occupying one district after another, and would eventually reach their own homes—such an idea never entered anybody's mind."

On March 20, 1936, the bedraggled army topped a rise in the hills and saw smoke in the valley below them. Haile Selassie, hearing of the disasters further north, had marched out from Dessye with his Imperial Bodyguard. Ras Kassa and Ras Seyoum hurried ahead to prostrate themselves before their Emperor and ask his forgiveness.

"Ras Kassa and Ras Seyoum are with us, but have not a single armed man with them," wrote Haile Selassie bitterly and not quite accurately that night.[8] "An army ... went to pieces without having suffered serious losses and without any attempt whatever at resistance. This is a grievous matter. Our army, famous throughout Europe for its valour, has lost its name. Brought to ruin by a few traitors, to this is it reduced."

---

[8] The letter is quoted from Italian sources, who claimed to have captured the courier taking it from the Emperor to Ras Imru. The author believes it to be genuine.

chapter thirteen

THE LAST ATTACK

It now seems clear that Haile Selassie, alone among the fire-eating rases, never expected to win the war against Italy. Not alone, that is. In the begnning he had sincerely believed that the League of Nations would find him a *modus vivendi* by which he could reach a settlement with Italy, a settlement in which he would at least receive a port on the Red Sea in exchange for some sacrifice of territory. When that possibility faded, he had put his faith in Great Britain, for, despite the warnings of his more cynical foreign advisers and friends— particularly the hard-headed British Minister, Sir Sidney Barton—he had believed every word of Sir Samuel Hoare's stirring speech of September 11, 1935.[1] When even these proved to be empty words, when even his legal right to purchase arms was sabotaged by the craven British, he went on believing that in the end someone with faith in right and justice—or, failing that, in their own future security—would intervene and help him halt the Italians. Otherwise he knew he was doomed. Knowing this, he had accepted the Italian challenge because there was no choice for him—after the first attempts at appeasement had failed, he would have earned the contempt of his countrymen and lost his throne if he had knuckled under to the invaders without a fight. But he spent most of the war like the beleaguered settler surrounded by the outlaws in a Western movie, listening for the hooves of the rescuing sheriff's posse. It was the era in Europe of idealistic voters and the cynical governments they kept on electing, and Haile Selassie was naïve enough to believe that the voice of the people was stronger than the hard men they put into power.

[1] Which even his Cabinet colleague, Anthony Eden, interpreted as an unequivocal pledge to "stop Mussolini."

201

By mid-March, however, he had realized that there would be no rescue in the last reel of this agonizing drama. The war was lost and the villains would win. The bombing and the gassing had terrified and effectively neutralized even the few foreigners who had come to help him. First his military missions had departed, called back by their governments, anxious not to get involved in a war with a fellow European power. Now, as the Ethiopian armies turned into a disorganized rabble, as bombs fell upon their Red Cross flags, the foreign medical missions began to withdraw from the front. In truth, in the circumstances, there was little any longer that they could do. They were running out of medical supplies and gasoline for their transport; they were operating without anaesthetics while being bombed by day by the Italians and attacked all night by the shiftas; their native personnel were deserting.

"This isn't a war—it isn't even slaughter," wrote Dr. John Melly of the British Ambulance Service. "It's the torture of tens of thousands of defenceless men, women and children with bombs and poison gas. They're using gas incessantly, and we've treated hundreds of cases, including infants in arms. And the world looks on—and passes by on the other side."

The Kenya orderlies belonging to the British Red Cross team pointed out that the terms of their employment did not include being bombed and gassed, and demanded their repatriation. So the British said good-bye to the Emperor and made south for Addis Ababa. So did all the other medical units. It wasn't cowardice. It was just the hopelessness of the situation, the impossibility of giving help to the wounded and sick in the midst of such painful chaos and confusion. Only one European, the Russian Colonel Konavoloff, stayed with him.

This was the period when Haile Selassie, the inevitable end of the struggle looming agonizingly before him, chose to move his troops forward rather than back. It was a decision which has since been criticized by European strategists as the crucial one that decided the fate of Ethiopia. "The Battle of Amba Aradam lost Ethiopia the campaign," they say, "and the Emperor's decision to attack lost her the war." It is possible. The Italians had come a long way, far beyond their supply dumps. The rains were beginning and in a week or two the Italian Army might have bogged down in the Ethiopian mud, unable to go on; and in the ensuing months of stalemate, perhaps the arms and the aid the Emperor needed would have come.

From Haile Selassie's point of view, however, there was really no choice. He decided to advance not with the idea of dramatically winning the war or even of "saving the situation." He realized only too well how dire that was. All he knew was that as an Emperor he must do what was expected of an Emperor by the Ethiopian people. It was a duty he had to perform if he was to continue as a leader, in the eyes of himself as well as his people. There must be one last full-scale attack upon the enemy. And, in the tradition, he must personally lead it.

He marched at the head of his Imperial Guard and set up his head-quarters in some caves corkscrewed into the hills in the valley of Aia, about 120 miles north of Dessye. Badoglio estimated his forces at 5,000 men in position at Aia itself, with some 30,000 troops behind, and calculated that of this force there were six battalions of well-trained and well-armed infantry and one battalion of artillery.[2] To Colonel Konavoloff, who had dinner with him at Aia on March 20, the Emperor was "thinner but nevertheless as determined as ever," and he did not seem to show any deep anxiety about the situation.

"It's all going normally," he said. "Up to now we have resisted as best we might and kept them back—I see nothing very dangerous in the situation."

But both he and the Russian colonel must have known that they were concealing facts and fears from each other. "I did not want to sadden the Emperor," wrote Konavoloff, "with the revealing details ... the ineptitude of the chiefs, the complete disorganisation and demoralisation of their forces ... to tell him how we, once tens of thousands against only thousands of Italians, used to abandon our positions at the first caprice of the chiefs or their soldiers, to hide in our distant camps, in caves and huts scattered mile over mile, until our armies became a chaos beyond my power to paint."

Haile Selassie saw "nothing dangerous" in the situation in his conversation with Konavoloff. But to Ras Imru he had written:

"For yourself, if you think that with your troops and with such local inhabitants as you can collect together, you can do anything where you are, do it. If, on the other hand, your position is difficult and you are convinced of the impossibility of fighting, having lost all hope on your front, *and if you think it better to come here and die with us,* let us know your decision."[3]

---

[2] In fact these battalions were the only reliable forces under the Emperor's command. The rest were Gallas who preferred to pick over the spoils from whichever side was defeated.
[3] Author's italics.

Colonel Konavoloff was the last European with the Emperor and his forces. All the rest—Red Cross field workers, doctors, military advisers and war correspondents—had made their painful and difficult way back to Addis Ababa and started to pack their bags for home. After months of privation in the mountains even Konavoloff was looking forward to a warm bath and a bed in Addis Ababa. But it was not to be. "As I was leaving next morning for the lorries, I was stopped. The Emperor wanted urgently to see me." He went across to Haile Selassie's cave and found him hovering over a small table.

"I have decided to attack the Italians at their camp near Mai Chow," he said, "before they have gathered in force. This is where they are."

He had a notebook with ornamented covers on the table and he pointed to it.

"I am no engineer like you, and you'll probably think my draft plan a wretched one." Konavoloff saw that he had drawn the perspective of a mountain on the page. "I want you to visit these mountains with three of our officers who were at St. Cyr and make a complete plan of the region occupied by the enemy, as well as a note of possible positions for us."

The colonel waved good-bye to the lorry that was to take him back to Addis Ababa, shrugged, and went in search of the three Ethiopian students from St. Cyr. He might as well stay; he had no passport with which to leave Ethiopia anyway.

On March 21, 1936, the Emperor sent a message by radio to the Empress in Addis Ababa. It was, of course, intercepted and decoded by the Italians. It read:

We are drawn up opposite the enemy and observing each other through fieldglasses. We are informed that the enemy troops assembled against us number, up to now, not more than approximately 10,000 men. Our troops amount to exactly 31,000. Since our trust is in our Creator and in the hope of His help, and as we have decided to advance and enter the fortifications, and since God is our only help, confide this decision of ours in secret to the Abun, to the ministers and dignitaries, and offer unto God your fervent prayers.

Badoglio told his troops to entrench themselves and get ready for the attack which now seemed imminent. The date his Intelligence calculated for the Emperor's assault was March 23. But on that day, the first of many things went wrong for the Ethiopians. The Emperor and his staff had moved to Aia and in the afternoon it was announced that a *gebir* or great feast would be given for the troops and that everyone, from chiefs to humblest soldiers, would be welcome guests.

"A cave about forty feet long, which looked as if carved in rectangular form, was covered with soft carpets," wrote Konavoloff, "while at its entrance employees of the Ministry of Public Works raised a wall of middling height with a door veiled by white silk stuff . . . the Emperor, seated on an improvised throne, had on either side the two Rases, Kassa and Seyoum. To the side, but sitting lower, were the other chiefs before the 'massobs', the baskets-with-feet which are the tables of Ethiopia. As I entered, the banqueters were eating their favourite dish, raw meat, offered at each table by a young man who was a servant of the Imperial household. Others offered tej in little cups or zinc receptacles."

At the end of the feasting the Emperor read and approved a draft of a battle order which Konavoloff had made. He seemed braced for battle. "Don't destroy the enemy who come over to us," he said to his chiefs, "but make them prisoner and send them to the rear." The attack, he indicated, would begin that night. "After the convocation of a council of elderly chiefs, however," wrote Konavoloff, "it was clear that the soldiers were not ready for the attack, that not all of them had reached Aia, and that lots of other things were missing. Obviously the old chiefs wanted to postpone the day of attack. They wanted the Italians to take the initiative."

In the next few days, the encampment was bombed repeatedly. Once a plane dived so low that it almost flew into the Emperor's cave. "They are really very brave," Haile Selassie said.

On March 26, with ample time for the Italians to pick up the message and act on it, the Emperor radioed his wife that he would attack "on Saturday (28th) or Monday (30th)." [4] Badoglio, with a shrewd soldier's instinct that this was about the right moment, told his troops to stand by. "With the object of consolidating our advanced line of defence, so as to break any further attempt against it by the enemy, I directed the suppporting divisions to close up," wrote the Italian commander, "and the troops occupying the western flank of our positions to be reinforced—thus on that side also I could resist with absolute security any possible enveloping movement. . . . I wished, in fact, to be in a position to take the initiative at any moment, whenever the enemy should abandon the attack."

March 28 came and still no attack. "What really was preventing

[4] Not even at the worst moments of the war did the Ethiopians ever fight on Sundays.

it?" asked Konavoloff, and learned that the Emperor's staff was
actually negotiating with the Azebu Galla—"the same Azebu who
had killed the Minister of War, Ras Mulugeta, his elder son and
many of his soldiers during their retreat from Makalle. Their corpses,
decomposing now, littered the road between Mai Chow and Lake
Ashangi." These same scavengers were now being bribed with "long
striped silk shirts and black satin capes, the complete outfit that is
given to petty chiefs. . . . They left the Emperor clutching in their
fists the ten or fifteen dollars he had just given them. In their striped
shirts with their filthy cotton rags underneath they looked savages
enough."

The hyenas had been given their instructions. They were to
scavenge this time on the flanks of the Italians, harrying them on
the morning of the offensive as the Emperor's troops moved in. Or
so, at least, the Emperor hoped.

On Saturday night the Shoan chiefs came and grovelled before
Haile Selassie as they pleaded with him not to attack the Italians.
They were not ready. They had not reconnoitered the terrain. "A
kind of military council was called by His Majesty," the Russian
colonel wrote, "but it was almost impossible to speak and utterly
impossible to hear. The soldiers, strung up by waiting so long for
the offensive, kept on firing their guns into the air. Some of the
nearer ones were arrested and beaten soundly, but that did not stop
the row."

The offensive was postponed until Tuesday.

On Monday the Emperor and a number of his chiefs climbed to
a hilltop overlooking Mia Chow and the Italian lines and examined the
slit trench Konavoloff had had dug for him. He got out, dropping
his black cape from his shoulders, and leaned against a tree, his eyes
on the enemy positions. "I looked at him. Slim, still young in appearance, very carefully dressed . . . he did not look like an Ethiopian
at all. The way he stood, motionless and concentrated, betrayed a
mind working hard. What was he thinking about? Perhaps the same
as me. Without conscious effort, almost involuntary, I saw again
those twenty years of fruitful government over Ethiopia during
which he had mastered every obstacle. The internal enemies who had
never ceased to give him difficulty had been defeated.

"But here was a new enemy, more terrible and stronger, which
had put itself in his way. He saw it from afar, three kilometres off,
behind the light fortifications in which, glittering in the sun, lay
pieces of broken glass to injure the naked feet of their enemy."

He had made up his mind, and the attack was to begin at last. The Ethiopians would assemble in three columns and make their way through the ravines to their start-off positions, and at dawn they would advance. That evening the Emperor summoned all his chiefs and told them that the columns would be led by Ras Kassa, Ras Seyoum and Ras Getachu, and Konavoloff was not the only one in the throng who groaned with frustration. "Why by them and not by others of greater energy and capacity?" he asked, and answered himself: "Because the sovereign had to reckon with his feudal seigneurs of the Empire although they had proved their ineptitude already and had lost the first part of the war. He had better men but he could not use them."

But for the unit commanders there was at least one pleasant surprise, and that was when the Emperor demonstrated to them from the mountain-top in which directions they were to go to attack the flanks of the enemy positions. For the first time in the campaign they had a chance to see where they were going and how they should direct their assault on the enemy lines. Konavoloff took a last look at them as darkness began to fall.

"The Emperor was very animated," he wrote. "He turned from side to side of the ring of chiefs, who listened to him in silence. Correct as ever in his European dress, his beard and moustache neat and trim, what a contrast he presented to the mass around him ... each dressed according to his fancy, most of them enveloped in their shammas and burnous, or with a muffler twisted round their necks." The Russian reflected that "there was a time when some of them had intrigued against the future Emperor, then Heir to the Throne. He had forgiven them. Others owed their career to him; they were chosen by him, educated and given high positions in spite of their obscure origin. But most of them were illiterate, ignorant alike of foreign languages and modern methods of warfare."

Only the Imperial Guard, about 5,000 rifles in all, had any real training. But it was now too late to worry about that.

"The night of March 30-31 passed quietly," wrote Marshal Badoglio. "At 5:45 A.M., almost simultaneously on the front of both the Pusteria Division and of the 2nd Eritrean Division, the alarm was given: the first hostile patrols had come in contact with our advanced posts."

The plan of battle had been worked out by the Emperor and had it been launched several days earlier the chances of success would have been considerable. The tactics were to launch a small but fierce attack against the Italian frontal positions but to drive home the main assaults to the flanks and rear; and five days before, when the enemy had only just arrived in position, his troops might well have been overwhelmed by the weight and fanaticism of the Ethiopian hordes. Delays and procrastinations, however, had enabled Badoglio not only to order the building of fortifications but to discover exactly where to put them. For the treacherous Azebu Gallas, having first taken guns, ammunition and dollars from the Emperor and promised to join in the attack when it began, went at once to the Italians, who doubled their bribes. The Azebu Gallas, having seen how the Italian guns and bombs had pulverized Ras Mulugeta's army, had no doubt of the outcome of the coming struggle and were resolved not to be among the victims of it. They told the Italian commanders in detail of Haile Selassie's plan and then infiltrated into the folds of the mountains—to watch and wait, and slaver with anticipatory greed over the looting to come. Badoglio built a low wall and trench system around his flanks and rear positions and manned it with artillery and machine-guns, and inside this protection he withdrew all but a few forward posts.

So it seemed, in the first few hours, that the Emperor's plan had succeeded and that a great Ethiopian victory was in sight. From his observation post on a mountain-top, waiting with his reserve, Haile Selassie could see fires burning behind the Italian lines; messengers arrived grinning with glee as they reported that the enemy had been beaten back, that the positions he had marked on his map to be taken were now in Ethiopian hands. The jubilant troops began firing their rifles in the air. "Victory!" they shouted, repeatedly.

A victory they certainly had—of a kind—of the kind, in fact, that Badoglio wanted them to have. For he knew the psychology of Ethiopian fighting men. "The Ethiopian soldier, if his assault succeeds," Menelik once said, "does not go on—he withdraws. He is capable of great bravery—but only for short periods."

The Italian commander had thoughtfully arranged for the Ethiopian assault to succeed by pulling back his men into their fortifications. As a result, the column commanded by Ras Seyoum, some 3,000 strong, occupied one mountain. Ras Kassa's men took and set fire to a small village on the opposite flank. Ras Getachu's column, stiffened with the infantrymen and machine-gunners of the Imperial Guard, found themselves battering against the most formidable of the Italian fortifications, in the rear.

Konavoloff, watching with the Emperor, reported that the Ethiopians had halted. "The bravest, some 900 men, struck at the redoubts. But the rest lacked courage to advance and crown their efforts with the capture of the Italian works. Under cover, they preferred to blaze away until their cartridge belts were empty. Then they withdrew."

Not at once, however. Badoglio records that at 9 A.M. the attack "reopened with renewed violence, its greatest weight being directed throughout against the left flank, where the enemy probably counted on the lesser capacity for resistance of our coloured troops. This time the whole of the Imperial Guard, supported by a lively fire,[5] moved against our positions, advancing in rushes and making good use of the ground, giving proof of a solidity and a remarkable degree of training combined with a superb contempt of danger."

He had a "veritable avalanche of fire" awaiting them, and those who succeeded in reaching the walls "were thrust back with the bayonet and grenades." By afternoon it was all over. "About 4 P.M. a fresh and desperate attack was attempted against both flanks of our line, but the concerted action of the two Eritrean Divisions and the firm stand of the 'Intra' battalion of Alpini on the right, supported by detachments of Blackshirts, decided the day.

"It was clear that the offensive had failed," wrote Konavoloff. And Badoglio commented: "This was the last action launched by the enemy, in a final effort."

That evening the Emperor radioed to the Empress in Addis Ababa: "From 5 in the morning until 7 in the evening our troops attacked the enemy's strong positions, fighting without pause. We also took part in the action and, by the Grace of God, remained unharmed. Our chief and trusted soldiers are dead or wounded. Although our losses are heavy, the enemy too has been injured. The Guard fought magnificently and deserve every praise. The Amhara troops also did their best. Our troops, even though they are not adapted for fighting of the European type, were able to bear comparison throughout the day with the Italian troops."

He ended: "The Gallas helped us only with shouts, not with their strong right arms."

He was much more cast down by the events of the day than his message indicated, for he knew that what had been lost was not a

---

[5] Konavoloff, of the Ethiopian artillery, wrote: "Our gunners had no idea of the objectives they were supposed to bombard. They shot at random and sometimes hit their own men. . . . The Emperor had said: 'Our men must hear their artillery shooting. It will give them courage and improve their morale.'"

battle—but hope. Only the enemy's outer positions had been occupied and no exhortation had been successful in persuading his forces to push on. He had spent most of the day deliberately exposing himself to enemy artillery and planes, in the hope that the sight of him would galvanize the troops, and in the final hours he had gone down among them and manned a machine-gun himself. But no one would mount a charge in the face of Italian grenades, shells and attacks from the air. They had made their effort. They had taken enemy positions. To ask them to do more, they made it plain, was too much.

That night Haile Selassie climbed back up the mountainside to the place where he had held his conference before the assault, and it was there, in a downpour of rain, that he spent the night. Next morning he said to Konavoloff: "I feel that we ought to renew the offensive," but one look down into the valley demonstrated how impossible that was. Already, with no prodding from the Italians, the Ethiopian troops were beginning to withdraw, of their own accord. No one had given them orders. They just drifted in behind their chiefs, and many of them came back empty-handed. They had simply left cannon and machine-guns behind, for the Italians to pick up. There was now only one Oerlikon gun left with the force.

Now Badoglio put his counter-attack into action. Now the great retreat began. And now the agony began too.

It had begun to rain heavily, and the news was bad. The Italians were moving forward swiftly and, from the mountainsides, the Azebu Gallas were preparing to pounce. "Ethiopian chiefs, mules, soldiers, the whole retreating army were climbing our slope," wrote Konavoloff. "The narrow path was filling up with a mass of people pushing and shouting at each other. Men posted there tried to shove the crowd back and keep them from coming near the Imperial cave, with blows of sticks to left and right."

Everybody was shouting and screaming. "What a disgraceful disorder," said the Emperor. "When we ought to be ready to stop the Italians from turning our flank. Fitaurari Taferi! Where is he? Bring him here!" A stocky Ethiopian chief with a sword scar across his forehead came forward. "You see that mountain covered with bush." The Emperor pointed. "You must occupy it with your men and stop the *ferengi* (foreigners) from taking it."

The Fitaurari hesitated and then went away. Two hours later he was still to be seen around the camp, chatting to his underlings. He had sent 50 soldiers forward, the only ones he could find, and had stayed behind himself "to be near the Emperor."

That evening the Ethiopian Army collapsed into disorder. Konavoloff reported that it was impossible to find a single man ready to obey an order or even in his proper place; the mountain was full of them. Just before darkness fell Haile Selassie decided to distribute to the men all the things he could not take with him—clothing, liquor and tinned food, cartridges and impedimenta of all kinds. At once his cave was jostling with soldiers fighting to grab what they could and the Emperor could get out only by having his bodyguard beat a way through the greedy mob with their staves.

The Imperial party took its place in the stream going southwards, away from the Italians. Behind them the troops were having a bacchanalia with the stores of gasoline, oil and ammunition, setting fire to everything inflammable and eating and drinking the supplies they could not carry. The Emperor left his radio behind with the rest of the abandoned supplies.

"The descent from our mountain was terrible, so dark was the night," recorded Konavoloff. "Every minute the road was jammed. When the Ethiopians march the main object of each man is to pass all the others. This mob of people trying to thread its way through donkeys, mules and hundreds of other Ethiopians created an incredible disorder."

It took them twelve hours of painful and terrifying marching to cover the seven miles that separated them from Lake Ashangi, and just after dawn down came the planes. "Before us is a hell which none of us can avoid. On one side of the road is the lake, on the other are the mountains. The pass is narrow and the human flood find it hard to press forward and through. . . . Here is another airplane which seems to be choosing its victims. One explosion, then another . . ."

As the Emperor and the hysterical troops pressed through, the Azebu Gallas opened fire on them from the hills. "These irregular units," Badoglio wrote of the treacherous bands, "deserve special mention. Warriors by instinct, particularly adept at surprise action, under the orders of their own chiefs [who had been well bribed by the Italians] and animated by a deep hatred of their Shoan rulers, they rendered signal service to our cause throughout the entire campaign." The Gallas would fire down upon stragglers and then descend upon the killed and wounded, stripping them of clothing, rifles and cartridges, and would then leave the mutilated victims to rot or to die. The road south stank with the smell of corpses and was loud with the groans of the dying, emasculated victims, while back to the Italians would go exultant Galla messengers, necks draped with grisly human trophies, to report yet more panic in the Ethiopian forces. Konavoloff called it "the valley inhabited by the terrible Azebu Galla."

There was no exaggeration in Badoglio's dispatch to Mussolini when he reported, on April 11, 1936: "The battle upon which the fate of the Empire depends is over. Of the Ethiopian Army which fought at Lake Ashangi nothing remains but a few groups of armed men, terror stricken by the losses they have suffered, scattered over a vast area, and for the most part heading for their own villages."

On that day Haile Selassie arrived, with a small entourage, at a sacred place northwest of Dessye called Lalibela. He had come to pray. A few days before, Konavoloff had reported that he seemed near to the end of his tether, his body and spirit shaken by a combination of weariness and horror, revulsion and despair, as he surveyed the painful chaos around him. It was raining steadily. The men were either mad or drunk and fired their rifles repeatedly into the air; the wounded and the gassed suppurated and coughed; the Azebu Gallas stalked them like jackals.

"I do not know what to do," said Haile Selassie. "My chiefs will do nothing. My brain no longer works."

He admitted to Konavoloff that he had given up hope of saving Addis Ababa or Ethiopia from the Italians.

"It is beyond our power to hold them back," he said.

So, over the Easter weekend, the Emperor decided to go to Lalibela and he did not seem to care that the enemy were pressing him and that it was off his route of retreat. He had ceased to think about martial matters and had embarked on a pilgrimage.

The eleven rock churches of Lalibela were first brought to the notice of the western world by the Portuguese priest, Alvarez, who discovered them during his travels in Ethiopia in 1520. He rightly described them as "the like of which, and so many, cannot be found in the world." They are intricately hewn out of solid red rock so that whole buildings, approached by tunnels and passageways, are literally part of the mountain itself. Alvarez wrote that "it wearied me to write more of these works, because it seems to me that they will not believe me if I write more, and because as to what I have already written they may accuse me of untruth, therefore I swear by God, in whose power I am, that all that is written is the truth, and there is much more than what I have written, and I have left it that they may not tax me with its being falsehood." [6]

Here in the cold damp depths of these ancient wonders of the Ethiopian Church, Haile Selassie was received by the priests and fell on his knees. For forty-eight hours he remained inside the holy mountain, drinking nothing but a little water, eating nothing but a roll of injera (the native bread); and never, one feels, was he more isolated from his fellow men, the evils, sins and sorrows of the world, and closer to his God.

On April 14, he rejoined what was left of the Imperial Guard and that evening their column entered Dessye, to find it deserted except for snipers hiding in the buildings. Overhead, Italian bombers circled. The Crown Prince, whom Haile Selassie had left in command of the Wollo Armies, had departed for Addis Ababa the same morning, leaving behind the news that his two chief lieutenants and their forces had gone over to the Italians.

The Emperor held a hurried conference and decided not to remain in the city, and it was just as well. The Italians arrived to occupy it the next morning and hung their flag from the Palace of the old warlord, Ras Mikael.

That night was spent in a rain-washed cave, and the next morning along a "river-bed full of corpses, naked and decomposing," past the debris of the retreating army and the smoking villages burned by looting troops, the trek south went on. At one point the Emperor called the remnants of his guard together and addressed them, saying: "Never forget what a soldier should be, especially at this present time. Up to now you have not all done your duty. Try to do it in future."

But Konavoloff added: "The great chiefs were losing little by little all their prestige. The rases and the seigneurs who usually traveled aloof from the crowd now mingled with the throng of soldiers. The Emperor himself was losing a great part of his authority." It was Death, wrote Konavoloff, "who followed us everywhere, and seemed to be stronger than the aristocratic power of the Emperor and his chiefs: he made us all equal, and it was he who drove us from the places where he was able to reign."

The soldiers raped, killed and pillaged as they made their way southwards, as if to show that they too could be as savage and bloodthirsty as the Azebu Gallas who still dogged their footsteps. The Emperor issued an order forbidding looting and ordering those caught at it

[6] *Narrative of the Portuguese Embassy to Abyssinia during the Years 1520-27*, Father Francisco Alvarez.

to be lashed. "The culprits lay down quietly on the ground to receive a dozen strokes." But everything, including discipline, was disintegrating. "What do you mean, soldiers?" asked one chief when questioned as to the whereabouts of his men. "Today there are no more soldiers; they are all brigands, for whom we no longer exist. Most of the chiefs have already flown."

On April 18, 1936, the Emperor and his entourage reached Fiche, 125 miles by lorry road from Addis Ababa, and there a car was waiting to take him to the capital. His eyes were burning with the sleeplessness that could no longer be helped by sleep, and his face was lined and mud-green with weariness.

He drove that night to his capital.

chapter fourteen

TRAIN TO JIBOUTI

HE ALREADY KNEW that the war was lost, but at least he could go
on fighting to the last. He would march westwards to the Gojjam
and there, with the help of his beloved friend Ras Imru and his men,
he would turn guerrilla in the Blue Nile gorges and make life un-
pleasant for the hated *ferengi*.

This was Haile Selassie's plan when he returned to Addis Ababa,
and at first nothing would swerve him from it. His Empress was to
leave Ethiopia and a special train was waiting to carry her away; she
pleaded with him to go with her. The rases agreed with her. Ras Kassa
addressed a meeting of them in the Palace and stressed the hopelessness of the position. Why fight on alone? Why not go with the
Empress to Geneva and there make one last appeal to the League of
Nations for help? The Emperor was eloquent and his personal presence might still persuade the powers to save Ethiopia.

The rases listened gravely and as gravely voted, and by twenty-to-
three decided that Haile Selassie should leave the country—with
themselves in attendance, of course. They conveyed their decision to
the Emperor.

His answer was to have his great drum of Menelik brought out
into the courtyard of the Palace, and for two hours it was beaten,
its boom even drowning out the throb of Italian planes hovering overhead. Into the Palace compound poured the army commanders and
their officers and to them he spoke. It was not over yet, he said. They
could still fight on, and he would do so. He would go westwards with
what forces he could get together; but first, to clear a path for him
and protect him from an enemy determined now to kill or capture
him, the army must march out and delay Badoglio's entry into the
capital. Ras Getachu would be in command, and 5,000 men were
needed. Who would volunteer?

It was no fighting speech, for he was weary and sick, but his gravity stirred a fire. Men began to shout and wave their rifles. Officers surged forward to prostrate themselves, declaring their readiness to fight and die. He ordered them away to a feast and told them to stand by for instructions to march.

They were instructions that were never given. For back inside the Palace, Ras Getachu was waiting for him, gold pince-nez perched on his podgy nose. He denied that, when the moment came, the men would move. The time for fighting was past. The struggle was over. While these words were being spoken, the Empress and Ras Kassa came in, and both of them seized their opportunity to persuade the Emperor of the hopelessness of his position. He listened to them wearily.

"It must have been then that the Emperor decided to go," wrote George Steer. "Reason, the appeal to the League, allied itself to the instinct for flight; reason in exhaustion found itself the weaker second to the partnership!"

Steer was waiting in the courtyard and he saw Haile Selassie come out after making his decision.

"He was dressed in khaki as a general. His aspect froze my blood. Vigour had left the face, and as he walked forward he did not seem to know where he was putting his feet. His body was crumpled up, his shoulders drooped; the orders on his tunic concealed a hollow, not a chest."

At twenty minutes past four o'clock on the morning of May 2, 1936, the Emperor of Ethiopia boarded a special train at Akaki, ten miles out of Addis Ababa, and began his journey into exile. With him were his Empress and her pet papillon puppy, his three sons, the Crown Prince, the Duke of Harar and Prince Sahle Selassie, his two surviving daughters, Princess Tenanye Werk Desta [1] and Princess Tsahai, and his most senior rases, including Kassa and Seyoum. He even had a prisoner with him, the inextinguishable Ras Hailu, who had been brought from his dungeon to accompany his old adversary out of the country and thus be kept out of the hands of the Italians, for whom he could make a useful puppet.

The train with its woebegone cargo chugged across the sodden, rain-washed plateau and across the swollen Awash River to Dire Dawa, where it halted for several hours. The Emperor had telegraphed an old friend, Mr. (now Sir) Edwin Chapman-Andrews, British

---

[1] Her husband was still fighting in the South.

Consul at Harar, to come to meet him, and his arrival was delayed by storm and flood. It was a time of frayed nerves, for Dire Dawa was full of rumors that the Italians were somewhere near. The Emperor and the Consul talked together for several hours and Haile Selassie unburdened himself. He did not want to leave his country in its moment of agony and he was already beginning to regret his departure from Addis Ababa. Perhaps there was still a chance that he might fight on in the South and help his son-in-law, Ras Desta, by raising the royal standard somewhere between Harar and Jigjiga.

"It took me some time to dissuade him, but it had to be done," writes Sir Edwin in a note to the author. "The military situation at this time was quite hopeless. If the Emperor had attempted to continue the fight I do not think he could have escaped death or capture."

The train started off again across the Danakil Desert, only an hour or two ahead now of the first Italian patrols coming in from Marshal Graziani's army in the South; and it was not until it was too late to turn back that it was discovered that Ras Hailu was missing. He had escaped from his escort, slipped off the train, and gone off to give his services to the enemy.

The war was over. Behind, in Addis Ababa, there was an interregnum while the city awaited the arrival of the conquerors. The news spread that the Emperor was gone. The soldiers reacted as Ethiopians always do when their leader falls—they panicked and then lunged out in an orgy of looting and killing. They turned in savage fury on the Palace itself, ripping its Harrods furnishings and Liberty fabrics for bonfires, and even shooting down the royal lions. They sacked the European shops and they began to rape and murder the Europeans.[2] This spoliation gave the Italians just the opportunity they needed to pose as the white civilizers of a barbarous people.

"We come to restore order!" Badoglio announced, as the victory parade filed through Addis Ababa.

It was May 5, 1936. At that moment Haile Selassie the First, Conquering Lion of the Tribe of Judah, Elect of God, Emperor of Ethiopia, was sailing into exile from Jibouti aboard the British cruiser *Enterprise*. He looked old, worn and pathetic. Few people who saw him then imagined that he would ever see his country again, and doubted that he wished to. He had had a lifetime's training in concealing his feelings. He would need all his skill in dissembling in the shabby days to come.

[2] One of those killed was Dr. John Melly, the British Red Cross missionary, who was shot in the stomach by a wounded rioter he had tried to help.

part four

EXILE—AND RETURN

chapter fifteen

A TIME FOR PATIENCE

ON MAY 9, 1936, Italy officially announced the annexation of Ethiopia and the conferring upon King Victor Emmanuel of the additional title of Emperor. The following day Marshal Badoglio was appointed Viceroy. Through the chancelleries of Europe and the corridors of the League of Nations one could almost hear the sighs of relief from premiers and foreign ministers as they remarked to their secretaries: "Well, that's that!" And *that's that* it might well have been if only Haile Selassie weren't still around. Why hadn't the little man got himself killed or disappeared into the wilds of Gojjam, where people would have forgotten about him? What with all the sentimental emotions welling over at the moment, he was going to be a positive embarrassment. And the British Prime Minister, Stanley Baldwin, was not the only one who profoundly hoped that the ex-Emperor (as they were already beginning to think of him, even if they hadn't yet recognized Italy's annexation of the title) would have the decency to keep his mouth shut.

In the meantime, they did their best to demonstrate that they were no longer too eager to be *officially* aware of his existence. He had his first taste of how quietly beastly British bureaucracy could be when he arrived in Jerusalem, and the High Commissioner quickly invented an unavoidable engagement in Sinai in order not to give him an official welcome. Many of the local consuls took their cue from this and sent their *vices* to the station. For the next two weeks he attended services on the roof of the Church of the Holy Sepulchre, which belongs to the Ethiopian Church, swam with his sons in the swimming pool of the YMCA opposite the King David Hotel, where he was staying, and consulted with his advisers about what he should do next to remind the world that he was still in the land of the living.

The answer to that came on May 10, when the League of Nations Secretariat received a telegram. The Members of the League, anxious to forget Ethiopia, eager to appease Italy, were fidgeting to get out of the agreements they had made to institute sanctions against the Fascist aggressor. Haile Selassie's telegram brought them up with salutary sharpness against the realization that they now had an angry scapegoat on their hands. In Ethiopia he had pleaded for help and been refused it; in exile he was demanding that the powers at least recognize what they had promised and how they had failed to deliver it.

"We now demand," wrote the Emperor, in his telegram, "that the League of Nations should continue its efforts in order to secure respect for the Covenant, and that it should decide not to recognize territorial extensions, or the exercise of an assumed sovereignty, resulting from an illegal recourse to armed force and from numerous other violations of international agreements."

It was sufficiently peremptory to persuade several sheepish governments, including the British, to postpone their plans to accept and officially condone Italy's occupation—for a time, at least.[1] The British Government was in a particularly fretful position, torn as it was between appeasing Italy and satisfying the clamant demand of public opinion to recompense the gallant Emperor for his sufferings. It could not do other than invite Haile Selassie to take refuge in Britain, and, when he decided to do so, to provide him with transport to his place of exile; but here the Baldwin mind took over. The cruiser *Capetown*, on her way from South Africa to Devonport for a refit, was diverted to Haifa to take aboard the Emperor and his family. There were rumors that Mussolini had plans to hijack the Emperor if he traveled through the Mediterranean by ordinary steamship, and this the brave British Government was certainly not going to allow. So he and his entourage were transported out of Haifa and told that they were being taken to Britain; and so the captain of the ship had been instructed when he took his distinguished passengers aboard. But somewhere between Haifa and the Atlantic Ocean, Baldwin began to have nagging doubts. If the Emperor arrived in Britain aboard a Royal Navy ship, might it not look as if the British Government was on his side? And might this not annoy the Italian dictator, Signor Mussolini—with whom Sir Robert Vansittart was still so anxious to be friendly? No, it would never do.

[1] The United States, Mexico, New Zealand and Soviet Russia will always be remembered with gratitude by the Ethiopians for never recognizing the Italian conquest. For the same reason, there are still sentimental ties between Ethiopia and Haiti, which never got around to recognition, either.

So at Gibraltar HMS *Capetown* docked, and stayed docked. To the fury of her crew, who were aching to get home after several years on foreign station, her captain announced that she needed repairs (which she didn't) and must delay her departure for the United Kingdom. No one knew how long she would remain in dock, and the Emperor was told by the unfortunate captain that it might be days and it might be weeks.

The shabby ruse worked. The Emperor and his family transferred to a passenger liner and he thus arrived in Great Britain as a private rather than an official guest. As for HMS *Capetown*, as soon as the Ethiopian monarch left her decks, she was discovered to be seaworthy again, and sailed for home.[2]

1936, even though it was a year of exile, was not too difficult to bear because there was still something to fight for. There were, of course, the humiliations to be swallowed. He was taken to the House of Commons to have tea on the terrace, and, with only the faintest grimace of distaste, watched the Prime Minister, Stanley Baldwin, whose apathy had contributed so much to his misfortunes, hiding behind a table so that he would not have to be introduced. But at least the people were on his side and made their sympathy plain; and there was still the League.

In that sad and sagging comity of nations Haile Selassie, despite the gentle warnings of his friends, still believed. It was for him the tribune of international justice where the world looked to its conscience, punished the wrongdoer, protected the weak and puny from the bully; where Italy might still be punished for her aggression and Ethiopia saved from conquest and domination. Upon his appeal to the League the Emperor put all his hopes at a time when his cynical fellow-members had long since abandoned them. He still believed that Britain, France and the non-Fascist nations of Europe could be rallied to his side from self-interest if not from more idealistic motives, and the proposal that the League should abandon sanctions now that Ethiopia was conquered gave him the platform from which to make a last appeal to their instincts for self-preservation.

His appearance before the tribunal of the League of Nations on June 30, 1936, has by this time won its place in history, and deservedly, for all those who saw it will never forget it. The stoop had not been ironed out of his back by the time he got to Geneva and

2 This will be the first time that Haile Selassie learns—though he may have suspected—why there was the delay at Gibraltar.

he was far from being in fighting trim as he marched to the tribunal. The Italian journalists who screamed insults at him as he stood before the microphone could hardly have done him a better service, for they won even the laggard nations to his side as he stood there, aloof from the epithets. "His behaviour was, as always, brave, calm and dignified," wrote Lord Avon (who, as Anthony Eden, was the chief British delegate). "In that great audience, his was probably the only mind at rest. He had done all he could, and gazed in quiet contempt at the hysterical Fascist journalists, hurling vulgar abuse, who had to be removed from the gallery. Titulescu [the Rumanian chairman] enraged at their conduct, rose in his seat, crying: '*Ala porte les sauvages!*' "[3]

Avon added: "These were wretched days at Geneva," and they were indeed for anyone with a conscience or a sense of justice. "One morning during an Assembly session about Abyssinia . . . I suddenly heard a report and saw a figure fall on the benches at my right hand. Until the police ran up I did not know what had happened. A Czech spectator had shot himself dead after a cry of warning, apparently about the fate of small countries."

But it was of the fate of large countries as well as small that Haile Selassie spoke, and there are passages in his speech worth recalling.

"I, Haile Selassie I, Emperor of Ethiopia, am here today to claim," he began, "that justice which is due to my people and the assistance promised to it eight months ago when fifty nations asserted that an aggression had been committed. None other than the Emperor can address the appeal of the Ethiopian people to these fifty nations."

The delegates shuffled and looked uneasy. He was speaking in Amharic rather than the French which they had expected, and the translation lacked the vibrancy of a personal appeal. He went on, moreover, to talk of bombing and gassing and the agonies of wounded Ethiopians, and this only made them feel guilty about the sufferings of black people far away. They looked at their feet and clucked sympathetically. But then, after a slashing attack upon the treachery of the French, he began to jab them where the skin was most tender.

"I assert," he said, "that the problem submitted to the Assembly today is a much wider one than the removal of sanctions. It is not merely a settlement of Italian aggression. It is collective. It is the very existence of the League of Nations. It is the confidence that each State is to place in international treaties, it is the value of promises made to small States, that their integrity and their independence be

[3] *Facing the Dictators.*

The Freedom Memorial in Addis Ababa, with the University College in the background

Haile Selassie in palace courtyard, being presented a flower basket by the Patriarch of the Ethiopian Church at the Feast of the Finding of the True Cross

Haile Selassie being greeted by U.N. Secretary U Thant upon the former's arrival at the world organization, October 4, 1963

Haile Selassie with Kenya's Premier, Jomo Kenyatta, on a state visit to Nairobi, Kenya, in 1964

respected and ensured. It is the principle of the equality of States on the one hand, or, on the other, the inevitability that they will be forced to accept the bonds of vassalship. In a word, it is international morality that is at stake. Apart from the Kingdom of the Lord there is not on this earth any nation which is superior to any other." He paused and then he went on:

"It is my painful duty to note that the initiative has been taken today with a view to raising sanctions. God and history will remember your judgment. Does this initiative mean in practice the abandonment of Ethiopia to her aggressor? Are the States going to set up the terrible precedent of bowing before force? Representatives of the world, I have come to Geneva to discharge in your midst the most painful of the duties of a Head of State. What reply shall I take back to my people?"

He stepped down from the tribunal to a sheepish scatter of applause, and he realized that he may have moved his listeners but he had failed to galvanize their decisions. He murmured then the words he was to use publicly later: "It is us today. It will be you tomorrow."

That summer the League of Nations voted to raise the sanctions it had imposed upon Italy, and though token membership was still accorded to the Ethiopian delegation, one by one the nations began to recognize the Italian régime in East Africa. News reached Haile Selassie that his son-in-law, Ras Desta, had at last surrendered to the Italians and that he had been murdered in prison. His old friend, Ras Imru, had been captured in Gojjam and transported to Italy.

The deadly dull days of waiting, with little to hope for, had begun.

chapter sixteen

THE ROAD BACK

IT WAS THE CITY OF BATH to which the British Government directed Haile Selassie when he returned from Geneva. There was an almost Freudian touch to their choice of a place of exile, as if they sheepishly hoped that the healing waters of the Regency spa would soothe his resentments, and, vicariously, wash away their own sense of guilt at their desertion of him.

For the first few weeks he, his family and his entourage lived in a wing of the Spa Hotel, and there was so much interest in him that special trips were organized from London for those who wished to catch a glimpse of him. One of those whose job it was to be close to him in those days writes: "The best place to see him was in the Pump Room. Apparently he had some colonic trouble and daily he went to the baths for treatment, Saturdays and Sundays excluded. He would arrive in the afternoon and then we had to do something about the crowds and also give him VIP treatment. He arrived by car, always dressed in his sombre clothes—a bowler hat and a dark suit with black cape. With him he used to bring his two sons, who were learning to swim." [1]

The royal party stayed in the hotel for about a month, after which a house, "Fairfield," was bought on the outskirts of the city and this became the headquarters of the Imperial household. "From the time of his moving into that house," writes the author of the note cited above, "the excitement of the Emperor's presence tailed off, until, in the end, he was of no more interest than many of the people who had retired to Bath. Frequently his little procession would be seen walking about the city, he walking ahead of two or three of his staff."

[1] In a note to the author from someone who does not wish to be named.

The writer of these comments admits that "the Emperor did not impress me favourably," and roundly declares that "his status was not, I fear, high, particularly with the tradespeople," and reports an incident in which the policeman on the beat outside "Fairfield" "could frequently see the Empress squatting on the floor of the greenhouse (no longer used as such) shredding cabbage leaves. No doubt that is a woman's job in her own country, but it struck the policeman as a little odd."

In fact the greenhouse had been turned into a chapel, and the Empress was praying. There were, of course, those in Bath who objected to the "fuss" being made over "a little colored man" and there were others who resented "all those black people in the place," but though Haile Selassie's memories of Bath cannot help but be sad ones, for tragic things happened to him while he was there, his memories of the friendships he made there are warm, and there are one or two old citizens of Bath who are still welcome guests at the palace in Addis Ababa.

But the winter of 1937-38 was, nonetheless, a black one for the Emperor and his family. "His treasure was brought from London," writes the author of the aforementioned notes, "but despite all the stories of the fabulous value of it, I have the distinct recollection that it all came down to a quantity of silver."

He is quite right. Ethiopian State funds in the Bank of England were blocked and the Emperor, contrary to reports circulated at the time of his departure from Ethiopia, had brought little money with him. The banqueting plate had to be sold off to buy "Fairfield," and in the hard winter of 1937-38 the household was rationed to one coal fire (for the Empress, who abhorred the climate and missed the sun), and the rest of the plate was being disposed of to pay the tradesmen's bills.[2]

"It must be realized," said the Emperor about this time, "that we have absolutely no income. We must live on what little capital we have. When one has a small capital and no income—when it is all out-going and no in-coming—there is bound to be anxiety. There is no secret about the money I was reported to have taken out of my country. When I came out of my country I hoped that I would soon return, with assistance from the League of Nations, and so I only brought what I thought would be sufficient for my immediate needs. That little has gone in assisting my people who are now refugees

[2] His credit was stopped at a local bookshop.

and in the litigation in which I have been involved in an effort to recover some of my money." [3]

One would have thought that the British Government would have come to the rescue and provided enough to pay for his coal bills. Sir Sidney Barton, the former British Minister to Ethiopia, who thought the official attitude to the Emperor was shameful, pulled every string within reach to get the Foreign Office to help, but with little success; Sir Sidney was not exactly popular in official quarters, either, for he made no secret of his detestation of Fascism, an attitude which the Government, at the most crawling moment of its career, found inconvenient. Finally, a private committee headed by Sir Norman Angell started a fund to aid Ethiopian refugees, and the response considerably eased the strain on the Emperor's private resources.

December, 1937, was probably the worst month. From all over the world Christmas greetings poured in upon the Emperor, and the Americans asked him to make a broadcast to thank his supporters. In the taxi taking him from Paddington Station to the BBC's headquarters at Broadcasting House, from which the transmission was to be made, he was involved in a collision. His collarbone was fractured —as X rays subsequently revealed—and he was in considerable pain when he made his broadcast, but he told no one about it. When the program was finished he telephoned a Harley Street specialist, the only doctor he knew in London, but he was away; so were the Bartons, whom he also called. He had an appointment to attend a Christmas party at the Great Ormonde Street Hospital for Children, where his second daughter Princess Tsahai, was working as a probationer nurse, and he did not let her down. Neither did he mention the accident or speak to any of the doctors about the pain in his shoulder. He waited until he had returned to Bath.

To his physical distress was added a mental one. For some months it had been growing obvious that if the Empress remained in Britain she would die. She found it hard to breathe in the damp, thick, misty English air after the thin clear sunshine of Addis Ababa and Harar. She was racked by rheumatism. She could not cope with the shortages around the house. It was decided that she would survive the winter only if she basked in a little sunshine again, and arrangements were made for her to go to an Ethiopian Convent in Jerusalem. She sailed with her youngest son, Sahle Selassie, and three priests on January

[3] In London he sued Cable and Wireless for £10,000 owed to him for cable fees. The Company admitted liability for the money but would not agree that it was due to the Emperor. He won the case but lost an appeal.

18, 1938.[4] It was one of the blackest moments of his life when the Emperor said good-bye to her and he took to his bed for several days after she was gone, all incentive to go on fighting drained from him. Politically speaking, the skies were dark too. Ethiopia's last supporter in the Cabinet, Anthony Eden, had resigned—though not over Ethiopia—and the régime, with Neville Chamberlain now at its head, was intent on ingratiating itself with Mussolini. It decided that the best way to win back the Duce's favor was by recognizing his conquest of Ethiopia. To do this the Government needed to persuade the League of Nations to abrogate the joint agreement whereby members had pledged themselves not to acknowledge the fruits of Italian aggression, and a proposal to this effect was put down for the May, 1938, session of the League. From every point of view, they could hardly have chosen a worse moment for their boot-licking expedition, for even the Italians themselves were beginning to admit that things were not going well in their conquered Empire, nor had savage reprisals succeeded in quelling a wave of unrest sweeping the country.

In 1937 an attempt upon the life of the viceroy, Marshal Graziani (who had succeeded Badoglio) had failed, but the reprisals were brutal. Practically all students in the country who had ever been outside Ethiopia, and at least half of those who had attained school certificate standard in Ethiopian schools, were executed. Local chiefs who had submitted to the Italians were asked to name victims from their areas, and the more bloodthirsty and vindictive of them had a fine time weeding out potential rivals. Among those nominated for the firing squad by Ras Hailu, now restored to the Gojjam, was a son of Ras Kassa. In all, some 125 students and well over 100 priests were shot, and in one month the cream of Ethiopia's educated youth was destroyed.[5] That year altogether 3,000 Ethiopians went before Italian firing squads.

Yet this bloodthirsty retaliation had exacerbated rather than relieved the situation for the Italians. The Abuna Kyril, foreign-born Archbishop of the Ethiopian Church, had sided with the conquerors after the Italian entry into Addis Ababa, and he was at Graziani's side—and also wounded—during the assassination attempt. He went to Cairo to recuperate and from there denounced the Italians and refused to return. They appointed an old priest, Abraham, half-blind

---

[4] The Crown Prince was studying at Liverpool University, the Duke of Harar was at school in Bath, Princess Tenanye Werk stayed with her father, and Princess Tsahai was training to be a nurse.

[5] Two senior bishops, Petros and Michael, had been shot the year before.

from cataract, as the new Abun, but the people spurned him and he was swiftly excommunicated by the synod of Alexandria. As if only now realizing what had happened to their country, the Ethiopians began to fight back against the occupiers. There were mass flights across the frontier into Kenya, where refugees waited in camps for arms and leaders to take them back; near Dessye a warlord named Ras Abebe Aregai claimed to have assembled an army of 10,000 men to menace the road back to Eritrea; in the Gojjam there were large communities, despite Ras Hailu, which refused to recognize the Italians as their overlords; and letters were flowing in to "Fairfield" from Ethiopian redoubts in the mountains asking for arms and outside help in the great revolt which, they said, was surely coming.

At such a moment, the British Government decided to tip their cap to Mussolini as conqueror of Ethiopia and recognize King Victor Emmanuel as Emperor, and the Duke of Aosta as the new viceroy.[6] The result of a favorable vote to Britain's proposal at Geneva would mean the departure, if not the expulsion, of Ethiopia from membership in the League; but more than that, it would crush friends and supporters of Ethiopia both inside and outside the country. Haile Selassie, suffering from acute depression, the aftermath of the physical and mental misfortune of the past few months, nevertheless roused himself and decided to fight back. To the Secretary-General of the League of Nations, M. Joseph Avenol, he addressed a telegram which read:

> I learn that the Ethiopian question will be placed on the agenda of the session of the Council of the League of Nations to be held in May next. According to the Covenant, if a question affecting a member of the League not represented on the Council is raised before the latter, the State concerned has the right to be represented therein. Consequently, and in order to defend the interests of my people which is fighting for its independence, I shall communicate to you in due course the names of my representatives for the Council, as well as for the Assembly, when any question concerning Ethiopia comes before the latter. Signed, Haile Selassie, Emperor.

The *Manchester Guardian* commented: "It is possible that the Emperor may come himself to Geneva as the Abyssinian representative," and the *Daily Express* added: "Dramatic moments are expected. The Negus is believed to be ready to defend his case to the last." The British delegation, led by Lord Halifax, the new Foreign Minister, made haste to indicate that "it was only right and fair that the

6 Aosta replaced Graziani in December, 1937.

Ethiopians should attend," well knowing that there would be trouble at home if they tried to prevent them.

But the fighting speech from the Emperor that the League had tensed itself for did not come from his lips. He was too ill. He came to the rostrum, a pale ivory figurine, and spoke a few words in French and then gave way to his spokesman, the able and supple-minded Lorenzo Taezaz, who read the Emperor's message:

I deeply regret that I must enter into conflict with the Government for which I feel the sincerest respect and which is according me hospitality. Very respectfully but very firmly I ask the British Government, whose loyalty is well known, to reconsider these proposals. Italy in Ethiopia controls only those cities and villages where there are garrisons, and there are many Ethiopian provinces where they have little or no control. . . . An implacable guerrilla warfare is being waged against the Italians and will continue until either they are driven out of the country or the Ethiopian people are exterminated. There is the maintenance of peace by law and there is the maintenance of peace at any price. A nation's independence cannot be sacrificed for the sake of appeasement in Europe. I ask that Ethiopia be allowed to remain among you as the living image of violated right. But should our appeal remain unanswered, our war against Italy will go on, whatever happens, until justice triumphs.

The tribunal cold-shouldered his appeal, and he returned to London. There was only one comfort—at the station the Empress, back from Jerusalem, was awaiting him. Next day, May 15, 1938, he was due to address a meeting of the Westminster Federation at Central Hall, London, but he sent word to cancel his appearance. "He is too sick in mind and body to attend," it was announced.

He recovered in body, but it was not until June 10, 1940, that his mental depression was dissipated. On that day Italy entered the war against Britain, and the attitude of the Government toward Ethiopia changed at once. Haile Selassie was a hero again—though not with everyone.

For many months there had been reliable reports from Ethiopia that the Italians, far from quelling the unrest among the people and consolidating their conquest, were continuing to lose their grip. The appointment of the Duke of Aosta, a cultivated and civilized man (and, incidentally, a great admirer of the British colonial system) as viceroy had failed to stem revolt and unrest. The new road which now ran between Addis Ababa and Asmara, a truly Roman achievement, was unsafe for use except in convoy. The Ethiopians who had failed to fight the Italians beside Haile Selassie in 1936 were hitting back now at them—or crossing the border to offer their services to the Emperor.

Haile Selassie was well aware of the state of his country from the report of one of his personal staff, Lorenzo Taezaz, who had made an adventurous trek through Gojjam and Begemeder in 1938-39, openly announcing himself to the people and bringing the Emperor's greetings. He returned to Bath to report to his master in the summer of 1939 that Ethiopia was ripe for revolt. In Cairo, too, there was a Briton with an acute knowledge of the trouble brewing for the Italians in their newest colony. Brigadier Daniel Sandford, who had lived and farmed in Ethiopia since 1914—except for war service and until the Italians took over—was now attached to Military Intelligence in Middle East Headquarters with special charge over news from Ethiopia. He had built up a small body of reliable agents and kept in touch with rebel chieftains; he had also been joined, with offices in Khartoum, by Major R. E. Cheesman, whose name has been mentioned before in this narrative (as British Consul to Western Ethiopia).

The combined intelligence work of these men enabled Cheesman to write later of the Italian administration: "Naboth's vineyard viewed from within was not what it had seemed from a distance. Minerals which could have justified the lavish expenditure on sea bases, public works, roads and bridges, had not been found in quantities that would repay the cost of the necessary machinery; the expected discovery of oil had not been made; trade was negligible; public security was nonexistent and revenue from agriculture could not be collected in consequence; nor did these conditions tend to attract foreign capital in spite of strenuous efforts by the Italian Government in this direction."

So sure were Sandford and Cheesman that Ethiopia was a liability rather than an asset to Italy, and that its people would be galvanized by news of approaching liberation, that they had already taken steps to exploit the incipience of rebellion. On May 10, 1940, Cheesman wrote and the Kaid, or Commander-in-Chief, of the Sudan (General Sir William Platt), signed a message which his agents took across the Ethiopian frontier to chiefs in Gojjam, Begemeder, Armachaho and Wolkait, saying: "Peace be unto you. England and Italy are now at war. We have decided to help you in every way possible to destroy the common enemy. If you are in need of rifles, ammunition, food or clothing, send as many men and animals as you can spare to the

place where our messengers will tell you. We can help you with your
requirements. It would also be wise to send your personal representative to consult with us and to arrange the best means of attacking
the common enemy."

At the same time, Brigadier Sandford called together what had
already been named Mission 101, a body of five British and five
Ethiopian officers, who were to infiltrate into Ethiopia and stir up
patriotic revolt against the Italians. Brigadier Sandford himself,
though now in his sixties, was to lead this hazardous expedition.

These were the plans, but neither in Cairo nor in Khartoum was
there, so far, any mention of what part the Emperor himself would
play in the operations. So far as the Governor General (Sir Stewart
Symes) and the Kaid (General Platt) were concerned, the activities
planned in Ethiopia by Sandford and any rases he could bestir would
merely serve to keep the Italians involved in anti-guerrilla operations
and therefore too preoccupied to invade the Sudan. There were even
those (among whom Symes must be numbered) who had already
concluded that Italian occupation of the Sudan was in any case inevitable. It was a moment when their fears were understandable
even if their defeatism was not; total military manpower in the Sudan
amounted to some 9,000 men, a few old planes, and not a single piece
of artillery. The Italians, on the other hand, had an army of over
a quarter of a million troops and a modern air force. On July 4
they crossed the frontier from Eritrea into the Sudan and occupied
the strategic town of Kassala and, further south, came in from Ethiopia to occupy a caravan center known as Gallabat. In Khartoum it
was presumed that this was the beginning of an offensive which
would culminate in the occupation of the whole of the Sudan, and
it is not unfair to add that it was a prospect viewed by Symes and
many British civil servants in the Sudan with a certain complacency.
They would regret being conquered, but they did not doubt that
they would be in good hands. The Duke of Aosta, the Italian Viceroy
of Ethiopia, had already communicated privately with the Governor-
General to give him unofficial assurance that the work of the British
administration in the Sudan would not be wrecked by the Italians.
As for the Ethiopians—over them there was a tendency to shrug
shoulders. The fonder a British official was of his charges in the Sudan
the less likely was he to be enthusiastic over the liberation of the
neighbors to the east. Naturally, like all civilized men, they agreed
that the Italian invasion and occupation of Ethiopia had been a brutal act of aggression, but they went on believing that the Ethiopian

(or *habashi*, as they called him) was a rascal, a poacher and a slaver. He had given trouble to the Sudan for years. He was a ruthless raider who murdered elephants and rhinos in the Dinder Game Reserve and invaded peaceful Sudani villages to kidnap young men and girls for the slave markets; and the Italian conquest had at least put a partial stop to this loathsome trade.

Therefore, faced by an imminent conquest by the Italians, there were many dedicated civil servants in the Sudan who were not cast down by their own weaknesses. Some of them honestly believed that Britain was going to lose the war anyway, and their principal anxiety was to ensure that Italy should assume control of the Sudan with as little unpleasantness as possible. Of course, the troops under General Platt would fight gallantly when the time came; but in the summer of 1940 they were a puny, under-equipped defensive force, waiting for the worst to happen. Who cared about Ethiopia in such circumstances? Only Dan Sandford and Robert Cheesman, and they were a couple of old white *habashis* themselves, anyway.

It was at this moment that the Emperor of Ethiopia descended upon them.

The decision had been taken in London and approved by the Prime Minister, Winston Churchill, that the Emperor should be flown out to the Middle East before the collapse of France and the intervention of Italy completely closed the Mediterranean. He departed from a blacked-out Paddington Station for Poole Harbour, on the south coast of England, on June 23, 1940, and there boarded a Sunderland flying boat for the journey across stricken France to Egypt. He traveled under the *nom de guerre* of Mr. Strong and he was accompanied by his middle son, the Duke of Harar, George Steer, who was to advise him on propaganda,[7] two secretaries, Lorenzo Taezaz and Walde Mariam, the Itchege and a number of servants. Only four people in the Middle East knew that he was on his way—Sir Miles Lampson (now Lord Killearn), the British Ambassador in Egypt, General (later Earl) Wavell, Commander-in-Chief of British Forces in the Middle East, Brigadier Iltyd Clayton, head of the Middle East Intelligence Office, and Mr. (now Sir) Edwin Chapman-Andrews, Assistant Oriental Secretary at the Cairo Embassy. Chapman-Andrews was, of course, the former Acting British

[7] Steer, formerly *The Times* correspondent during the Italo-Ethiopian War, had campaigned vigorously on Ethiopia's behalf both by speech and writing during the Emperor's exile. He had married Esme, the daughter of the former British Minister to Ethiopia, Sir Sidney Barton. Steer was later killed in Burma.

Consul in Harar, an expert on Ethiopian affairs, and a friend of the Emperor. He would act as the Emperor's political adviser.

Haile Selassie and his party landed in Alexandria harbor late in the afternoon of June 25, 1940, and were met there by Clayton and Chapman-Andrews. Strict precautions were taken to conceal the Emperor's presence, for Alexandria had a large population of Italians, none of whom had yet been rounded up by the authorities. They spent that night in the wash room [8] of the Italian Yacht Club, the only part of the club which was blacked out, and the flying boat took off again at dawn the following morning, with Chapman-Andrews as an additional passenger. It was only after they had landed on the Nile at Luxor and taken off again toward the Sudan frontier that a cipher telegram went from Cairo to Khartoum to inform the Governor-General and the Kaid that the Emperor was on his way. Consternation does not quite describe the reaction of the two of them when they got the news. Sir Stewart Symes was panic-stricken at the effect the presence of the dethroned Emperor would have on his friendly Italian enemies. General Platt was furious. Both of them decided that they wouldn't have the Emperor in their territory at any price, and Symes sent off a telegram instructing the flying boat to land at Wadi Halfa—on the Sudan frontier—and stay there until further notice. When they landed, Chapman-Andrews was told the reason for the delay, but did not pass it on for the moment to Haile Selassie, for the Emperor was buoyed up and invigorated by the prospects before him and the hostility awaiting him from his allies would have been a shattering blow.

On the first night of their stay in Wadi Halfa he asked Chapman-Andrews to walk with him and they left the Grand Hotel and strolled down to the banks of the Nile. The river was beginning to rise and the telltale streaks of yellow from Blue Nile silt were beginning to muddy the clearer waters of the White Nile flow. The Emperor led Chapman-Andrews down the bank to the water and leaned down, took a handful from the stream, and let it run slowly through his thin, delicate fingers.

"*C'est l'eau de mon pays,*" he said, softly.

Two days later Chapman-Andrews flew on in the flying boat to Khartoum to talk to Symes and Platt. He saw the Kaid and Robert Cheesman, both of whom stressed that the Emperor could hardly have arrived at a more inconvenient time. Platt talked angrily about

[8] "First time I've ever had a party with an Emperor in a lavatory," commented Steer.

provocation and said that the Emperor's presence would "invite reprisals" and "stir up a hornet's nest." Chapman-Andrews responded by implying what was a half-truth—that the Emperor was back at the special wish of Winston Churchill, and added: "There'll be a hell of a row. If you don't let him in, he'll go back to Britain."

At this the Governor-General gave way and Chapman-Andrews, accompanied by Sandford, flew back to Wadi Halfa to tell the Emperor his path had been smoothed.[9] The Emperor, who had been sweating out nearly a week in conditions of great heat, adequate comfort but great uncertainty, was hardly encouraged by Sandford's report to him. He had expected to hear that an army was awaiting him in Khartoum which he would lead back across the frontier to the liberation of his country. Sandford told him the truth. There was no army. Nothing had been prepared for his arrival. The Sudan authorities didn't really want him.

Haile Selassie arrived in Khartoum from Wadi Halfa by train (the pilot of the flying boat wasn't prepared to risk his craft again to the acquisitive hungers of the RAF in Khartoum) in a vastly different mood from the belligerently optimistic one in which he had started out from England. It did not take him long after arrival to get the message that he was unwanted. He was tucked away in a villa outside Khartoum with a heavily armed guard, without even a telephone, at first. He had an interview with General Platt but, for security reasons, was given no information about the military situation and could not understand why it seemed so funny to some of his white Sudan advisers when he asked for artillery and anti-tank guns to be set aside for "my army." No one was prepared to tell him that there were no such weapons in the Sudan.

The author flew from Cairo to Khartoum about this time and saw the Emperor at the so-called Pink Palace, outside the Sudan capital, to which he had recently been moved. He was in an unhappy frame of mind. As ever polite and uncomplaining about his personal comforts—and they left much to be desired—he managed to convey the intense distress he felt at the way in which he was being snubbed by the Sudan administration, and at the tricks which he believed were being played upon him.

---

[9] In the process of arguing with Symes and Platt, Chapman-Andrews almost lost his flying boat. Air Commodore Slattery, GOC the RAF in the Sudan, tried to requisition it as a bomber against Ethiopia. He was only dissuaded when it was pointed out that bullet holes in the bottom of a Sunderland—of which they could expect plenty over Ethiopia—turned her into a sieve and she would not survive more than one operation.

He spoke, for instance, of the stream of deserters which had begun to arrive from Ethiopia, from which he hoped to form his body-guard and his army. It was true that those who had come across the frontier into the Sudan had been put into camps and told that they would be armed and trained. But those escaping across the frontiers in the South into Kenya had not been so fortunate. They had been requisitioned by the Kenya Government and put on roadwork, and Kenya refused to release them on the grounds that they were subjects of *Italian* Ethiopia, therefore prisoners of war, and, according to the Geneva Convention, only to be used for non-combatant labor.

The censorship was strict but word of these difficulties was conveyed outside the Sudan, and it was arranged that Chapman-Andrews and Lorenzo Taezaz should go south to Kenya and organize the refugees into combat battalions with British officers. Before setting off on this task, Chapman-Andrews flew to Palestine with the Emperor's seal, which he presented to Ras Kassa, Ras Biru and Dejazmach Makonnen Endelkatchu, three warlords who had been ekeing out the months in the cheap warmth of Jericho—for their allowance was puny—and asked them to attend his Imperial Majesty in Khartoum. They arrived just in time to hear Haile Selassie demanding to be allowed to accompany Sandford and Mission 101 into Ethiopia, since a full-scale military expedition was impossible at the moment. Sandford gently persuaded the Emperor that this was impossible; he could hardly be expected to cast an Imperial glow over the circumstances of his return if he went back in such a hole-in-the-corner manner. Sandford and his Mission departed and were soon reporting that they had established promising relations with the warlords of the Gojjam—Ras Hailu, now an Italian puppet, excepted.

This was all very well, but Haile Selassie still remained a half-resented, semi-prisoner of the British administration in the Sudan, and his advisers encouraged him to rebel against the situation. Was he or was he not an independent sovereign? Where was the army the British had promised him? In a fit of unaccustomed irritation, he allowed himself to be persuaded into protesting formally and forth-rightly about the way in which he was being treated, and with a shrewd judgment of British susceptibilities he asked for something calculated to stir the civil servants into action—a long-term treaty of alliance and friendship between Ethiopia and Britain. This request for a political rather than a military problem to be solved had an almost immediate effect. The British War Minister, Anthony Eden, was in Cairo and he came hurtling down with General Wavell, the

Commander-in-Chief. There were three days of turbulent conferences in which General Platt [10] sought to win his fellow Britons over to his way of thinking against the arguments of the Emperor, but was roundly rebuffed by them. Platt's view was already well known. He did not approve of proposals whereby a thousand or so soldiers, "in two or three packets," should be launched "into the mountains of Abyssinia, against a European led enemy vastly superior in the air, in ground numbers and in armament, on nebulous information with no known local chieftains to rely on for support and insurrection." He stated frankly to Eden that if the Emperor went into Ethiopia, he should do so "as part of my baggage," and was surprised and hurt by the vehemence of Eden's reply and his warm praise of the Emperor's qualities, courage and importance. Eden's heated advocacy of the Ethiopian monarch was so forcefully stated that Platt was momentarily crushed, but resentful. "How they must hate me," the War Minister wrote in his diary that night.

The upshot of the meeting was no treaty but an agreement to recognize Haile Selassie as leader of a war of liberation, to be given full freedom of movement, and to be kept in touch with every development which concerned Ethiopia. The Ethiopian refugees were to be armed and trained and known as the Patriot Army. The rebellion was to be encouraged with arms and money and coordinated by a trained staff, which Eden promised to send down from Cairo. He kept his word. In Cairo he confirmed the choice General Wavell made of two officers to go south to join the Patriot Army, one, Major Tuckey, from the Deputy Quartermaster General's Department, and the other an artillery officer named Orde Wingate.

Orde Wingate, as readers of the author's biography of him, *Gideon Goes to War*, may already know, was one of the controversial military figures of the Second World War. He was a Scot by birth, a religious zealot, and, though not a Jew himself, an avowed and perfervid supporter of Zionism.

He had arrived in the Middle East after a bruising time at the hands of the War Office—which had placed an embargo on his reentry into Palestine and turned down his proposal to raise an anti-Nazi army among the Jews—and was at first lukewarm to Wavell's proposal that he should join the Ethiopian patriots. But then he caught fire. He had begun by browsing through the files at GHQ Middle East, and what first quickened his interest was a letter he found

[10] Sir Stewart Symes had by this time been removed.

there gathering dust. It had been sent by a lieutenant and four sergeants in the Australian Army, on service in the Middle East, who had spent a leave in Jerusalem. There they had met a number of Ethiopian priests and refugees (among them Ras Kassa) and talked to them about their dreams of liberating their country. They were deeply impressed and they wrote a naïve but moving letter to their commander, who forwarded it on, in which they said: "For the first time this war begins to make sense to us. We have all read about the conquest of small countries by big ones, of the brutal aggressions of Hitler and Mussolini. But in Jerusalem, from these simple Ethiopians, we learned for the first time from the lips of the victims what conquest can mean, and what liberation can mean too. We began to see that we are in the Middle East for a reason, and that we have a part to play. We hope that the part we play will be concerned with the liberation of Ethiopia. Hence this letter. It is a formal notification that the undersigned are prepared to volunteer for service, in any circumstances or conditions which you may designate, in any operation planned for the liberation of Ethiopia. We should be honoured to fight with any army pledged to bring the Emperor and his exiled followers back to their capital."

Wingate read the letter and was uplifted. He sent a memorandum to Wavell with the letter attached and ended it with the words: "I should like to have these men report to me at once. They shall be my first volunteers."

It so happened that the author was with Wingate in the plane which took him south from Cairo to his new duties in Khartoum, and I found him reticent about what he was going to do. I wrote at the time: "He sat at the window of the flying boat either staring fixedly at the Nile below us or reading a Bible. During the halt at Luxor he rushed swiftly away to walk around Karnak on his own and had to be fetched to rejoin the flight. It was my first view of him: in a mussed-up gabardine uniform around which a Sam Browne belt was loosely fastened, an old-fashioned solar topee on his head, a fly whisk on one finger and an alarm clock on another, his face jutting from his shoulders like the carved head of an American hero on one of those cliffs in the Far West. It was a face too big for the body below it, and its top-heavy look was increased by the luminosity of the large blue eyes. On this day they were half glazed and brooding, as if part of their candle power had been shuttered off from inside. He was very calm and amiable with the other passengers, but it was obvious that he hardly knew they existed. He sat in the plane like a torpid eagle, relaxing in a broody somnolence while there was still time."

Twenty-four hours after his arrival he was the talk of Khartoum. The tendency at first was to make fun of him, for he cut a strange figure. He had chosen as his chief aide Captain Douglas Dodds-Parker, an immaculate officer of the Grenadier Guards, who happened to be at least five inches over six feet tall. To see these two men, one as straight and tall as a birch tree, the other as small and bent as a desert shrub, walking down a corridor of GHQ in Khartoum was a laughable experience. At each door a Sudani *syce* would rise and salute, and get a slam-bang reply, in the best Guardsman tradition, from Dodds-Parker, while Wingate would flick a preoccupied and flaccid hand to his topee. His shorts hung below his knees and his bush-shirt was ill-fitting. His stockings had wrinkles in them and his pocket buttons were undone. Those who started by laughing at him ended by being irritated, particularly by the fly whisk—in a country which prided itself on an absence of mosquitoes and flies—and scandalized by stories that he dined on bowls of onions eaten raw and brushed himself all over with a toothbrush rather than bathed. He was also apt to receive visitors to his room completely naked, except for the alarm clock on his finger.

But Wingate endeared himself to Haile Selassie by reporting to General Platt and immediately having a row with him—though Wingate at the time was a mere major. He said to the Kaid: "I am appalled by the lack of progress which has been made in implementing our promise to the Emperor. He has been told that we would help him to reconquer his country, but nothing has been done."

The Commander-in-Chief, taken aback, replied that every feasible means had been utilized to help the Ethiopian cause. What about Sandford? Was he not inside Ethiopia stirring up revolt?

"And what has happened to him?" asked Wingate. "No one here cares whether Sandford and his Mission are alive or dead. None of his appeals for help has been answered. I cannot help coming to the conclusion, sir, that the conduct of the revolt so far shows poverty of invention combined with an intention to limit its scope below what is possible and desirable."

The Kaid looked at him in astonishment and then said: "Perhaps, Major Wingate, your arrival in the Sudan will change all this. No doubt you have plans."

"I have," replied Wingate, evenly. "I hope I may count on your cooperation in carrying them out."

He left GHQ and climbed into a car which took him to the Pink Palace beside the Nile where the dispirited Haile Selassie was waiting for him. It was typical of Wingate that he had taken care to learn beforehand how many times to bow to the Emperor as he approached him, and the soft brown eyes twinkled with a suspicion of cynical amusement as the untidy figure approached, making its exaggerated obeisances. Wingate had brought a prepared statement which he read:

I bring you most respectful greetings, Sire. In 1935 fifty-two nations let you and your country down. That act of aggression led to this war. It shall be the first to be avenged. I come as adviser to you and the forces that will take you back to your country and your throne. We offer you freedom and an equal place among the nations. But it will be no sort of place if you have no share in your own liberation. You will take the leading part in what is to come.

The Emperor reflected upon Wingate and his words. "What part can I play?" he finally said. "Nothing is being done. They have even prevented my fugitive people from coming here from Kenya. I sit here and time passes. I am being used as a pawn."

Wingate said: "That is not so. You will play your part. I remind you of an ancient proverb: 'If I am not for myself, who will be with me?' You must trust to the justice of your cause."

Haile Selassie smiled. "Yes, Major Wingate. But can I also trust the justice of your superiors?"

"You have my word on it," said Wingate.

But he knew when he left that first audience that he had spoken with more confidence than the facts warranted. It was not only bad faith with which the Emperor had to contend but also with incompetence and lack of vision, and sometimes with downright spite. For instance, there was the matter of the Umbrella. Someone in the Sudan Civil Service had written a memorandum pointing out that the Emperor of Ethiopia always ceremonially marched under the canopy of a state umbrella. The administration sent to India and ordered one to be made by the contractor to a maharajah. In Khartoum the umbrella was decorated with sequins and the Ethiopian colors and put into a jewelled box and delivered to the Pink Palace.

Fortunately, just before George Steer handed it over to the Emperor, he looked inside. Some Government House wit had enclosed a verse:

A little gift, a puny thing,
Meet for a small but royal head.
In gold and silver, laid in red,
Umbrella, one, in case, for King.

It was rather like delivering a royal scepter with a jokey poem to the Queen of England.[11]

The refugees were shipped north from Kenya and sweated at bayonet drill under the hot Sudan sun and the abrasive voices of British sergeants. Envoys had begun to come across the frontier from Ethiopia in response to the call from General Platt and they were sent back with arms and ammunition. At Gedaref they saw the Emperor, in a General's uniform, review a battalion of Ethiopian infantrymen and returned to their own country to broadcast the news that Janhoi, their Majesty, was back among them with a vast force at his disposal. (It was, in fact, not yet two battalions strong.) British, French, Kenyan, South African and Australian volunteers were coming forward to officer the Ethiopian companies. They were a heterogeneous band of scholars, writers, adventurers, white hunters, scamps and drunks. Among their steadier and more respectable element were such men as Allen, a history don, Laurence van der Post, who divined for water, the Comte de Sibour, who had flown for the Emperor back in 1930, and Wilfred Thesiger, a Roman-nosed giant whose father had befriended both Menelik and Tafari. Wingate galvanized them with continual conferences at which he stalked his room in the Grand Hotel, Khartoum, naked and toothbrushing himself. He was bitterly dissatisfied with the paucity of the weapons provided for his Patriot Army by the military authorities, but he made a virtue out of his weakness. He had made a fuss after the Gedaref review because pictures had been published in the newspapers of the Emperor taking the salute of the Patriots from a car.

"There are some of you who still wonder why I became enraged at the photograph of Haile Selassie in the car. I am told the little man himself thinks I am trying to stop him getting publicity and crabbing it for myself. Not so. I have repeatedly pointed out that

---

11 Wingate, incidentally, was annoyed that the umbrella had been given at all, on the grounds that the Italians had made mockery of such attributes of majesty. He had the umbrella taken away. Haile Selassie surreptitiously got it back.

we are engaged on a campaign in which Haile Selassie is David and the Italians are Goliath.[12] The smaller and weaker Haile Selassie seems, the better. The Ethiopians must believe, to secure their co-operation, that their Emperor comes not on the backs of the British but by his own efforts and courage—and that, if they care for it sufficiently, they will fight for their freedom too, no matter what the odds."

One of his aides, Douglas Dodds-Parker, one of the few who dared to talk back to Wingate, said quietly: "I can't help thinking, Orde, that you are making a sob-story out of necessity. I am all for human courage and David versus Goliath, but I wish we could just get enough elastic to provide David with a sling."

In the midst of these preparations, something happened to plunge the Emperor's spirits into the depths from which they had been slowly lifting. News reached him, probably through George Steer, that a certain Colonel Brocklehurst had arrived in Cairo in December, 1940, and had had talks with General Wavell. Brocklehurst was an ex-game warden who had conducted safaris in Ethiopia and had conceived, for no explicable reason, a hatred of Haile Selassie and a firm belief that neither he ·nor any other Amhara had the right to rule the Ethiopians. He appears to have had the backing of certain elements in Kenya and Rhodesia who were already dreaming of a postwar East African Federation—under British colonial control—and were not averse to including in it a large slice of land from Southern Ethiopia, where the earth was fertile and hospitable. Brocklehurst succeeded in convincing Wavell, for a time, at least, that the Galla tribes would never be persuaded to rise against the Italians if they had to do so under the aegis of Haile Selassie and that the spur necessary to get them moving was a promise that they would be given an autonomous Galla state after the war, independent of Amhara exploitation.

Now it is true that some of the Gallas in the North, particularly the Azebu Gallas, had been bribed to fight against the Emperor during the Italo-Ethiopian War; but the Azebus were one of the few Galla tribes which had not intermarried with the Amharas and Shoans. Many others had adopted the Ethiopian Church and long since intermingled their blood with the rest of Ethiopia. They had come first to the land as conquerors, had been conquered in their turn by Menelik, and had now been absorbed. When he heard the

12 Wingate was fond of equating himself or those associated with him with biblical characters.

news of Brocklehurst's mission, the Emperor began to suspect that once more Britain was letting him down—or, even worse, perhaps conspiring against him for their own selfish reasons. But for a time he did nothing about it.

Someone, however, told Wingate, who rushed to the Emperor and roused him to action. "The theory of the Brocklehurst Mission means dividing Ethiopia against herself. You must get into touch with London and tell them that you suspect the motives behind this move and smell a colonial plot."

Haile Selassie sent a telegram to Churchill conveying his alarm and suspicion, and from Wavell came an assurance a few days later that Brocklehurst and his cohorts would be warned off the Gallas and left to sweat it out this side of the Ethiopian border. The Emperor's spirits rose again—and even higher when he learned shortly afterwards that the time had come to move.

chapter seventeen

STATE ENTRY

ON JANUARY 20, 1941, at forty minutes past noon, Emperor Haile Selassie crossed the frontier from the Sudan into his own country for the first time since 1936 and raised the Ethiopian flag once more on Ethiopian soil. The author was one of those present and a reading of the dispatch I wrote as the special correspondent of *The Times* makes it seem like a most impressive martial occasion. For that the censorship authorities in Khartoum can be thanked. Unlike Wingate, they were anxious to suggest that this was a ceremony full of majestic panoply, and all references to its more humble and touching moments were eliminated from my dispatch. So this is how *The Times* report reads, in part.

"We who had been informed of [the Emperor's] courageous decision preceded him, travelling by camel across a great tract of wild country to the airfield on which his machine was to land. It was just after noon when we who were waiting on the frontier heard the roar of airplane engines announcing the Emperor's arrival from Khartoum [*in fact he had arrived from the adjacent village of Roseires*]. Soon, while a fighter escort wheeled overhead, Haile Selassie's machine shaved the treetops and side-slipped to a landing on the airfield which had been hacked out of the jungle. [*The use of the words 'side-slipped' must have indicated that this was no modern machine; it was in fact an old Valentia troop carrier with a maximum speed of 100 mph. The 'fighter escort' consisted of two biplane Gloucester Gauntlets.*]

"The frontier between Abyssinia and the Sudan at these points is marked by a dried river bed in which rocky pools, still infested with crocodiles, are the only signs that the river in the rainy season is a roaring torrent. [*The place was Um Iddla, on the Dinder River,*

*in the midst of the Dinder Game Reserve, and the original word to
describe the pools was 'stagnant' as those of us who had to share water
from it with our camels came to know; we had no disinfectants so
we wiped off the scum and laced it, the Emperor included, with
whisky.*] Thick jungle, in which elephant, lion, giraffe and buck
roam, crowds down to each side of the steep banks. Storks were circling overhead in the noonday blaze as the moment for the Emperor's
arrival approached. It was exactly 12:40 that Haile Selassie set his
foot on the runway down to the river bed and began the fifty yards'
walk across the sand back into Abyssinia. In the exact centre of
the river bed a flagpole had been erected, and behind, under the command of a British major, was a company of Ethiopian troops to
welcome their sovereign. He was dressed in khaki drill and sun
helmet and behind him were his two sons, the Crown Prince and the
Duke of Harar. His entourage of British Army advisers [*Chapman-
Andrews*] and members of his Court followed. Among them was that
famous warrior, Ras Kassa, who led Abyssinia's northern army in the
campaign against Italy in 1935.

"As the Emperor reached the bottom of the runway a British
officer detached himself from the delegation awaiting him and bade
him Godspeed on the hazardous journey lying before him. [*It was
Wingate, who was to go with him; General Platt was attending to
military operations against Eritrea and could not spare anyone.*]
Haile Selassie, speaking in Amharic, said in reply: 'I wish to thank
you for your message. I am now entering Ethiopia with full confidence of the assistance of the British Government in order to crush
our common enemy. It is a great task which lies before me, but I
hope to carry it out successfully with the aid of Allied forces. I thank
those British officers who are already fighting for me inside my
country. Before I go I would like to say that I shall never forget the
sympathetic feelings which the British public have shown me in my
hours of painful tribulation. I understand, and I am grateful to them.'

"A high dignitary of the Ethiopian Church [*the Itchege*] then
blessed the Emperor's project and Haile Selassie, leaving his entourage
behind him, marched out of the shadow of the river bank into the
sun. When he reached the flagpole just across the border he hauled
the flag to the top of the pole. The red, green and gold standard,
with the Lion of Judah inset, fluttered in the light breeze. As it
did so, and as Haile Selassie stepped back, the troops awaiting him
came to the salute and the Ethiopian bugler blared a triumphant

welcome to Abyssinian soil." [*In fact there were several minor mishaps; the troops were ragged in their drill, the smell of camel dung was heavy in the air, the bugler collapsed halfway through, and someone had forgotten to bring the champagne from Khartoum. The toast to Ethiopia was drunk in some bottles of beer rescued from an officer's kitbag.*]

The following day Wingate set out to blaze a trail across the bushland of the Ethiopian frontier into the highlands of Ethiopia. The object was to take the Emperor to a tableland kingdom, known as Belaya, which had never been conquered by the Italians and still acknowledged the Emperor's suzerainty. Wingate was using maps, provided by Major Cheesman from his days in Western Ethiopia, on which certain tracks were marked; and there followed a series of disasters the responsibility for which it is now not necessary to determine. A fellow correspondent named Kenneth Anderson, representing Reuter's Agency, followed Wingate (who was on a horse) in a lorry. A platoon of Ethiopian Patriots came behind and then the Emperor was supposed to follow in another lorry.

"We had a rendezvous with Ethiopian tribesmen on Belaya," said Anderson,[1] "but nobody in our lot really knew quite where Belaya was nor where, in fact, the Italians were. The only available maps were those made by the RAF from the air [in fact, Cheesman's]. Wingate was leading the way, guiding himself only by instinct and a compass. I drove my truck for eight days through such dense bush that we averaged only five to six miles a day from sun-up to sun-down." Wingate, tireless, riding his beast until it had saddle sores, tried to goad them on. Anderson went on: "He was certainly one of the most ruthless chaps I have ever met. Absolutely fearless, tireless and at times uncouth. He never bothered to shave or wash. On the rare occasions when we came to a waterhole, he would lower his trousers and squat with his bottom cooling in the water. But that was as far as he went with his ablutions."

At the end of the eighth day the lorry shook itself to pieces. Wingate rode on ahead to Belaya and then, having exhausted his horse and a camel, continued on foot. He reached his rendezvous on January 31 but did not send back to the Emperor any indication of the ordeal that was awaiting him. Instead of going along beaten paths, Wingate had either followed the faulty map or gone on a

[1] In a note to the author.

compass bearing, and the terrain was appalling—a mixture of volcanic rock, dust bowl and scrub. Nevertheless, he assured the Emperor that the route was open and should be followed. In his message Wingate indicated that he was at that moment at a pool where the elephants water ("you can tell it by the droppings") and calculated that he was only twenty miles from the Massif of Belaya, which could easily be reached by motor transport.

In the author's biography of Wingate, the following passage seems to be justified.

"It was one of [Wingate's] moments of whopping over-optimism. The lorries carrying Haile Selassie, Chapman-Andrews (his political adviser) and his retinue were led by Major Boyle, commanding the 2nd Patriot Battalion. The first day they did well over 30 miles through heavy underbush and almost stupefying heat, and were forced to camp in the bush without water; and next day, the lorries, without water, covered an even smaller mileage. It was two and a half days before they reached the 'Elephants' Water Hole' and there they found water aplenty and took heart. The Emperor even demonstrated how to fish in the pool with a mosquito net and provided the party with its supper for the evening. He looked pale and frail, and the ebony colour of his face was beginning to have a queer green glow, but he never complained about the hardships and put his shoulder to the chassis when a lorry overturned or got stuck in the sand."

On February 2, forty-eight hours after Wingate had calculated that they would reach Belaya, the Emperor's party found the dried river bed where Kenneth Anderson had abandoned his lorry. Across the plain was Belaya, lifting into the brassy Ethiopian sky like a beckoning hand, so clear that its cool green heights looked only a few miles away. But by this time Chapman-Andrews was beginning to grow skeptical both about the distances on this pitiless plain and about Wingate's route to the cool heights. He rode out with a fellow major to look for tracks; they realized that from here on there would be no more trail-blazing by Anderson's lorry. They met Wingate coming in to meet them, pushing his exhausted horse hard to make speed. He looked near to exhaustion himself; his hair was tangled and his face yellow with mud. He admitted in a few words to the Emperor that he had made a mistake and that the massif was still fifty miles away. It was decided that Haile Selassie should ride back with him to Belaya—for a lorry would never get through—and three more days went by. The route was fetid with the smell of dead or dying camels.[2] It was a black and scorched landscape, skies filled with vultures, ground scuffed and trampled by ravening hyenas, the air and everyone's sweaty skin abuzz with blowflies. Of that phase of the Emperor's return all the censor allowed me to say was: "Haile Selassie is now 300 miles inside his kingdom."

On February 6, 1941, at last, they reached Belaya. On the last few hundred yards of the journey Wingate kept prodding the Emperor's horse to make it go faster. At last Haile Selassie fell back, saying: "You go first, Colonel Wingate. And let us hope that the people will recognize which one of us is their Emperor."

It had been a journey that would have killed any man who was really as frail or as supine as the Emperor looked.

A smart Alfa Romeo limousine with a liveried Ethiopian chauffeur arrived at Wingate's headquarters outside Debra Marcos, the capital of the Gojjam, on April 4, 1941. Thus far had the Patriot Army fought its way and either overcome or forced the Italians into flight. The car belonged to that impermeable old rascal, Ras Hailu, and had been sent to bring the commander of the Patriot Army to his headquarters. Wingate was shrewd enough to refuse the soft seat of the Italian car and ride in by lorry, but neither he nor his British assistants were clever enough to withstand the blandishments that followed. One of Wingate's officers, Hugh Boustead, was instructed to remain behind and accept Hailu's surrender. He was received by the old man clad in an Italian uniform, a picture of quietly confident dignity, and roundly told that Hailu had been mainly responsible for the Italian retreat, and that he had it in his hands to keep the Gojjam quiet or spur it to civil war. Boustead was fool enough to believe him. In fact his control over the Gojjam was finished and he was recognized by the people as a pathetic Italian puppet.

But the damage was done. The British protective arm was wrapped around the traitor's shoulders, and Haile Selassie had to accept it. He drove into Debra Marcos on April 6 to accept Ras Hailu's surrender and was kept waiting for half an hour before the old man appeared. The ceremony bewildered the populace, who expected to looloo ecstatically over the Emperor's return and the exhibition of their former ruler with a chain around his neck, instead of which they got only Ras Hailu's formal bow and his retirement with what George Steer

[2] Wingate used 25,000 camels on his expedition. All of them died, probably due to overloading, before they reached Addis Ababa.

described as "a graven scowl on his face." The Emperor accepted this obviously casual act of contrition—for the time.[3] At the moment he had other things to worry about. It was obvious that the war in Ethiopia was almost over. A fortnight or so earlier, he had received a visitor from Khartoum who had flown to the airstrip now constructed at Belaya to tell him of British plans for Ethiopia once the campaigning was concluded. In Cairo a plan had been drawn up for the administration of Ethiopia, which would come under military control. The military administration would be known as OETA, otherwise Occupied Enemy Territory Administration. It was a fatuous name to have given to the administration of what was obviously *liberated* territory—for Ethiopia had not ceased to be Ethiopia just because the British Government had cravenly accepted its conquest by the Italians—and only a dunderhead or someone antipathetic to the Emperor and the Ethiopians would have ignored this fact. The envoy charged with the task of telling the Emperor what was planned was Brigadier Lush, a Sudan Civil Servant who was also Brigadier Sandford's brother-in-law. Sandford had a heated argument with Lush in which he told him that the Emperor would never accept such an insult, and Lush finally consented to fly back and get some adjustments made.

Meanwhile, as the Emperor was addressing his subjects in Debra Marcos, a radio message reached Wingate from Khartoum. It informed him that the South African armed forces under General Cunningham, having pushed up from the south—against next to no opposition—were that day entering Addis Ababa. He was ordered to halt all further operations for the moment. His reply was to request that a plane be sent immediately so that the Emperor could be flown to his capital and so receive the homage and welcome of his people. The request was refused. He was sternly ordered to keep the Emperor where he was. When he protested, he was told: "There are 25,000 Italians in Addis Ababa. White people. If the Emperor arrives, the natives will panic. They will go wild and start looting and raping, and the Italians will all be killed. So keep the little man out."

This was followed by peremptory commands from General Cunningham telling Wingate to halt any impulse of the Emperor to approach Addis Ababa by "everything short of force." It was, however, the sort of instruction not likely to sway Wingate, who distrusted the generals, the Middle East Command, and the South

[3] But he kept Ras Hailu in semi-confinement near at hand for the rest of the old warlord's life.

African troops in Addis Ababa. He hardly needed to encourage Haile Selassie, who was anxious to reach his capital as soon as possible; he also suspected white plots, and wanted to be in his capital to frustrate them.

The Emperor made his state entry into Addis Ababa on May 5, 1941. He had paused en route to pray at Debra Libanos, where two of the sons of Ras Kassa and two hundred monks had been shot by the Italians for sheltering patriots. He halted again to pray at the church of St. Mariam, on a hill overlooking the city. Then his procession formed up for the triumphal entry. Wingate rode a white horse (and got his knees severely chafed, for he had no riding breeches and rode in shorts) but Haile Selassie typically chose a less gaudy entry. He sat in the back of the Alfa Romeo car that Ras Hailu had turned over to him.

On a rostrum in front of the old palace General Cunningham and a guard of King's African Rifles were waiting for him, no hint on the General's face of his irritation at the Emperor's premature arrival.

Haile Selassie solemnly acknowledged the loolooing greeting from the ecstatic crowds and then sniffed the air, taking in that scent of eucalyptus and spice which is the peculiar body odor of Addis Ababa. He looked very small beside the British officers around him, but somehow loomed very large.

"On this day," he said, "which men of earth and angels of heaven could neither have foreseen nor known, I owe thanks unutterable by the mouth of man to the loving God who has enabled me to be present among you. Today is the beginning of a new era in the history of Ethiopia. . . . Since this is so, do not reward evil for evil. Do not commit any act of cruelty like those which the enemy committed against us up to this present time. Do not allow the enemy any occasion to foul the good name of Ethiopia. We shall take his weapons and make him return by the way he came."

The crowd shrieked anew, but there was only joy and no hate in them. With a few words Haile Selassie had quelled with his presence what General Cunningham had thought it would most likely provoke —a riot against the Italians. The crowd stayed around for several hours, and then drifted away to celebrate but not to loot.

That night the Emperor gave a small party for Wingate and his men, and for Cunningham and the officers of the South African Army.

Toward the end, for the first time, the hint of tremendous feeling was noticeable in what a hostile Englishman in Bath had once called "that dead pan face." Outside, in the cool blue night, fires flickered all over the hills, as bright as the bonfires of Maskal. The smell of eucalyptus smoke was pungent now.

"*Vraiment,*" said the Emperor, "*j'ai été très émotionné.*"

It was just five years to the day since Marshal Badoglio and the Italian Army had marched into Addis Ababa.

part five

HARSH REALITY

chapter eighteen

LIBERATED—OR NOT?

THE WAR IN ETHIOPIA dragged on for several months after the capture of Addis Ababa, but by the end of 1941 it was all over and the last Italian garrison (at Gondar) surrendered. Wingate had been recalled to Middle East headquarters in Cairo, his achievements and inspiration unrecognized by the military machine. Haile Selassie, who owed him so much and was deeply conscious of it, never had a chance to express his gratitude personally, for Wingate went on to die in Burma; but he made what was, for him, no empty gesture by becoming the god-father of Wingate's only son.

This was the most difficult phase of the Emperor's postwar reign and a new kind of War of Liberation began—against his Allies.

In February, 1941, two weeks after the Emperor had re-entered Ethiopia, Mr. Anthony Eden, who was always to be Haile Selassie's friend in the British Government,[1] read a statement in the House of Commons in which he said: "His Majesty's Government would welcome the reappearance of an independent Ethiopian State and recognize the claim of Emperor Haile Selassie to the throne. The Emperor has intimated to his Majesty's Government that he will need outside assistance and guidance. His Majesty's Government agree with this view and consider that any such assistance and guidance in economic and political matters should be the subject of international arrangement at the conclusion of peace. They reaffirm that they have themselves no territorial ambitions in Abyssinia. In the meantime the conduct of military operations by Imperial forces in parts of Abyssinia will require temporary measures of military guidance and con-

[1] A purely intellectual amity, I may say. They had little personally in common and never established a rapport during their meetings.

trol. These will be carried out in consultation with the Emperor, and will be brought to an end as soon as the situation permits."

It was a welcome statement but it was vague. What, for instance, did "temporary measures of military guidance and control" mean and to what extent would they be carried out "in consultation with the Emperor"? Haile Selassie soon discovered that all General Cunningham had been told from GHQ Middle East was to "establish an administration" and so far as he was concerned Ethiopia was conquered, and not liberated, territory. It was therefore put under the control of the OETA (Occupied Enemy Territory Administration) which had been established in Nairobi by a talented but vastly superior ex-Colonial Governor named Sir Philip Mitchell. Sir Philip did not have any specialized knowledge of Ethiopia but he did know how to deal with native chiefs, having been Governor of Uganda, and the problem of handling Haile Selassie, in spite of his high-sounding title, did not seem to him to present any particular difficulties; after all, they had colored "kings" in Uganda, too.

In a book which he wrote after the War, Sir Philip (a South African by birth) maintains that the bitter tug-of-war which began between his administration and the Emperor in 1941 was entirely due to a misunderstanding on the part of Haile Selassie.

"It has to be admitted," he wrote,[2] "that the Emperor became suspicious of our intentions and resentful of what he—sincerely, no doubt but mistakenly—supposed to be our designs on his full sovereignty. I dare say the fact that I had been a colonial governor had some effect on his mind. Our intentions were, in fact, exactly what the Emperor himself desired."

Immediately after the Emperor's return the first clash came. To Haile Selassie the situation was simple. He had returned to his kingdom and resumed his rightful position on his throne, and he was Emperor again. His first move was to announce the appointment of seven Ministers to head his new Government. At once, on Sir Philip Mitchell's instructions from Nairobi, his representative in Addis Ababa, Brigadier Lush (a Sudan Civil Servant in time of peace and no lover of the *habashi*) hurried to the palace to berate him for presumption.

To Walda Giorgis, Haile Selassie's chief aide, he made the astonishing statement; "His Majesty cannot fully reassume his status and powers as Emperor until a peace treaty has been signed with Italy.

[2] Sir P. Mitchell, *African Afterthoughts* (Hutchinson & Co.).

Until that happens the King of Italy remains the legal ruler of Ethiopia."

The Emperor received this announcement at first with disbelief and then with anger and he roundly refused to accede to the demand that he annul his appointments (though eventually he did agree to term them Minister Designates). From this first encounter began what might be called the War of the Patriots and the Cromerites. The Patriots were led by the Emperor, of course, aided and advised by his old English friend, Brigadier Sandford, a perfervid fighter for Ethiopian independence in peace as well as in war. The Cromerites had as their leaders Sir Philip Mitchell and his chief representative in Ethiopia, Brigadier Lush, who, as has been mentioned, was Sandford's brother-in-law. In her biography of the Emperor, Mrs. Sandford, no doubt for family reasons, mentions nothing of the bitter arguments which took place between her husband and her brother, but Sir Philip writes: "It is a characteristic of the Briton in such circumstances that he develops a sort of apostolic fervour and there were occasions, in the months that followed, when I sometimes wondered if Brigadier Sandford, in his devotion to the Emperor's interests, was really going to break off relations with Great Britain!"

It was, however, a rather more sinister situation than Sir Philip's light-hearted remarks would indicate. Lush and his staff, all of them either from the Sudan or Kenya,[3] left those who listened to them in little doubt that they were not going to let Haile Selassie get his hands on Ethiopia again if they could help it. Gordon Waterfield, who was in charge of propaganda in Addis Ababa at this time wrote: [4] "British officers in charge of the political administration, a rapidly growing organization, were talking openly of establishing control over Ethiopia on the Sudan model with political officers throughout the country. Feeling ran high between the two parties. . . . All the old arguments were brought up about the benefits of British control. They did not like to see the Italian improvements, which had cost millions of pounds, go down the drain under the Ethiopian administration; besides that, Ethiopia was regarded as a rich pendant to the Sudan, including as it did Lake Tsana and the source of the Blue Nile."

The suspicion grew, and not only among the Ethiopians, that Sir Philip Mitchell was thinking of utilizing the confused legal situation

---

[3] Where the *Standard* in Nairobi was reporting: "Suddenly we have had a very large addition to our African Empire."

[4] G. Waterfield, *Morning will Come* (John Murray).

to have himself appointed Viceroy of Ethiopia, a rather far-fetched possibility, since he, an Englishman, would have been *vice* to the King of Italy; but certainly the Emperor had strong reasons for believing that a party was building up among the British to push him off his throne, or failing that, to turn him into a puppet dancing to strings pulled in Nairobi.[5]

Sir Philip Mitchell did nothing to allay these suspicions by his actions in the middle months of 1941. He flew to Addis Ababa on his way to London and had his first meeting with the Emperor at the palace on May 23. It was a meeting both frigid and formal and Haile Selassie must have found his "dead pan face" useful on this occasion, for a cynical smile might otherwise have passed over it as Sir Philip explained that he was flying to London to obtain "clarification" of "the next phase" of Anglo-Ethiopian relations. The Emperor knew from his own sources that the chief of OETA was going to London with one object only—to sabotage any plan the Cabinet might have for an Anglo-Ethiopian Agreement. It is true that he took with him a number of requests from the Emperor which he promised to submit to the Cabinet, chief of which was the production of a draft Treaty.[6] But Sir Philip spent most of his time, after his arrival in London on May 31, 1941, in trying to persuade Mr. Anthony Eden that no draft Treaty should be produced for some considerable time to come. In this he was unsuccessful, for Mr. Eden was determined to demonstrate to the world by example in this, the first territory liberated by the British in the War, that there were no strings attached to British cooperation.

Even so, the negotiations took time and relations between the Ethiopians and the British in Addis Ababa ebbed in the interim. Some of the South African troops in the city did not help to endear the pink skins to the brown, for they had entered Ethiopia not only as conquerors but with their knapsacks stuffed with prejudices about colored people. The Ethiopians were just another race of kaffirs, only much more arrogant and presumptuous, and there were many painful incidents when, liquored-up with tej or whisky, they began tossing Ethiopian officers from bars and Ethiopian rases from the sidewalks. It was the rases (and particularly Ras Abebe Aregai, who had fought

[5] "At just about this time I received a signal from the War Office," wrote Sir Philip, "saying that ... Italian sovereignty remained until formally terminated by HM Government. It seemed to me that I was over-establishment in sovereigns."

[6] The others were: 1, that he be helped immediately to establish an army; 2, that he be given financial aid; 3, that he be sent advisers to his ministries, and 4, that he be helped to establish his provincial administrations.

on against the Italians through the occupation) who began to question the Emperor's patience and wonder aloud whether he was really the strong man the country needed; his subservience to the British, Aregai suggested, was humiliating. Haile Selassie decided that he could allow the British to procrastinate no longer, and without informing any member of OETA (who expected to be kept in touch) of his intention, he sent a telegram direct to Winston Churchill in London asking why the treaty between the two countries was not forthcoming. The British Prime Minister replied that the delay was due entirely to the desire of the British Government to ensure that nothing remained in the agreement "which could be interpreted as interfering with your sovereign rights or the independence of Ethiopia." The Emperor hastened to the radio to publicize the message and emphasized that "if there are any anxious people who feel that the British now wish to restrict our independence, let them realize their error when they consider this note from the Prime Minister."

His warlords were silenced for the moment. But one cannot escape the feeling that the Cromerites, once they realized that their cause was lost, were motivated by most spiteful intentions toward Ethiopia, as if, failing to gain control of the kingdom, they wished to demonstrate how badly it would do without them. The Anglo-Ethiopian Agreement was signed on January 31, 1942, and it was, considering that the war was far from won, a generous one. The British made it clear from the start that they regarded Emperor Haile Selassi as undoubted Head of the State. He was to be given financial and military aid and the help of British advisers, but with the minimum political control whatsoever. True, they asked and were conceded supervision of the railway from Addis Ababa to Dire Dawa (the outlet through Jibouti was, at the time, blocked by the Vichy French), a strip of land alongside French Somaliland, and military control of the whole of the Ogaden. This latter concession was most reluctantly conceded by the Emperor, who was always to be particularly sensitive about any suggestion that the Ogaden (controlled from his beloved Harar) or any part of it should pass, even temporarily, from Ethiopian control.[7] But finally he gave way, and the agreement was signed. Sir Philip Mitchell wrote in his diary: "January 31, 1942. 8 P.M. to 11 P.M. Reception at the Palace. Very cordial indeed; all the Ministers

---

[7] He has not yet forgiven a British Under-Secretary for presuming on old friendship (he had served on Wingate's staff during the War) to try to persuade him to cede part of the Ogaden to Somalia after that country gained its independence; and he has, of course, reacted swiftly to more recent Somali infiltrations.

and Rases assured me they were delighted by the Agreement and the atmosphere could not have been better. The Agreement was read to a group of Rases and Notables yesterday and greeted with applause. There can be no doubt that it is genuinely welcomed. I found the Emperor, Empress and the Princes and Rases all beaming smiles."

But there were others who felt less cordial. There was, for instance, the position of the Italians in Ethiopia. These now numbered some 70,000 in the whole of Ethiopia (not counting Eritrea), of whom some 30,000 were now concentrated in Addis Ababa. In many quarters at home, and among the British and South African military in Africa, there had been lively fears that the Ethiopians would use this body of enemy nationals as a convenient whipping boy for the sufferings they themselves had endured at the hands of the Italians during the occupation. Rape and slaughter were expected once the Patriot troops were allowed into Addis Ababa, and for this reason Ras Abebe Aregai was told by General Cunningham that only 700 of his men would be allowed to line the streets when the Emperor rode back in triumph. Aregai ignored the order and paraded 10,000 of his men, but they went quietly back to the camps when ordered to do so by the Emperor. Even Miss Margery Perham, a good friend of the Ethiopians, had anticipated the shedding of Italian blood at the hands of vengeful Ethiopians, and she had written to *The Times* early in 1941: "Let us ask ourselves whether we should not bitterly regret to learn that there had been massacres of women and children or mutilation of prisoners which action on our part might have prevented. The word 'Abyssinia' covers not only the Emperor and those of his civilized assistants who escaped Graziani's massacre but such wild tribesmen, thirsting for revenge or loot, who may constitute themselves his auxiliaries and therefore our allies. If terrible things are done by these men which might have been prevented, the memory of them will add another chapter to the vendetta between the two peoples, and will cloud the reconciliation we must hope to have with our ill-guided enemy."

If such a perceptive, knowledgeable and civilized student of African affairs could express such forebodings, the fears of the wilder whites in Ethiopia are to be imagined. They forecast rivers of Italian blood and the screams of ravished Italian women. They were somewhat taken aback when the slight increase in murders in Addis Ababa in which Italian corpses figured turned out to be those committed either by Greeks or Armenians seeking revenge upon their former occupiers, who had ruined them, or by Italians themselves. In the course of 1941 and 1942 several hundred nubile Italian women in Addis Ababa and other Ethiopian cities found themselves the objects of sexual attentions—but in almost all cases the enemy soldiers they eventually lay down with were white Allied troops eagerly offering them protection and food.

The surprise the Cromerites felt at Ethiopian good behavior gave place to irritation when it was noticed that they and their former enemies, far from hating or fearing each other, were getting together to share mutual grumbles about the British. "A certain number of influential Italians," wrote Gordon Waterfield, "were in daily touch with the Palace through Ethiopian officers, and Rases in the interior were using Italian officers and men to train Ethiopians in warfare. Distrust had been created in the minds of the Italians as well as in the minds of the Ethiopians which it was difficult to eliminate."

So, since the Italians seemed quite happy and contented to remain in Ethiopia, and since the Ethiopians had refrained from killing or ravishing them, the Cromerites decided to expel them from the country. The British commanders of OETA announced that a message had been sent to Mussolini telling him to send ships, under a flag of truce, to East Africa whence his Italians would be shipped back to him. Meanwhile they would be rounded up and placed in camps to await transport back to Italy. A wail of dismay arose from both sides. Since Graziani had massacred, among the 3,000 victims of his reprisals, all the skilled native technicians in the country, the Ethiopians relied upon the Italians to keep the mechanical side of the administration going—the telephone and electricity services, road maintenance and transport, mills, factories, hotels and shops. Without their help millions of dollars' worth of Italian enterprise would slowly run down to a standstill. The Cromerites shrugged their shoulders; one almost heard them saying: "Yah! Serves you right for not letting us take over."

Brigadier Sandford, who had made up his quarrel with his brother-in-law once the Anglo-Ethiopian Agreement was signed, went into battle with Brigadier Lush once more. He pointed out that not only did the Ethiopians need Italian help but that the Italians themselves were anxious to stay. (It was true. Hundreds of them went into hiding in Ethiopian homes the moment they heard of the British plans for their evacuation, and stayed under cover until it was safe to come out again.) But this time Lush was adamant. He and his two chief assistants, Lieut. Col. Belcher and Major Rennell (later Lord Rennell) Rodd set to work to round up the Italians and ship them out of the country. They organized a system of priorities so that, in Lush's words, "Addis Ababa will only die slowly."

It had not even definitely been decided where the 70,000 Italians would be sent, for East Africa was already crammed with prisoners taken from Libya and Cyrenaica and Somaliland, there was not enough shipping to send them to India, and Mussolini failed to send the ships he had promised.

"There was a period of real anxiety in April, 1942," reported Waterfield, "when thousands of Italian women and children had already been kept too long in the intense early summer heat at camps in Dire Dawa and Mandera in British Somaliland. Children were sickening; there was a shortage of water and green vegetables, and Italians were refusing to be evacuated and going into hiding, often helped by the Ethiopians. Many of the women were also recalcitrant. Opinion was very divided whether they wanted to go back to Italy."

But now that the disastrous decision had been taken no one was willing to admit that it was an act of folly if not spite. Slowly service began to sag in telephone exchanges and electricity stations, potholes appeared in the roads, buses ceased to run either from shortage of gasoline, of drivers or of mechanics to keep them in order; shops, dance clubs, hotels closed down. Appeals were made to Sweden for expert help, but the Swedes were too busy making money out of the war to spare mechanics for Ethiopia.

"It was our blackest time," said Taffera Work, now the principal aide to the Emperor. "We were desperately short of trained men. We were even more desperately short of money, for our financial requests from the British had been turned down.[8] We had little food and no petrol—for it cost two gallons of petrol to bring one gallon from the coast to the capital."

There was one other decision by the British which was hardly helpful to the Ethiopians in their difficult days of rehabilitation. It was the removal of all surplus war material from the country. Enormous amounts of it had been captured from the Italians, and it might have been thought that since it had been taken on Ethiopian soil it might have been left behind for the Ethiopians to use—especially transport, bulldozers and arms. The material was old-fashioned and

---

[8] The British refused to make a loan unless they were told how it would be spent and allowed to participate in the program of spending. The failure of the negotiations—conducted on the British side by Lord de la Warr—ended in Ethiopia's reversal to her own Maria Theresa currency instead of the East African shillings introduced by Britain. There were rumors of British operations against the M. T. Dollar as a reprisal; certainly, its value fluctuated thereafter.

the British had no intention of using it elsewhere; and the rifles alone would have been invaluable to the Emperor in rebuilding his army. But no. If the Ethiopians were going to be so arrogant and self-sufficient, they must suffer for it. So the whole of the material was taken out of the country, and much of it was left to rot on the roads south into Kenya and across the deserts of the Sudan.

chapter nineteen

INDEPENDENT AGAIN

IN THE MIDST of these political trials the Emperor was hit by a personal tragedy which affected him deeply. His twenty-year-old daughter, Tsahai, died. Until 1942 she had been in England training as a nurse and was on the verge of taking her final examinations at Guy's Hospital when Haile Selassie summoned the Empress to join him. She was too nervous to make the journey alone and so the Emperor ordered his daughter to accompany her; they were to travel in a hospital ship. Her old matron, Miss Emily MacMannus, writes:[1] "The Princess was very sad about this. She so badly wanted to become a State Registered Nurse of England so that, when she returned to her own country, she could hold an important position in her nation's health service. However, as always, she was her father's most loyal daughter.... Lady Barton (wife of Sir Sidney Barton) particularly had Princess Tsahai's career in her care. The Princess was already a State Registered Children's Nurse, trained at Great Ormonde Street Hospital, and she was to travel with her mother as a Red Cross nursing official. Lady Barton quite rightly said that the Princess must have some emblem on her shoulder straps; she must not look inferior to the Senior Red Cross ladies who would be travelling with them. Yet as she had not yet completed her training she was not entitled to any of the badges. 'I know,' said Lady Barton. 'The Lion of Judah. She shall wear that on her shoulder.' But when we told Princess Tsahai she said: 'No, that is my father's emblem. I know he would let me wear it but I cannot without his permission. But my mother's emblem —the Queen of Sheba—that I can wear!' So it was arranged."

Some months after her return to Addis Ababa she was married to

[1] In a note to the author.

a young warlord from the North, Colonel Abiye, of whom much was expected.[2] She died from a hemorrhage and a miscarriage some months later, and the first her parents knew of her death was when her husband led a wailing cortège of mourners who carried her body into the Palace. The Emperor dressed himself in his oldest clothes, covered himself with mud, as is the Ethiopian custom, and wept over her bier.

Tsahai was the second of his daughters to die in tragic circumstances —and that would not be all.

There was, however, one event that year to lift his heart. When the Italian armies began to collapse on their home ground the Emperor asked the new British Minister, Mr. Howe, to make inquiries about the whereabouts of his old friend, Ras Imru, who had been taken to Italy as a prisoner and hostage at the end of the Italo-Ethiopian War. Howe telegraphed the request to London and Churchill ordered a search to begin.

"Ras Imru's discovery was dramatic," wrote Major Cheesman in his diary. "A young British officer was rounding up Italian prisoners in a small village in Tuscany when he noticed a dark figure who, when questioned, gave his name as Ras Imru. It took a little time for the name, which seemed familiar, to sink in, and then the officer gasped: 'Why, you are the man the whole of our army is looking for.' "

Imru was taken to Rome and put on a plane for Ethiopia. The Emperor met him on the airfield and embraced and wept in the arms of his childhood friend. The first question he asked the Emperor was: "What have you done with that villain Hailu?"

"Oh," said the Emperor, "I keep him hanging around the palace all day, where he can't do anyone any harm."

It was perhaps inevitable that the deliberate slights inflicted on him by the Cromerites should have soured Haile Selassie's feelings toward Britain, but the arrival of a new Minister with friendly feelings toward Ethiopia did much to restore the situation. The disappearance of the OETA officers to a new headquarters in Harar removed an obvious irritant—though they still kept control of the Ogaden—and much of the goodwill was restored by an entirely unofficial action of Major Cheesman, by this time a member of the British Military Mission.

Those surly and bloodthirsty Gallas, the Azebu, who had betrayed their country to the Italians in 1936, were still as truculent as ever

[2] He was Governor-General of Eritrea (1960-63).

in 1943. Tigre province had been taken over by Ras Abebe Aregai as a reward for his guerrilla work under the Italian occupation, but he was now starved of men and guns and the Azebu defied all his attempts to bring them to heel. It was decided to arm a small body of Ethiopians under British officers and send them north to deal with the rebels. On moving out of Dessye they encountered more resistance than was expected, and in one engagement a British officer was killed. This setback fanned the flames of rebellion and the Emperor, thoroughly alarmed, asked for the assistance of British airplanes. The Minister knew that the nearest planes were in Aden but were under East African Command in Nairobi, and he was all for asking the Commander there, General Sir William Platt, for permission. Cheesman, knowing full well that they wouldn't get it, persuaded him to allow a direct request to go through to Aden instead. Three Blenheim bombers arrived the following day and the same afternoon dropped bombs around the rebel encampment.

Twenty-four hours later Platt stormed into Addis Ababa to find out what was going on, but by that time it was all over. The Azebu had broken and fled and their chief had gone into hiding in the Semien Mountains. The Emperor sent a warm expression of gratitude to "my friend the British Minister," and Anglo-Ethiopian relations were more friendly from then on. Nevertheless, in 1945, when Roosevelt came to Cairo, Haile Selassie flew to a meeting with the American President on a warship off Suez. He recited Ethiopia's problems and they were listened to with sympathy and understanding. As a result, Roosevelt invited the Emperor to visit him after the war [3] and in the meantime promised to send an economic mission. This was followed by a loan to the Ethiopians, an oil concession to the Americans, and the replacement of several British advisers by Americans.

Thanks to the ham-handedness of Sir Philip Mitchell and Brigadier Lush, the British were never to achieve a dominant influence in Ethiopia again. In the new Anglo-Ethiopian treaty of 1944, almost all exclusive British privileges were eliminated. The Franco-Ethiopian Railway from Jibouti was handed back. The British monopoly over the air service was relinquished—all services are now run by Ethiopia in association with Trans World Airlines of America—and only part of the Ogaden remained in British control.[4]

Ethiopia was independent again, back in the Emperor's hands. Henceforth no foreigner would have a say in the destiny of the

[3] Eisenhower was President by the time he arrived, in 1954.
[4] It was handed back in 1955.

country, except as an adviser and never as a dictator. The land would be Ethiopian and no foreigner could own an acre of it (except Dan Sandford, of course, who was a special exception). Even the Church must be purely Ethiopian from now on. The Abun Kyril had returned from Alexandria with the liberation and Haile Selassie, anxious not to start a religious controversy, had accepted him on sufferance—but only if the Ethiopian Church in Cairo agreed that with his death an Ethiopian would take his place. (He died in 1950 and was succeeded by an Ethiopian.)

The legalists had tried to prevent Ethiopia from joining the United Nations until after peace was signed with Italy, but Haile Selassie had insisted on it; and Ethiopia in 1942 became one of the Charter Members. The same hair-splitters (British, alas) tried to prevent his being a signatory to the Peace Treaty—on the grounds that his country had been conquered before the "proper" war began—but once more the Emperor threatened a hubbub of such proportions that they gave way. Ethiopia signed alongside Britain, America, France and the other Allied nations.

Independence! He had it now and time to develop his country without the hot breath of an aggressor breathing down his neck.

What would he do with his opportunity?

EPILOGUE

THERE IS A temptation among writers about present-day Ethiopia to take a standpoint for or against the régime and then make a convincing case accordingly—citing the remarkable improvements which have been made if one is pro, the dismal and dismaying lack of development if one is con. On only one thing do these writers agree: the Emperor is to be praised or blamed for everything.

It is unlikely that Haile Selassie would disagree with this. There are recurring rumors that he would like to democratize his State, see a genuinely popular parliamentary body elected to govern, and turn himself into a constitutional monarch on British lines. The author's observations of the Emperor force him to the conclusion that though he may once have desired to do so, it is now a most doubtful possibility, and one which Haile Selassie would accept only over his (literally) dead body.

In the years since Ethiopia slipped the last shackles which bound her to her wartime ally, the one remaining constant in the kingdom has been the benevolent despotism of the Emperor. The revised Constitution which Haile Selassie gave to his people in 1955 was described as a blueprint for the modernization of the State, and it did in fact promise the people equal rights under the law, plus a vote. But those observers who expected its promulgation to be followed by a surge of democracy were doomed to disappointment. The Constitution did indeed set out the privileges of Ethiopian citizenship, but one-third of its articles referred specifically to the monarchy and made it clear that the Emperor was relinquishing none of his traditional prerogatives.

"By virtue of His Imperial Blood," read one of the clauses, "as well as by the anointing which He has received, the person of the Emperor is sacred. His dignity is inviolable and His power indisputable. He is, consequently, entitled to all the honours due to Him in accordance with tradition and the present Constitution. Anyone so bold as to seek to injure the Emperor will be punished."

He retained control of the Army and of foreign affairs, the power to initiate and ratify treaties with foreign governments, to frame legislation and proclaim laws, to issue notes and coin, to make grants of land, to confer titles and honors—and to withdraw them. He let it clearly be understood that he remained an absolute monarch in every sense of the word and that a decree signed "We, Haile Selassie," [1] was to be regarded as holy writ the length and breadth of the land.

An absolute monarch, with absolute power; but not one corrupted by it. To those who have not lived in Ethiopia it may seem godlike arrogance of the Emperor to believe that it is only his regal presence, his symbolic influence and his personal intervention in almost every affair of State, which keeps his country together; and that ambition for his people as well as self-aggrandizement is what makes him so eager to hold on to every vestige of power.

A writer in the *Manchester Guardian* in December, 1961, described his disappointment at finding the secret of the Emperor's grip on his country to be "not, as I had fondly supposed before I came to Ethiopia, merely by the exercise of his avuncular feudal fascination. He has done it by force, frankly employing the techniques of a sort of medieval police State." But he adds later, somewhat to his own surprise: "Nobody I have met in Ethiopia wishes to see the monarchy abolished. Except perhaps among the less mature of the student body, it is universally recognized as the proper fulcrum of this weird and beguiling Empire."

The author is under no illusions that Ethiopia is ever likely to be a democracy so long as Haile Selassie lives, but I am reasonably certain that it will not be a democracy after he is dead. It is the liberal element in the land today (largely composed of those who owe their education and status to the Emperor) who urge a relaxing of the régime, a speeding-up of modernization, an end to feudal privileges and traditions. But it is a much cleverer and more malevolent group of self-seekers who are waiting in the wings to strike the moment Haile Selassie ceases to act like an all-powerful king. He has lost the admiration of the young élite by the sluggishness of his reforms and his insistence on feudal privileges, but he stands to lose his throne the moment he improves conditions too radically.

There are many young Ethiopians (who still only number about 2,000 in all) who are disappointed with the Emperor's achievements since the war. They have been to Britain, France, Germany, America

[1] The frequency of the royal plural prompted a witty Englishman to suggest that the Emperor's motto should be: "*L'état, c'est nous.*"

and the contrast between these countries and their own appalls them. Ethiopia has school places today for only 280,000 children out of a population of 18,000,000, and 90 percent of the nation is illiterate; but they forget that when Haile Selassie went to school there were school places for only 291. There are 54 hospitals with 5,774 beds to cater for a population among which leprosy, tick fever, tapeworm, smallpox and syphilis are endemic. There is only one *free* hospital in the whole of the country, in Addis Ababa, to which patients drag themselves or are carried, on journeys which sometimes last weeks, from all over the country. But as recently as 1940 there were no hospitals at all and no Ethiopian doctors.[2]

There is still no road from the capital to Dire Dawa which is open all year round, and hyenas and jackals are the garbage disposal units in all the cities. But aircraft link cities and provinces which were once weeks away by mule, and no longer can the feudal ras tyrannize his subjects in the knowledge that the Emperor cannot reach and punish him. The days of the rapacious rases are not yet over, but at least Haile Selassie has cut them down to size. They are no longer invulnerable provincial barons but rather bad landlords squeezing as much as they can, but aware that the Emperor's eye is upon them—and that he has a national army now to deal with them if they get too big for their breeches.

Since Ethiopia became free again, Haile Selassie has made his mistakes, and the worst of them nearly cost him his throne. But this one was a mistake he would have found it difficut to avoid. He rewarded the chiefs who stayed behind and fought during the Italian occupation, and he elevated the chiefs who officered his Patriot Army. He was not the first to discover that a wartime hero is not always a peacetime paragon. The principal recipient of the Emperor's favor was Ras Abebe Aregai, who did enormous damage to the Italian occupation authorities. Haile Selassie made him his Minister of Defense and gave him a province as well, and he proceeded to prove that he could exploit his own people just as well as he had done the enemy. He squeezed his province until the people groaned and the pips squeaked. As Minister of Defense he held out his hand to arms salesmen from all over the world.

There were others who were just as corrupt, but it was Aregai who worsted them all. The readers of this story will not be surprised that the Emperor, though he must have been aware of the corruption going on around him, did nothing about it. The great constant of his

[2] There are five today and another fifty are in training.

career has been his inability to remove from office anyone, no matter how incompetent or venal, who has once done him a service; and this Aregai and the others certainly had. So he stomached them.

His new army did not, or at least part of it. In December, 1960, while the Emperor was on a State visit to Brazil, the Royal Body-guard mutinied and its commander, the chief of security and a pro-vincial governor formed a triumvirate to take over the State. It was probably the most reluctant revolution in history and it had some typical Ethiopian touches. The leaders of it made no elaborate prepara-tions but decided to revolt while the Emperor was out of the country "so that he should not come to any harm." They stressed that they deeply admired him but thought he was not dynamic enough. They arrogantly neglected to inform the members of the Royal Bodyguard what they were mutinying against, and most of them believed, until they learned otherwise, that they were putting *down* a plot against the Emperor.

The first thing that Addis Ababa knew of the plot was a speech over the radio from the Crown Prince, Asfa Wossen, in which he indicted the corruption and nepotism of the régime—without men-tioning his father's name—and promised to serve the nation on a fixed salary. The listeners did not realize that he was reading the statement, and a further one which he made later, as a prisoner of the rebels with a gun in his back.

There was a spontaneous demonstration from a number of students at the news that the Emperor had been dethroned, but it was small in numbers and lacking in fervor, and there was little other reaction either in the city or in the countryside. The rebellion had no popular backing. It turned out that it had no army backing, either, for the rest of the troops—other than the Royal Bodyguard—were on the Emperor's side. There were a number of clashes but the regular Army was much better armed than the Bodyguard (who began to desert their leaders when they knew they were attacking rather than defending the Emperor) and it was all over three days after it started.

In a way, the rebellion did the Emperor a good turn. The rebels had arrested all the members of the Royal Family and they held all the Ministers, including Abebe Aregai, as hostages. They gathered the Ministers together in the palace while the American Ambassador, Mr. Arthur Richard, attempted to arrange a truce between the rebels and the Army. It was a brave but abortive attempt to referee a mad Ethiopian contest in which no one quite knew on which side he was fighting.

When the Army made it clear that they would accept no compromise, were unequivocally for the Emperor, and would not parley
the rebels decided to cut and run. Before doing so they turned their
machine-guns on the hostages and killed them all. There were some
honest men who died alongside Abebe Aregai and his fellow-villains,
and the unfortunate American Ambassador might have been involved
in a sticky diplomatic incident had he not fortuitously found a
window to jump through; but the result of the abortive rebellion
was to "clean the rats out of the hen house," as the American Ambassador put it. Haile Selassie, who had been warned of the revolt
by way of a British Embassy message from Addis Ababa to the
Foreign Office, flew from São Paulo to Khartoum. The Ethiopian
Chargé d'Affaires in Khartoum was the brother of Ato David, Ethiopian Minister for Foreign Affairs, whom the Emperor had left behind
in Addis to keep his eye on the Crown Prince. The Chargé d'Affaires
had kept in telephonic touch with the Governor of Eritrea, General
Abiye, a son-in-law of the Emperor and a loyal supporter. Abiye
himself had been in radio contact with Ethiopian Army forces outside
Addis Ababa and discovered not only that the bulk of them were
against the revolt but that the Ehiopian Air Force was loyal and its
landing grounds usable.

In the circumstances, the Emperor was all for flying direct to
Addis Ababa and dealing with the situation, but Sir Edwin Chapman-
Andrews, by now British Ambassador to the Sudan, dissuaded him.
"Having discussed things previously with General Abbood [the Sudan
President] I advised the Emperor to fly to Asmara rather than to
Addis Ababa," he writes in a note to the author. "The situation was
not by any means desperate but it was thought not only safer but
more satisfactory if the Emperor could assess the situation with
Abiye before moving into the capital. The Emperor accepted this
advice, though he said he had no doubt that he could equally well
go straight to Addis. The only thing was that at the time he did not
know exactly the cause of the trouble. He was rather puzzled by the
whole thing, though not for one moment was he in the slightest
doubt about what he should do or his ability to straighten things out.
What struck me at the time was his utter and complete calm confidence. He was puzzled but by no means alarmed about the Empress,
the Crown Prince, and his family. It was the same during the War.
In fact, I have never known him in any circumstances other than
calm, quiet—serene, even. Anxious I have seen him, but never

frightened or in any doubt about what he should do and what he was going to do. This was never clearer than at that moment."

The Emperor flew to Asmara and thence to the capital. When Addis Ababa awoke at last to the knowledge that there had been (*a*) a revolt, (*b*) it had been put down, and (*c*) the Emperor was safely back among them, he was given a hero's welcome. He did not even have to worry about his corrupt Ministers any more, for both the good members of his Cabinet (including Ato David) and the bad (including Aregai) had been shot by the rebels. The rebels also obliged. Two killed themselves, and their corpses were hung from gallows erected in the Piazza in Addis Ababa. The third rebel leader, General Mengistu, Commander of the Royal Bodyguard, was wounded and captured. He was tried for treason and hanged in March, 1961.

The Crown Prince prostrated himself before his father and asked forgiveness for having, albeit unwillingly, joined the uprising. He was forgiven, though what he had done would not, of course, be forgotten.

Since the 1960 revolt Haile Selassie has worked hard to erase from the minds of his subjects any memory of that melancholy event. It was only reluctantly that he was persuaded to have a public trial of General Mengistu, the principal rebel; the principal British adviser who convinced him that it was necessary, Sir Charles Mathew, has since retired from his position as senior judge.

A little disillusioned by the disloyalty of a number of his army officers, aware of the unrest among the students whose education he sponsors so fervidly, the Emperor has begun to make a direct appeal to the masses for the support he needs for his slow but steady program of reform. He has begun to emulate Western leaders and make radio talks to his people. He has appealed to their sense of pride by shopping abroad for prestige both for himself and Ethiopia. In this he has had some remarkable success. The Organization of African Unity has established its headquarters in Addis Ababa, as has the United Nations Economic Commission for Africa. The meeting of the Heads of State of the new African nations which established OAU in Addis Ababa in 1963 was a great personal triumph for the Emperor and his was undoubtedly the most statesmanlike of the speeches. His State visit to the United States at the end of 1963, his appearance before the United Nations in New York to a tremendous ovation, his successful intervention in the quarrel between Algeria and

Morocco, and the American appreciation of his presence at President Kennedy's funeral—all these events have achieved their object in persuading his subjects that Ethiopia is a power in the world, and that they have him to thank for it.

So if another threat to his throne comes, it will almost certainly not be from the people. And since 1961, he seems to have learned how to defend himself against threats from his liberal intellectuals and his diehard army officers. "He maintains the hegemony of his throne," says one study of his present régime,[3] "by playing off factions and groups against one another. He chooses his advisers, his officials and their subordinates less on the basis of their personal abilities than on the basis of how their appointments contribute to the balance of power among factions within the government."

This is sad, and the Emperor recognizes it as retrogressive. But he follows this defeatist policy as the only way to keep himself in power and save the country from chaos and revolution until the elements of stable government are created, and can be trusted.

"The power of any individual," says the HRAF study, "is measured in terms of the relationship with Haile Selassie. Each faction must constantly seek to maintain and improve its connection with the throne. Closeness to the Emperor means having access to him, being able to obtain audience with him, having him endorse members of one's faction for better and more influential positions, and being able to parry moves by opponents and to undermine rivals. Competition is great. It absorbs most political energies and leaves little opportunity to formulate political demands and further political goals. Survival often becomes the chief preoccupation."

Writers from abroad study this method of government and roundly condemn it as archaic, despotic and ruthless. But it works, and for the moment the only alternative is likely to be anarchy, terrorism, and an eventual return to the chaotic days of the tyrannizing rases.

Haile Selassie is seventy-two years old. He works a twenty-hour day, sleeps for three hours and prays during the other. There is little doubt that he prays not so much for himself as for Ethiopia. It has come a long way under his guidance, but it is still coated with a veneer of civilization; there is much about it that needs praying for.

He is a lonely man, and since the Crown Prince joined the revolt against him—though unwillingly—he is a worried man too. Should he still recognize his eldest son as his heir? Does his eldest son, a mild and unambitious man, really want to shoulder the tremendous burdens

[3] George A. Lipsky, *Ethiopia* (Human Relations Area Files).

of the throne? But if not Asfta Wossen, then who? His eldest grandson, Prince Iskinder Desta—an amiable, intelligent, Westernized sailor but perhaps a little too Anglicized for Haile Selassie's taste today? His second grandson, the Duke of Harar—son of his favorite son, killed in a motor accident in 1957? Or someone outside his family— like his efficient former soldier son-in-law, General Abiye, Governor-General of Eritrea?

The problem taxes him heavily, for he knows that one day he will die. But those who forecast that he will die violently by a plot against his life do not number among them the Emperor himself, for the precautions he takes when he rides abroad are far less than those of a Western leader. His car will halt for him to listen to the petition of a litigant. He still personally hears the grievances of his subjects in the Palace on one day each week. The author has seen him stop to pick up the body of a sick peasant lying by the roadside and convey him to the free hospital. He eschews his bodyguards at informal gatherings and poses for batteries of amateur cameramen. His brown eyes are sad, but they lack the apprehensive glint that is noticeable in the eyes of some African leaders.

One senses that, in some way, he will not mind dying. He badly misses the comfort and advice of his Queen, Menen, who died in 1962. He goes often to visit his future tomb in the Church of the Trinity in Addis Ababa, where the Queen and the Duke of Harar are already lying; and as he prays he is surrounded by frescoes of events in his tempestuous life—his lonely appearance before the League of Nations, his arrival by mule in the Gojjam in 1941, his first grand review of his army, his presence among a group of young students.

Exactly what he prays is his own business, but the author would not be surprised if the prayer included the first words of the Ethiopian National Anthem:

> Oh Ethiopia be happy,
> By God's power and your Emperor.

It is the sort of prayer that his mentor, the great Emperor Menelik, probably said too.

APPENDIX

The Solomonic Legend, or how the Queen of Sheba was seduced, and the first Emperor of Ethiopia conceived.

As translated by Sir Wallis Budge from the *Kebra Nagast.*

And when the Queen sent her message to Solomon, saying that she was about to depart for her own country, he pondered in his heart and said, "A woman of such splendid beauty hath come to me from the ends of the earth! What do I know? Will God give me seed in her?" Now, as it is said in the Book of Kings, Solomon the King was a lover of women. And he married wives of the Hebrews, and the Egyptians, and the Canaanites, and the Edomites, and the Moabites, and from Rif and Kurds and of Damascus and Syria, and women who were reported to be beautiful. And he had four hundred queens and six hundred concubines. Now this which he did was not for the (sake of) fornication but as a result of wise intent that God had given unto him, and his remembering what God had said unto Abraham, "I will make thy seed like the stars of heaven for number, and like the sand of the sea." And Solomon said in his heart, "What do I know? Peradventure God will give me men children from each one of these women." Therefore when he did thus he acted wisely saying, "My children shall inherit the cities of the enemy, and shall destroy those who worship idols." And King Solomon sent a message unto the Queen saying, "Now that thou hast come here why wilt thou go away without seeing the administration of the kingdom, and how the meals for the chosen are eaten after the manner of the righteous, and how the people are driven away after the manner of sinners? From seeing it thou wouldst acquire widsom. Follow me now and seat thyself in my splendour in the tent, and I will complete thy instruction, and thou shalt learn the administration of my kingdom; for thou hast loved wisdom, and she shall dwell with thee until thine end and for ever." Now a prophecy maketh itself apparent in this speech.

And the Queen sent a second message saying, "From being a fool I have become wise by following thy wisdom, and from being rejected by the God of Israel I have become a chosen woman because of this faith which is in my heart; and henceforth I will worship no other God but him. And as concerning that which thou sayest, that thou wishest to increase in me wisdom and honour, I will come according to thy desire." And Solomon rejoiced because of this and he arrayed his chosen ones and he added a double supply to his table, and he had all the arrangements concerning the management of his house carefully ordered, and the house of King Solomon was made ready. And he made it ready with very great pomp and joy and peace and wisdom, and in tenderness with humility. And then he ordered the royal table according to the law of the kingdom.

And the Queen came and passed into a place set apart in splendour and in glory, and she sat down immediately behind him where she could see and learn and know everything. And she marvelled exceedingly at what she saw and heard and she praised the God of Israel in her heart. And she was struck with wonder at the splendor of the royal palace which she saw. For she could see, though no one could see her, even as Solomon had arranged it in wisdom for her. He had beautified the place where she was seated, and had spread over it purple hangings and laid down carpets and decorated it with marbles and mishcat and precious stones, and he burned aromatic powders and sprinkled the oil and myrrh and cassia round about, and scattered frankincense and costly incense in all directions. And when they brought her into this abode, the odour thereof was very pleasing to her, and even before she ate the dainty meats therein she was satisfied with the smell of them. And with wise intent Solomon sent to her meats that would make her thirsty, and drinks that were mingled with vinegar, and fish and dishes made with pepper. And this he did and he gave them to the Queen to eat. And the royal meal had come to an end three times and seven times (they had eaten ten courses) and the administrators and counsellors and the young men and the servants had departed, and the King rose up and he went to the Queen and he said unto her—now that they were alone together—"Take thou thine ease here for love's sake until daybreak." And she said unto him, "Swear unto me, by the God, the God of Israel, that thou wilt not take me by force. For if I, who according to the law of men am a virgin, be seduced, I should travel on my journey home in sorrow, affliction and tribulation."

And Solomon answered and said unto her, "I swear unto thee that

I will not take thee by force, but thou must swear that thou wilt
not take by force anything that is in my house." And the Queen
laughed and said unto him, "Being a wise man why dost thou speak
as a fool? Shall I steal anything or shall I carry out of the house of
the King that which the King hath not given me? Do not imagine
that I have come hither through love of riches. Moreover my own
kingdom is as wealthy as thine, and there is nothing that I wish for
that I lack. Assuredly I have come in quest of thy wisdom." And
he said unto her, "If thou wouldst make me swear, swear thou to
me, for a swearing is meet for both, so that neither of us may be
unjustly treated. And if thou wilt not make me swear, I will not
make thee swear." And she said unto him, "Swear to me that thou
wilt not take me by force, and I on my part will swear not to take
by force thy possessions." And he swore to her and made her swear.

And the King went up on his bed on the one side and the servants
made ready for her a bed on the other side. And Solomon said unto a
young manservant, "Wash out a bowl and set in it a vessel of water
whilst the Queen is looking on, and shut the doors and go to sleep."
And Solomon spake to the servant in a tongue which the Queen did
not understand, and he did as the King commanded, and went and
slept. And the King had not as yet fallen asleep but he only pretended
to be asleep, and he was watching the Queen intently. Now the
House of Solomon the King was illumined as by day, for in his
wisdom he made shining pearls which were like unto the sun, and
the moon and the stars in the roof of the house. And the Queen
slept a little.

And when she woke up her mouth was dry with thirst, for the
food which Solomon had given her in his wisdom had made her
thirsty, and she was very thirsty indeed, and her mouth was dry;
and she moved her lips and sucked with her mouth and found no
moisture. And she determined to drink the water which she had
seen, and she looked at King Solomon and watched him carefully,
and she thought that he was sleeping a sound sleep. But he was not
asleep and he was waiting until she should rise up to steal the water
to slake her thirst. And she rose up and, making no sound with her
feet, she went to the water in the bowl and lifted up the jar to drink
the water. And Solomon seized her hand before she could drink the
water and said unto her, "Why hast thou broken the oath that thou
hast sworn that thou wouldst not take by force anything that is in
my house?" And she answered and said to him in fear, "Is the oath
broken by my drinking water?" And the King said unto her, "Is

there anything that thou hast seen under heaven and earth that is better than water?" And the Queen said, "I have sinned against myself and thou art free from thy oath. But let me drink water for my thirst." Then Solomon said to her, "Am I perchance free from the oath which thou hast made me swear?" And the Queen said, "Be free from thy oath, and only let me drink water." And he permitted her to drink water, and after she had drunk water he worked his will with her and they slept together.

And after they slept together there appeared in a dream to King Solomon a brilliant sun, and it came down from heaven and shed exceedingly great splendor over Israel. And when it had tarried there for a time it suddenly withdrew itself and flew away to the country of Ethiopia and it shone there with exceedingly great brightness for ever, for it willed to dwell there. And the King said, "I waited to see if it would come back to Israel but it did not return. And again while I waited a light rose up in the heavens, and a sun came down from them in the country of Judah, and it sent forth light which was much stronger than before? And Israel because of the flame of that sun entreated that sun evilly and would not walk in the light thereof. And that sun paid no heed to Israel and the Israelites hated him and it became impossible that peace should exist between them and the sun. And they lifted up their hands against Him with staves and knives, and they wished to extinguish that sun. And they cast darkness upon the whole world with earthquake and thick darkness, and they imagined that the sun would never more rise upon them. And they destroyed His light and cast themselves upon Him and they set a guard over His tomb where they had cast Him. And He came forth where they did not look for Him, and illumined the whole world, more especially the First Sea and the Last Sea, Ethiopia and Rome. And he paid no heed whatsoever to Israel and He ascended His former throne.

BIBLIOGRAPHY

There are scores of books about Ethiopia. This list contains some of those which the author has read himself and found useful. There are many, many more.

The Government of Ethiopia. Margery Perham. A study, first published in 1948, of every facet of Ethiopian life, history and society, written by a friend of the country but none the less honest and clear-eyed.

Ethiopia. "Survey of World Cultures." George A. Lipsky and collaborators. A study of Ethiopian life from all angles made by a team sponsored and subsidized by the Human Relations Area Files Inc., New Haven, Conn. Critical but shrewd, perceptive and telling.

A History of Ethiopia. A. H. M. Jones and Elizabeth Monroe. A short history of the land, admirable in its early chapters but marred by a bias and lack of hind sight in its dealings with the Italo-Ethiopian War.

Mission to Menelik. Lord Edward Gleichen. A splendidly easy and unaffected travel diary of a journey to Ethiopia in 1897.

In the Country of the Blue Nile, and *Unconquered Abyssinia as it is Today,* by C. F. Rey. Both written with observation and humor about a country which the author loves and finds strange but congenial. A writer with a sense of humor to match that of the Ethiopians themselves.

Lake Tana and the Blue Nile, by Major Robert E. Cheesman. A small masterpiece of the literature of exploration. A Consular report to make one realize that the diplomatic services are not what they were.

Caesar in Abyssinia. By George Steer. An incomparable account of the blood, tears and frustrations of the Italo-Ethiopian War, seen by *The Times'* correspondent. Having watched the humiliation of Ethiopia at first hand, he lived to write a book about her liberation, called *Sealed and Delivered,* of less impact since it was the postscript to the tragedy. Steer was killed in Burma in 1944. Alas.

The Lion of Judah Hath Prevailed. Christine Sandford. She also wrote *Ethiopia Under Haile Selassie,* and is a close friend of the Emperor (together with Brigadier Dan Sandford, her husband) with an unabashed and uncritical admiration of Haile Selassie.

The Ethiopians. Edward Ullendorf. A thorough, authoritative survey of the land, its people, and its history by a British expert of Ethiopian life and customs. The author fills the chair of Ethiopian Studies at London University.

Living in State. Beatrice Russell. The memoirs of a State Department wife in, among other places, Ethiopia.

Ethiopian Paradox. C. Jesman. A Czech's study of the problems and paradoxes of Ethiopian life and policy.

John Melly of Ethiopia. Edited by Kathleen Nelson and Alan Sullivan. The diaries of a British doctor-cum-missionary who came to Ethiopia during its crucial years and formed a Red Cross unit to help victims of the Italo-Ethiopian War. He was killed by an Ethiopian drunk he was trying to help, just before Italy occupied Addis Ababa.

The War in Abyssinia. Pietro Badoglio. A soldier's well-written and emotional account of a military campaign to conquer a country.

Anno XIII. Emilio de Bono. The earlier Italian commander's less restrained account of the strategic plan to annihilate Ethiopia.

The Ethiopian Crisis. D. C. Heath and Co. A summary of opinions and afterthoughts on the Italo-Ethiopian War.

Ethiopia: A Cultural History. Sylvia Pankhurst. A survey of the artistic life of the nation.

The Day of the Lion. Roy McGregor Hastie. An Italian-based life of Mussolini with some interesting asides about Haile Selassie.

African Afterthoughts. Sir Philip Mitchell. An account of a former Governor of Uganda's experiences as head of Occupied Enemy Territory in Africa.

Morning Will Come. Gordon Waterfield. An amiable account of life as a wartime information officer by a peacetime foreign correspondent.

Alvarez. Narrative of the Portuguese Embassy to Abyssinia, 1520-27 (translated by Lord Stanley), which contains a splendid account of the rock temples of Lalibela.

Chronique Du Regne De Menelik II. Guebre Selassie. A muted account of the rule of an extrovert monarch who changed the shape of Ethiopia.

Travels in Ethiopia. David Buxton. A felicitous account of both country and people.

INDEX

Abata, Ras, 54-5, 107-8
Abdullahi, Emir of Harar, 19
Abiye, Colonel, 264, 272, 275
Abuna Mattheos (Archbishop), *see* Mattheos, Abuna
Addis Ababa, palace, 36-7; "roads," 37-8; schools, 44, 269-70; raiders, 61-2; roads, 121-2; slaves, 126-7, 173; funeral, 129-30; trade and transport, 131, 270; shanty town, 155-6; feasting, 157-8; lack of amenities, 172-3; Italian road plans, 174; hospitals, 270
Adowa, 22-3, 193
Aia, Battle of, 203
Ali, Ras, 94-6
Ali, Wodaju, 186
Alvarez, Father Francisco, 212-13
Amba Aradam, Battle of, 196-8
Anderson, Kenneth, 247
Angell, Sir Norman, 228
Aosta, Duke of, 230-1
Aramayo, Lake of, 70
Aregai, Ras Abebe, 230, 258-9, 265-6, 270-3
Avon, Lord, *see* Eden, Anthony
Azebu Gallas, the, 208-9, 211-12, 243

Badoglio, Marshal, 181, 194-9, 204-5, 207-12, 217, 221
Balcha, Ras, 50, 57-9, 83, 89-90, 92, 132-5

Baldwin, Stanley, 182, 221-3
Barton, Sir Sidney (British Minister), 180, 191, 201, 228
Bekr, Achmed bin Abu (Emir of Harar), 18
Belaya, 247-9
British Mission, *see* Mission, British
Brocklehurst, Colonel, 243-4
Burton, Richard, 15-16, 18, 24
Buxton, Lord Noel, 173

Chamberlain, Neville, 229
Chapman-Andrews, (*later* Sir) Edwin, 216-17, 234-7, 272
Colli, Count (Italian Minister), 83, 97
Cora, Giuliano (Italian Minister), 140, 146
Cheesman, Major R. E., 144-5, 157, 164-6, 173, 232, 234-5
Churchill, Winston, 182, 234, 236, 259, 265
Crown Prince (Asfa Wassen), 216, 229n, 246, 271-4
Cunningham, General, 250-1

De Bono, Marshal, 175-6, 185, 193-4
Demissie, Ras, 91, 107-8
Desta, Princess Tananya Work, 216, 229n
Dodds, Major (British consul in Harar), 72-3, 89-90

Dodds-Parker, Captain Douglas, 240, 243
Doughty-Wylie, Major C. H. M., 184

Eden, Anthony (*later* Lord Avon), 176, 182, 191-2, 201n, 224, 229, 237-8, 255, 258

Getachu, Ras, 215-16
Giorgis, Hapta, 54-5, 60n, 61-2, 82-3, 86-7, 91-6, 107, 109-11, 114, 117-18, 126-9
Giorgis, Walda, 54, 58, 63, 65-6, 81, 91, 94, 101, 104-5, 256
Gleichen, Lord Edward, 23-6, 28-31
Graziani, Marshal, 229, 260-1
Gugsa, Haile Selassie (no relation to Haile Selassie or to Ras Gugsa), 184-7, 193
Gugsa, Ras, 102-4, 114, 132, 144-50

Haile Selassie, parents, 16; birth at Ejarsa Gora, 16-17; named (Lij) Tafari, family name Makonnen, 16-17; at school, 25; childhood, 31-2; to Menelik's court, 32-3; title of Dejazmach, 33; appointed Governor of Solali, 35; squire at court, 35; temperament, 43-4; school at Addis Ababa, 44; affection of Menelik for, 43-4; appointed Governor of Sidamo, 52; nominated Governor of Harar, 57; as administrator in Sidamo, 58; marriage with Waizero Menen, 59; in danger from Lij Yasu, 64-5, 69-70, 78-9; to capital, 77; move against Yasu, 80-1, 83-5; appointed Heir to Empress Zauditu, 85-6; battle at Sallale, 92-7; Taitu's plot, 103; need for arms ignored, 104-5; Magdala, 108; enemy Taitu died, 113; influenza epidemic, 114-15; Ethiopia joins League of Nations, 118; travels to Aden, to London, 118; return to Ethiopia, 120; built school, 122-3; letter to League, 124-6; attitude to slavery, 126-7; Regent paramount, 132; 1928 plot, 136; status of Negus, 137-8; trade, 140; revolt by Ras Gugsa, 146-50; proclaimed H. M. Haile Selassie, Emperor of Ethiopia, 150-1; coronation, 155-9; reforms, 159; break-up of feudal powers, 162-3; Lij Yasu's escape, 169; Wal Wal incident, 176-8; appeal to League against Italy, 178; Italo-Ethiopian War, 187-217; exile, 216; to England, 223; tribunal at Geneva, 223-5; at Bath, 226; at Council of League, 223, 230; to Middle East, 234-5; return to Ethiopia, 245; to Addis Ababa, 251; Isahai dies, 264; Independence, 266-7; rebellion, 271; present-day government, 268, 273-5
Hailu of Gajjam, Ras, 91, 102, 116-17, 118-19, 143-5, 162-9, 216-17, 229-30, 249-50
Harar, 15-18, 23-5, 126
Harar, Duke of, Masfin Makonnen (son of Haile Selassie), 216, 229n, 234, 246, 275
Hoare, Sir Samuel, 180-1, 201
Hoare-Laval Agreement, 181, 189

Igazu, Bitwaded, 110, 112-14
Ilg, M. (Swiss engineer), 26-7, 30, 33, 49
Imer, Ras, 109-11

Imru Haile Selassie, cousin and friend
  to Tafari (Haile Selassie), 77-8,
  96, 170, 195, 198, 215, 265
Italo-Ethiopian War, 187-217

Jones, A. H. M. and E. Monroe, 174,
  179-80

Kassa, Ras (became Emperor John),
  48, 92-6, 109-10, 117, 129, 134-5,
  143, 145, 162, 166-8, 189, 195-6,
  198-200, 205, 207, 229, 239, 246
Konavoloff, Colonel, 199, 202-13

Lalibela, 212
League of Nations, 117-18, 123-6,
  180-2, 222-5
Lush, Brigadier, 256-7, 261-2, 266

MacMannus, Emily, 264
Mad Mullah, the, 68, 71-2, 77, 79
Makalle, 184-7, 193, 196
Makonnen, Ras (Governor of Harar,
  father of Haile Selassie), 16, 24;
  leadership under Menelik, 19; as
  plenipotentiary to Europe, 19-20;
  founded hospital at Harar, 20;
  against Italians at Adowa, 21-3;
  death, 33-4
Makonnen, Tafari (boyhood name of
  Haile Selassie), see Haile Selassie
Mattheos, Abuna, 65, 81-4, 104, 113,
  129-30
Mathew, Sir Charles (judge), 273
Melly, John, 172-3, 202
Menelik, King of Shoa, captured
  Harar, 19; crowned self Emperor
  of Ethiopia, 19; defeat of Italians,
  22-3; reception at Addis Ababa, 29;
  appearance, 29-30; power of feudal

rases, 29; routine, 40; feast, 41-3;
  marriages, 45-6; failing health, 49;
  named heir, 51; death, 64
Menen (became Empress), 59, 77-80,
  97-8, 115, 118-9, 136, 204, 209,
  216, 227-8, 231, 264, 275
Mengistu, General, 273
Mikael, Ras (son-in-law to Menelik),
  33-4, 47-54, 64-7, 87-8, 90-7, 101
Mission, British (to Menelik's court,
  1897), 23-31
Mitchell, Sir Philip, 256-9, 266
Monroe, Elizabeth, and A. H. M.
  Jones, 174, 179-80
Mulugeta, Ras, 149, 181, 187-9,
  195-9
Mussolini, 139, 174-6, 178, 181-3,
  193, 222, 229-30, 261-2

Occupied Enemy Territory Administration (OETA), 256, 258-9, 261,
  265
Ogaden, 32, 68-9, 72, 78, 89-90, 192,
  259, 265-6

Perham, Margery, 260
Platt, General Sir William, 232-3,
  235-6, 238, 266

Rey, C. F., 117, 120-3, 127-8, 130-1,
  141
Richard, Arthur (American Ambassador), 271
Rodd, Rennell, 23-4, 28-30, 261

Sallale (on Plain of Sendafa), 92, 95
Samuel, Aba (tutor to Tafari), 44,
  70-1
Sandford, Christine, 136-7, 257
Sandford, Brigadier Daniel, 136, 232-
  4, 236-7, 261, 267

Seged, Lul (husband of Menen before Tafari), 59-60, 79-80, 88, 91, 97-8

Selassie, Emperor Haile, *see* Haile Selassie

Selassie, Prince Sahle, 216, 228

Seyoum, Ras, 91, 118-9, 145, 184-6, 199-200, 205, 207-8

Steer, G. L., 161, 188-9, 192-3, 197-8, 216, 234, 242-3

Symes, Sir Stewart, 233, 235

Tafari, *see* Haile Selassie

Taitu, Queen (Menelik's consort), 30-1, 33-4, 42, 44-55, 60-3, 102-3, 110, 112-4

Tesemma, Ras, 52-3

Thesiger, Wilfred (British Minister), 52-5, 60-4, 67, 69-75, 77-84, 91, 104-5, 107-8, 111-12, 114-15, 140

Times, The, 118, 157-9, 260.

Tsahai, Princess, 216, 228, 264-5

Ullendorf, Edward, 160-1

Vansittart, Sir Robert, 191, 222

Victor Emmanuel, King, then Emperor, 221

Vinci, 187

Wangel, Waizero Sabela, 165-6

Waterfield, Gordon, 257, 261

Wavell, General, 234, 237-9, 243-4

Wingate, Orde, 238-51, 255

Wollye, Ras, 114

Work, Taffera, 262

Yasu, Lij (son of Ras Mikael and Menelik's daughter, Shoaraged), 47-9; named heir to Menelik, 51, 56; character, 60-7; interest in Islam, 68-72, 76; "alliances," 73; deposed, 85; arrest, 88-90; at large, 102, 106-7; ill, 109-10, 112; hostage, 116-17; death, 169-71

Ydlibi (Turkish consul-general in Harar), 68, 89

Yeshimabeit, Waizero (mother of Haile Selassie), 16-17

Yilma (step-brother to Haile Selassie), 16, 32, 34-5, 50

Zaphiro, M., 58

Zauditu (Menelik's daughter, *later* Empress), 47-8, 54-5, 64, 85-6, 101-4, 112-17, 120, 122, 126-30, 132, 136-8, 144-5, 147, 150, 155

Zeila Agreement, 179